Impact
THIRD EDITION

A Guide to Business Communication

MARGOT NORTHEY
University of Western Ontario

Prentice Hall Canada Inc.
Scarborough, Ontario

Canadian Cataloguing in Publication Data
Northey, Margot, 1940–
  Impact : a guide to business communication

3rd ed.
Includes bibliographical references and index.
ISBN 0-13-452541-8

1. Communication in management.   2. Commercial correspondence.
3. Business report writing.   I. Title.

HF5718.N67 1992   651.7   C92-095318-2

Prentice-Hall, Inc., Englewood Cliffs, New Jersey
Prentice-Hall, International, Inc., London
Prentice-Hall of Australia, Pty., Ltd., Sydney
Prentice-Hall of India Pvt., Ltd., New Delhi
Prentice-Hall of Japan, Inc., Tokyo
Prentice-Hall of Southeast Asia (Pte.) Ltd., Singapore
Editora Prentice-Hall do Brasil Ltda., Rio de Janeiro
Prentice-Hall Hispanoamericana, S.A., Mexico

ISBN 0-13-452541-8

Acquisitions Editor: Marjorie Munroe
Developmental Editor: Maryrose O'Neill
Copy Editor: Jocelyn Smyth
Production Editor: Valerie Adams
Cover Design: Sharon Matthews

  2   3   4   5   AP   97   96   95   94   93

Printed and bound in Canada by The Alger Press

Contents

Preface

In business today, communicating well is more important than ever. As organizations shift from autocratic to participative management, as more individuals work together in teams, people have to be able to get results not simply by commanding but by explaining, persuading and inspiring. They need to understand how to adapt their writing and speaking to suit the occasion. Yet many business students feel unprepared for this challenge.

If you are wary about writing, this book can help you gain confidence and competence in putting words on a page. It will take you through the steps of planning and producing good letters, memos and reports. It will reveal strategies for attacking common business-writing problems — ways to address different kinds of readers for different kinds of purposes. You will learn how to avoid common grammatical faults and how to write with a clear, concise and vigorous style.

You will also discover when and how it is best to talk — what to do for an oral presentation, and how to handle a job interview and run an effective meeting.

Good writing and speaking reflect good thinking. The explanations and exercises in *Impact: A Guide to Business Communication* will show how thinking through a task and making informed choices will bring you better results. It's a practical approach since, after all, business is a practical subject.

Acknowledgements

With this third edition of *Impact*, I again appreciate the advice of Dr. Margaret Proctor of the University of Toronto, whose extensive knowledge of language is matched by her understanding of student needs. I am also grateful to those students at Western Business School who have shared with me their diverse communication experiences, to Lynn McClary, who helped with her technical skill, and to Martin Walker of Price Waterhouse for his comments. A special thanks goes to those instructors across Canada who made suggestions for this edition.

Valerie Adams of Prentice Hall was conscientious and helpful throughout the writing and editing process, and I appreciated the energy and enthusiasm of Maryrose O'Neill and Marjorie Munroe.

Finally, I want to thank my husband, Patrick Northey, for his continuous support in this and other projects.

About the Author

Margot Northey is Associate Professor in the Western Business School at the University of Western Ontario, and a specialist in management communications. Formerly, she was Associate Professor of English and Director of the Writing Program and Teaching/Learning Centre at the Erindale Campus, University of Toronto. Professor Northey is the author of two other books, *The Haunted Wilderness: The Gothic and Grotesque in Canadian Fiction* and *Making Sense: A Student's Guide to Writing and Style*. As a consultant she has advised diverse organizations and given seminars on communication to businesses across the country.

Note to Instructors

This third edition of *Impact: A Guide to Business Communication*, like the previous ones, was written to help Canadian business students communicate better. It reflects my experience as a teacher of undergraduate and graduate business communications and as a consultant to business and government. Since business students typically are practical, results-oriented, and attuned more to numbers than to words, the book is deliberately lean, giving them the least they need to know to do the job well. A good reader will take only a few hours to go from cover to cover. I've tried to follow my own advice to produce a clear, concise, and forceful text that students will want to read and remember.

The approach to the book is based on three assumptions:

— Thinking through a communications problem is more effective than simply learning a formula.

— Writing well is less a matter of right or wrong than of making choices between better and worse.

— Inexperienced writers pay too little attention to planning and editing.

Since reading about a problem is no substitute for addressing it, the chapters have exercises, most with an oral as well as written component. The exercises are at two levels of difficulty. Those in Section A are generally more specific or technical than those in Section B, which require a broader range of decision-making skills.

This third edition of *Impact* includes:

— added exercises;

— more discussion of electronic communication tools;

— a greater emphasis on communication differences among various cultures;

— an enlarged section on listening skills;

— a sample of a formal report as well as of an informal one.

These additions and other changes incorporate the suggestions of readers and the findings of recent research. They also reflect my own sense of communication needs in the changing business environment.

When students have mastered the material in *Impact*, they should be able not only to handle the particular problems discussed in the text, but also to apply the principles to any other writing or speaking task. Whatever the business challenge, they should be able to think their way through to effective communication.

Thinking About Communications

The prospect of having to write fills many business people with dismay. Owing to the emphasis on quantitative methods in business courses, many students and recent graduates have had little practice writing or speaking formally. As a result, some feel more at ease working with numbers than with words. Yet the ability to communicate effectively is important in getting to the top in business.

Why is writing so important? The reasons can be summed up in three words: flexibility, power, clarity.

Writing Gives Flexibility

Let's suppose you have an idea for a new product that you want to propose to the managers of marketing and production, two busy and more senior people. You make appointments to see them. First you go the marketing manager's office and enthusiastically make a brief presentation. Unfortunately, she has had a bad day. The president has come down to see her about declining profits, the latest sales figures are discouraging, and she has just finished arguing on the phone with a major distributor. She responds half-heartedly, makes a few nit-picking points about your proposal and, politely showing you to the door, vaguely says she'll think about it.

When you start to talk to the production manager, he is even more distracted. He says one of the expensive new robots in the factory has just broken down, causing a production crisis. He apologizes that he is really too busy to think about new ideas at this time. You leave, feeling unhappy and defeated.

Now let's suppose you had put your ideas in writing. The two managers could have set your proposal aside to read at a time when they were feeling less harassed. One might even have taken it home to study quietly in the evening. Since the managers would be reading the proposal at their convenience, they would have been in a more receptive mood — ready to see your suggestion as a possible benefit rather than another headache.

Writing allows this kind of flexibility. It allows readers to decide when and how much they want to read. They have a chance to reread if necessary and to reflect upon a message or proposal.

Writing Has Power

The old saying, "The pen is mightier than the sword," suggests the enormous influence the written word has had over people, both individuals and groups. Martin Luther's Ninety-five Theses, which ushered in the Protestant Reformation, or Karl Marx's *Das Kapital*, laboured over in the damp rooms of the London Museum, have had more influence than the armed might of most rulers. On an admittedly far less profound level, writing in a business setting can also be a powerful force.

To begin with, it has staying power. Often a written proposal or report will be shelved because it is ahead of its time or not in line with current policy. Later, sometimes several years later, when conditions are more favourable, the same document can be picked up and made the basis for company action. To stay alive, the spoken idea relies on memory — a notoriously unreliable vehicle — whereas the written word needs only an adequate filing system. It provides a permanent record.

Writing also has travelling power. Young employees of medium to large businesses are sometimes surprised to discover that a memo or report they have written has made its way into the president's office before they have. Clearly written ideas or information will often travel quickly up the rungs of the corporate ladder. It is not unusual for good writing to catch the eye of a senior manager and lead to speedier promotion for the writer.

Writing Helps Clarify Thinking

Writers often say that the act of putting things down on a page not only records what they have in mind but helps them to sort out their thoughts. Consider a letter sent to Ann Landers several years ago. It began:

> I have written you dozens of letters in the last 10 years and I have never mailed one until now. Yet I can truthfully say you have helped me a great deal. Let me explain.

> When I ran into trouble in my life, I would sit down and write you about it. In order to put my thoughts down on paper, I had to think in a logical manner and figure out how the trouble started. By the time I got to the end of the letter, I could see many aspects of the problem that I hadn't seen before.[1]

---

[1] Courtesy Ann Landers, News America Syndicate, *Toronto Star*.

Although the context differs, you will find — or may already have found — that you can analyze complicated business problems more clearly when you try to sort things out on paper. Beyond being a medium of communication, therefore, writing becomes a tool for understanding. It's a tool worth learning to use well.

Communicating in Organizations

It's perhaps not surprising that Marshall McLuhan, the most influential communications expert of this century, was a Canadian. As a nation, we have been preoccupied with forging communication links among a sparse, widespread population. The old Canadian one-dollar bill, with its line of telephone poles receding to the distant horizon, illustrates this preoccupation. Year after year we strive to maintain a national radio and television broadcasting system in the face of foreign competition. We have been aggressive in entering the international high technology market with our telecommunications equipment.

Nevertheless, while we have put our imaginations to work on the technological aspects of communicating, we still have a distance to go in recognizing the importance of communications on a day-to-day level. Business as a whole is just beginning to appreciate what the successful Japanese and North American companies have known all along — that excellence comes not only from technological know-how but from handling people well. Good managers are usually good communicators, whether the process of communication is systematic or informal.

Communication Systems

As they expand, most businesses institute systems or mechanisms for communicating inside and outside the organization with people who are important to their success. Shrewd managers aim to set up an effective communication system, not as and end in itself, but because it is a way of improving overall performance and exploiting opportunities. They recognize the usefulness of both formal and informal systems in helping achieve their corporate goals.

Formal Systems

Both internal and external methods of communication tend to become more structured or formal as an organization grows. Internal communications are designed for company employees, and can include newsletters and magazines, departmental reports, regular group meetings, opinion surveys, and suggestion boxes for employees' ideas. Increasingly, businesses are realizing the need for systems encouraging two-way communication between management and subordinates.

External communication aims to inform through various written and spoken communications outside stakeholders in the organization, whether they are shareholders, governments, customers, or the public at large. Building good relations with the media also matters. The growth of public relations departments illustrates the increasing dependence of business on a favourable public image — and the recognition that an organization cannot operate independent of its environment.

Informal Networks

Conversations over coffee, spontaneous meetings, and even casual access to the boss's office down the hall all contribute to an informal communications network. Peters and Waterman's research revealed that companies they consider to be excellent are, in part, characterized by a rich network of open, informal communications.[2] Management by "wandering around" contributes to the sense of openness. However, this kind of informal communication can't be based simply on aimless chitchat; it must engage employees in purposeful talk about their concerns and ideas.

The "grapevine" is a major source of information in most organizations. News about hirings, firings, or layoffs is more apt to reach people first through the grapevine rather than through formal channels. Grapevine information may be distorted or based on rumour, but it always travels fast. Managers can learn who the key people in this informal network are and make use of them. They can also anticipate what's likely to spread by rumour and give the official version first.

Whether communication is channelled through formal structures or an informal network, employees have information needs that must be met if they are to continue giving of their best. Roger D'Aprix suggests employees want answers to three questions:[3]

1. How am I doing and does anybody care? (The need for personal evaluation.)
2. How are we doing? (The need to know group or company performance measures.)
3. How can I help? (The need to contribute meaningfully.)

Managers who are good communicators see that those who report to them have answers to these questions. However, creating good communication in an organization isn't a one-shot effort. Rather, it's a continuous process, requiring continuous management commitment.

The Flow of Information

An organization with good communications has an efficient flow of information in three directions: downward, upward, and lateral.

Downward Communication

This flow of communication follows the hierarchical route from superior to subordinate. It may take place at any level. Top executives often use this route to explain corporate strategies, to instill loyalty, or to rouse employees to greater effort. Lower-level managers often give job instructions, details of policy, and feedback to employees about employee performance.

---

[2] Thomas J. Peters and Robert H. Waterman, *A Search for Excellence: Lessons from America's Best-Run Companies* (New York: Harper & Row, 1977).

[3] *A Conversation with Roger D'Aprix*. Videotape. Towers, Perrin, Forster & Crosby.

Downward communication often is serial — that is, it is transferred from person to person through several levels. The more links in the chain of command it passes through, the more distorted it becomes. According to Pace and Boren, serial communication has several tendencies:[4]

- The original message can become simplified, with some details, such as qualifiers omitted and the remaining parts highlighted or "sharpened;"
- Some details are changed according to the predisposition, communication style or status of the interpreter;
- The order and details of events are adapted according to what is plausible. What one expects to have happened overrides what actually happened.

Serial communication is more likely to be distorted if it is oral, but changes in meaning can occur in any message. A good practice, therefore, is to monitor important messages — to check on how they have been received after passing through several levels, so that any distortion can be corrected.

Upward Communication

Communication from subordinate to superior can increase productivity and help create a team feeling. Yet too many companies still pay only lip service to it. Participative management, which the Japanese have used so effectively, does not mean that subordinates make all the decisions, but that they provide input into the process.

Upward communication takes two forms:

1. requested feedback to superiors on policies, practices, or performances;
2. unsolicited ideas or suggestions.

For either form to work, there must be a climate of trust. Subordinates must feel free to make critical comments or suggest changes without being considered troublemakers. Without a climate of trust, employees will say only what the boss wants to hear.

Lateral Communication

This kind of communication moves horizontally across areas that are on the same level in the hierarchy, or sometimes diagonally to a different level. In complex organizations, such communication helps coordinate activities across functions or departments and can produce a spirit of cooperation. When there is little lateral communication — when "the right hand doesn't know what the left hand is doing" — departments often operate at cross purposes. Often companies trying to be more productive reduce some of the layers of management. In this "flattening" of the organization, lateral communication becomes even more important, since each manager will have a wider span of control — that is, a greater spread of people to manage.

4 W. Pace and R. Boren. *The Human Transaction*. Glenview, Illinois: Scott, Foresman, 1973.

Some Help From Communications Theory

A growing body of research and theory is emerging about various aspects of communications, from semiotics (the study of signs), to linguistics (the study of language), to cognitive psychology and persuasion theory. For communications specialists, these are fruitful areas to explore. However, for those of us interested in the individual acts of writing and speaking in business, the most important feature of modern communications theory is its description of communication as an exchange. Rather than thinking of communication as only the delivery of a message, we should envisage a process in which the receiver of the message matters as much as the sender.

This idea is not new. The ancient Greeks had at the centre of their education system the art of rhetoric. Students learned various techniques for communicating ideas; they practised ways of swaying an audience to the speaker's point of view by appealing to both reason and emotion. In more recent times, however, with the Western world's emphasis on reason, we have tended to overlook the importance of the listener in the communication process. The thinking has often been that since people are reasonable, they will agree with your conclusions, as long as you address them with a reasonable argument. You need concentrate only on the logic of your message.

In the twentieth century we began to correct this mistaken approach. The insights of psychology have made us realize that human reactions are much more complicated than we once thought. In our dealings with others, a simple reliance on reason will not work. Moreover, the insights of linguistics, especially in the area of semantics, have made us aware that meaning itself is a complex matter. Words do not have a fixed meaning; they are only symbols and their meaning may differ with different users and in different contexts. The word *cool* may mean one thing when a meteorologist refers to "a cool temperature"; it has another meaning when a politician bemoans "a cool reception" for his speech, and yet another when a teen-ager talks about a friend being "a cool guy."

Modern communications theory builds upon these and other insights in studying the ways we express ourselves. It analyzes communication on several levels, beginning with the individual and extending to the interaction among large groups and cultures. It explores the different ways, verbal and non-verbal, that we communicate with each other, from written messages and oral presentations to gestures and body language.

In a book of this size it is obviously impossible to explore the intricacies of communications theory; what follows is simply a summary of some of the key concepts that affect our ability to write and speak effectively as individuals in business.

The Communications Model

In 1949, Claude Shannon and Warren Weaver published a mathematical model of communications based on Shannon's work in the Bell Telephone laboratories. It described a one-way communications process going from sender to receiver. As might be expected, it used terms associated with electronics. Subsequent changes to this basic model have described a two-way process and have a more behavioural emphasis, dealing less with the message itself than with the way people perceive it. Figure 1-1 illustrates a simple two-way model. To accomplish a purpose, a sender encodes a message into signals (words, numbers, or pictures) which are transmitted by a channel (for example, telephone lines, air waves, or the nervous system) and a medium (such as a telephone, magazine, television, computer, or even a voice). The receiver gets the signal directly, either through the ear or eye, or indirectly, through the medium of technological equipment. The receiver decodes and reacts to the message, and in turn gives feedback, through the same process of encoding and transmitting a signal.

FIG. 1-1   A Simple Two-Way Communication Model

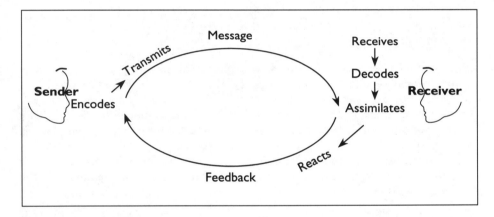

Barriers to Communication

Interference can disrupt any stage of the communications process. Here are the most common types:

Technical Interference

Most people have experienced static on telephone lines, a breakdown of television transmission, or a computer "crash." Older people may have to cope with faulty hearing aids or inadequate eyeglasses. We all know that even minor physical ailments can affect communication. If the boss has a headache when sending a memo, the message may be unintentionally abrupt or snappish.

Semantic Interference

The problem here stems from words themselves. When faulty diction muddles a sentence, the message may be misinterpreted. "Bypassing" occurs when the same word means different things to different people. For example, if you describe someone as a "detail artist," you may mean "thorough," but the listener may interpret the phrase negatively as "nit-picking."

Environmental Interference

Often these barriers have to do with individual or group attitudes. We tend to filter information according to our perception of reality, and that perception may differ from one person or group to the next. Consider these possible sources of environmental interference:

1. **Age**   The term *generation gap* reflects the fact that a difference in age can cause people to see things in a different light. Teen-agers are well aware of this phenomenon when communicating with parents.

2. **Sex**   Jokes or comments acceptable to males may offend females, and vice versa. In addition, perceived sexist attitudes may cloud the reception of a message that ostensibly has nothing to do with sex.

3. **Physical Appearance**   The underlying premise of "dress for success" lessons is that people are judged partly by the clothes they wear. We may not like this kind of typecasting by appearance, but it is not likely to go away. If applicants for a job turn up in untidy or inappropriate clothes, they send an unintentional message. So may someone with smoke-stained fingers, especially if the prospective employer is a non-smoker.

   Interference is not confined to human appearance. A sloppy-looking letter filled with crossouts may annoy some readers enough to deflect their attention from the ideas.

4. **Cultural Attitudes**   Cultural attitudes, even aside from obvious racial and religious prejudices, can cause interference. People's ways of seeing things — their perceptual maps — differ from the ways of others in a different cultural group, and can affect the reception of a message.

   For instance, attitudes to time vary from culture to culture. North Americans are concerned about being on time. In business, "on time" means precisely at the scheduled hour, perhaps even the scheduled minute. North American executives who have to cool their heels for an hour in the waiting room of a South American associate could be infuriated about "wasting time" if they didn't realize that their ideas about time are not always shared by others.

   Attitudes to space also vary. Research in proxemics — the study of the space between people — shows that different cultural ideas of what is "private space" may cause communication problems. For example, South Americans and southern Europeans like to move close when they talk to each other. Northern Europeans and North Americans, by contrast, like to keep about a metre apart in business relationships, moving in only if the relationship becomes more intimate. The British, with their customary reserve, have the reputation for being the most "standoffish."

It's easy for people from these different cultural groups to give offence unknowingly when talking to one another, by moving in during a conversation or by backing away. Most groups in our multicultural society share common types of behaviour, yet we can still see subtle differences based on cultural background.

All these potential barriers to communication show that there is more to speaking or writing well than using correct grammar or sound logic. Grammar and logic certainly matter, but they are not enough to ensure complete understanding. Effective communication depends as much on attitudes and perceptions, especially those of the receiver.

Non-Verbal Communication

Many of the barriers discussed above are non-verbal. Although the primary focus of this book is verbal communication, it's important to recognize the part that non-verbal communication plays.

One research study has found that over ninety percent of the effect of a message on a listener is conveyed by non-verbal means.[5] Although the influence of non-verbal elements is certainly less in written communication, presentation still matters. Layout, typeface, and colour can affect reader response, as experts in direct mail know.

Non-verbal communication can be classified in various ways, but it falls most easily into two divisions: setting and gesture.

Setting

The colour of an office or its decor can be an important element of communication. For example, we know that the colour green, which used to be so prevalent in hospitals, helps create a relaxed atmosphere. By comparison, red, a feature of many restaurant decors, is a stimulant.

The way furniture is arranged can also affect communication. Managers who want to emphasize their status can do so by talking to others from behind an imposing desk. Managers who want to put visitors at ease will move from behind the desk and talk in a conversation area where chairs are arranged more casually. Similarly, if the person chairing a meeting sits at the head of a long table, he or she will more easily dominate the discussion. In contrast, a circular table will encourage conversation between all the participants.

Gesture

We all react, often unconsciously, to the signals that people send by their expressions or actions. If we are in the middle of making a point and we see our listener has raised eyebrows, we infer that he or she has doubts. Similarly, we interpret a frown or scowl as a negative reaction. We wouldn't take long in an argument to move away from a clenched fist or to interpret a handshake as a sign of a truce.

5 Albert Mehrabian, "Significance of Posture and Position in the Communication of Attitude and Status Relationships" in *Psychological Bulletin*, 71 (1969), 363.

Kinesics is a relatively recent field of research that explores the science of gestures. It has given us helpful insights into the messages people send by the ways in which they use their bodies. Unfortunately, some popularizers of the subject have made far-reaching claims that are not supported by research. In trying to develop our unconscious understanding of non-verbal signals to the level of conscious interpretation, we should remember two provisos:

1. Individuals may not fit a common pattern. Just as racial stereotyping distorts the truth about individuals, so does the reliance upon a single, prescribed interpretation of a gesture. For example, a listener's crossed arms may often signify opposition, but they may also be just in a comfortable position. To be interpreted reliably, a specific gesture needs to be considered in the context of other knowledge, as part of a pattern.

2. Gestures can have different meanings in different cultures. When people in western cultures nod their heads up and down in a conversation, they are generally showing agreement. For some Africans, the same nod means disagreement. Looking a person in the eye also has varied meanings. A young person in most western cultures is coached to look an adult in the eye as a sign of respect. However, a young North American Indian or West Indian may be taught that this is disrespectful.

As a communicator, you can make many gains by being receptive to non-verbal signals as long as you are aware of these limitations. The key to non-verbal communication is to be observant and sensitive to subtleties. Remember also that the better you know people, the more likely you are to be able to "read" them correctly.

Listening and Questioning

Approaches to Listening

Listening is probably the most underrated of all the communication skills, probably because it seems so easy. Yet a common complaint from subordinates about managers at all levels is that they don't listen. Research has shown that managers generally rate themselves as better listeners than their employees rate them.[6]

Often a manager's poor listening behaviour reflects the old notion that a manager's job is to tell others what to do and see that they do it. Although good managers do indeed have to spend time talking to others — instructing and advising them — increasingly they recognize the need to involve employees throughout the organization in making suggestions and problem-solving, as a way of improving performance and productivity. Such effective upward communication depends on management's willingness to listen.

---

[6] J. Brownell, "Perceptions of Effective Listeners: A Management Study," *The Journal of Business Communication* 27:4 (Fall, 1990), 401-415.

What are the guidelines for effective listening? First of all it helps to understand Carl Rogers's distinction between passive and active listening.[7]

Passive listening means listening without giving a response, other than the odd nod or show of comprehension. It's appropriate when the talker merely wants to let off steam or muse out loud. *Active listening*, by contrast, creates a constant interaction between speaker and listener. By directly responding to what the speaker says, through comments and questions, the listener helps direct the conversation. An active listener can, in fact, retain control of a conversation.

If you want to be an active listener, according to Rogers, you need to have "empathy" — an understanding of the speaker's perspective and feelings. Empathy is not the same as sympathy or feeling sorry for the speaker, but rather implies awareness. Four kinds of "mirroring" techniques will help you show this awareness:

1. **Paraphrasing**, in which you restate in different words the speaker's point: "You mean. . . ."

2. **Clarifying**, in which you ask for a restatement or fuller explanation: "What exactly do you mean by. . .?"

3. **Reflecting feelings**, in which you respond to the emotions behind the words: "It sounds as if you're feeling. . . ."

4. **Summarizing**, in which you pull together the speaker's points: "What I hear you saying is. . . ."

Beyond mirroring the speaker's remarks, here are some other ways to become a good listener:

1. **Stop talking** — sometimes a hard thing for busy managers to do, especially those used to giving orders. Don't be afraid of silence. Give others time to collect their thoughts. If they take time getting to the point, be patient. Don't interrupt to finish sentences for them. Wait until they pause, and then clarify or try to draw them out.

2. **For a lengthy discussion, pick a spot** where neither of you will be distracted by telephone rings or other disruptions. Clear your mind of other matters enough to concentrate on the conversation.

3. **Show by your posture and expression that you are attentive.** Leaning forward, for example can show concern for the other person, as can facing the speaker squarely rather then turning partly away. Eye contact also helps signal that the listener is attentive, although staring or glaring will certainly not encourage relaxed conversation.

4. **Be open** rather than judgmental. Try not to let preconceptions or biases about the speaker shape what you are hearing. Concentrate on the substance rather than the

---

7 Carl Rogers, *On Becoming a Person* (Boston: Houghton Mifflin, 1961), 226.

style. At the same time, try to get some sense of the pattern of the speaker's remarks and where they are heading.

5. **Be alert to non-verbal cues.** The speaker may betray deeper or more conflicting feelings than the words indicate. The non-verbal cues can often tip you off to areas where you should probe deeper — to a hidden message.

Sometimes we assess the speaker by the pace of the speech. A fast talker may be impatient with a slow talker, or a slow talker suspicious of someone who speaks at a fast clip. The typical difference in speed between "fast-talking" Northerners in the United States and the slower "drawl" of Southerners has affected attitudes in many a conversation. On the whole, a listener who matches the speed of the speaker's talk will produce a more positive atmosphere in the conversation. There are exceptions, however. For example, people who are upset or excited often talk faster than usual, sometimes at a breathless pace. We can help calm them down by responding in a slower, more moderate way — a technique doctors use with agitated patients.

Listening to Understand

Although much of this discussion about listening has do with strengthening a relationship with others, there are times when the point of your listening is simply to understand some information, as when you are receiving instructions, finding out background information to a problem, or attending a speech or lecture. In these instances, note-taking is helpful, as long as getting down details doesn't prevent you from catching the overview or "big picture." Don't try to put everything into notes, unless you are skilled at shorthand or are able to review your short-form scribble immediately afterward. Instead, try to concentrate first on understanding the flow of the talk and on noting the main lines of the argument or instruction.

It can be helpful to keep the points in one column on a page and the examples or justifications in a column to the right. You might also try leaving space at the right of the page to fill in your own comments after the talk. That way, at a later date you can easily review at a glance the speaker's ideas and your response to them. Personalizing the information will help you to remember it.

Listening as a Critic

Occasionally your task as listener will be to evaluate — to assess the information critically. For example, you may need to assess a marketing or sales proposal, or to review other corporate plans. The danger here is that you can become so intent on finding weak spots or problems that you don't really hear what is being said. Sometimes your own biases and emotions can get in the way, so that you unwittingly "tune out" the speaker's message. In either case, the result is distortion or misunderstanding.

Instead, try to concentrate on full understanding before you reach evaluative conclusions. Brief note-taking can help. You might also jot down beforehand questions that are central to your assessment, so that after you are sure you have understood the presentation you can use them as a guide for your evaluation. If you have only a general idea of what the topic will be, here are some basic questions that can help you evaluate:

• What is the main strength of this idea?

- Are there any factual errors or distortions of fact?
- How balanced is the point of view? Is there an underlying bias?
- What are the alternatives to the proposal, and have they been adequately considered?
- What are short-term and long-term implications of the ideas?
- How could the ideas be implemented practically? What are the barriers to their implementation and could they be overcome?
- As a result of this speech, what needs to be changed, re-examined, or explored further?

Remember that a speaker cannot talk as fast as your brain can process the information. There's a lot of "empty time" when, as a listener, you can easily be distracted. A more useful alternative to day-dreaming is to use that time to review or summarize the sequence of ideas, to consider implications, and to anticipate where the talk is heading. It's worth reiterating, however, that your first duty, even as a critic, is to listen carefully to what is being said.

Approaches to Questioning

Effective questioning clearly fits hand-in-glove with effective listening. Asking the right questions helps reach the right answer or solution to a problem. Some kinds of questions ease the flow of communication; others hinder it. This list illustrates the effect of different kinds of questions:

1. **An open question** allows the receiver to respond in a variety of ways. It often begins with *How*, *Why*, or *In what way*. It helps to probe the listener's opinions, eliciting a thoughtful or in-depth reply:

   How can we improve this set-up?
   Why do you think this is a problem?
   What would you like to accomplish?

2. **A closed question** asks for a limited response — often yes or no. It's useful for getting specific information or for checking the accuracy of something:

   Are you saying you'd like more support?
   Should we mail the report?
   Have we covered all the dimensions of the issue?

3. **A hidden-assumption or "loaded" question** makes it difficult for the receiver to answer without admitting something. It's a trap that puts the receiver on the defensive, and journalists often use it to try to get business leaders or politicians to acknowledge an error or weakness. Clearly, it impedes free-flowing communication:

   Why haven't you done anything to stop this massive pollution?
   Is it really that difficult to keep to a budget?
   When will we get a report from you without mistakes?

4. **A hypothetical question** asks "What if?" It is a useful sort of question when people are doing free-form planning or trying to think up creative ways to address an issue. For example: "What would you do if your budget were cut by fifteen percent?" Or "If you were in charge of this factory, what changes would you propose?"

   On the other hand, a hypothetical question can be troublesome if it is directed at you as a kind of accusation. A question such as "If your product is found to contain dioxin, what do you intend to do about it?" leads away from the known facts to supposed ones, and can deliberately inflame an issue.

5. **A two-part question** is really two questions in one. It can confuse or make it difficult for the receiver to know which part to answer:

   How should we react and is this really the whole problem?

   How can we better deploy our sales force as well as increase our promotional efforts?

   The questioner would be better to split the question and ask each part separately.

EXERCISES

● Section A

1. Analyze two company magazines or newsletters. How would the contents improve internal communications, whether upward (employees to management), downward (management to employees) or lateral (among equals)?

2. Popular cartoons and comics in the daily newspapers often focus on communications problems. Find one or two such cartoons or comics and analyze the interference in the communications process.

3. Give a brief outline or a one-minute talk disclosing the oral and written communications skills needed in one or two of the following jobs:
   — insurance sales representative;
   — doctor;
   — computer programmer;
   — internal corporate accountant;
   — store manager;
   — payroll and benefits supervisor;
   — affirmative action counsellor;
   — bank manager.

4. Although non-verbal communication is not an exact science but rather a source of useful clues, what would you suspect from the following actions:
   a) While you are talking to a client, she starts drumming her fingers on her desk.

b) You are a new employee attending your first group meeting. When a man arrives after the meeting has started, others stand up to offer him a chair.

c) When you make a suggestion at a group meeting, a colleague rolls her eyes.

d) You need to see the internal controller. When you enter his office, you see that he sits with his back to the door, facing the window. He motions you to sit down and continues working for a minute before turning to face you.

e) At a meeting you've requested with your boss, she closes the door after you've entered and presses the telephone call-forward button to her secretary.

f) A prospective employee sits facing you. She hunches her shoulders, fiddles with her ring, and bites the side of her mouth throughout the interview.

g) You hear there is a new engineer your age down the hall, and go to his office to welcome him. While you sit talking to him across his desk, he continually rocks back in his chair and presses his fingers together in a "church steeple" position. He smiles with his mouth but his eyes don't crinkle.

h) Three days after you have reprimanded an employee, she refuses to look you in the eye when you meet in the corridor. She returns your greeting in a clipped voice.

5. Identify the mirroring technique shown in each of the following conversations:

   a) "When I suggested that idea, no one responded, but when Beth suggested it, the same people were enthusiastic."
   "You feel that you don't count?"

   b) "The problem with this project flows from the group dynamics."
   "I'm not sure what you mean."

   c) "I mentioned he was a good prospect two weeks ago, and no one has contacted him yet. It's the same with other leads. We have to get more action."
   "You want us to follow up on leads a lot faster."

   d) "This department can't handle the workload. They want us to increase the number of direct mail campaigns and add to the number of special events. We can't possibly do all this with our present resources. We're strapped in this department, and if they're going to keep dumping stuff on us like this, we need a lot more money."
   "To do the added work effectively, you need an increase in the departmental budget."

6. Suppose that in some organization you belong to — such as a business, athletic team, social club, student group, or voluntary association — you have been asked to help hire a part-time employee. Create a list of four or five attributes needed to do the job well. For each attribute, create an open question for candidates that will help to reveal whether they have that attribute.

7. Select a partner, and each take careful notes during a lecture you both attend. A day or week later, review your notes together. Do they still make sense to you? Did you miss any important points? Could they be better organized or laid out so that key ideas stand out from less important details? Have you made any evaluative comments, personalized the ideas or considered practical implications beyond those presented by the speaker?

8. Compare the barriers to communications in the worst classroom you have studied in with the conditions that make communication easier in another room of the school — whether a classroom, the cafeteria or a student lounge. Consider the size and shape and colour of the room, lighting, seating arrangements, acoustics, and other influences.

9. Increasingly, businesses are paying attention to public relations and to fostering a good corporate image. Examine the advertisements in a mass-market business publication (for example, *Canadian Business*, *The Financial Post*, *Fortune*), paying attention to those that are not selling a specific product. Assess three or more advertisements. What do you think is the particular message of each ad, and what perceptions on the part of the reader is it trying to influence or correct?

● Section B

1. Think of someone you have worked for in any organization (perhaps a business, a school activity, or a volunteer group). Analyze the effectiveness of communications between you. Consider these questions:
   — What direction did the flow primarily take?
   — How formal or informal was the communication?
   — How at ease were you in the communication and why?
   — How relevant was this communication to your concerns on the job?
   — To what extent did the organization foster good internal communications?

2. Give a three-minute oral presentation or write a few paragraphs discussing how one or more of the following changes might affect business communications, either inside the organization or with the public:
   — increased decentralization in business;
   — increased business competition from Japan;
   — greater job-security provisions in contracts;
   — affirmative action programs;
   — promotion or recognition of multicultural goals;
   — increased public suspicion of business.

3. Select two people in the class who hold opposing views on an emotionally charged political or social issue; for example, universal old-age pensions, free health care, the death penalty, abortion on demand, an adoptee's right to information, the need for unions, or a terminally ill patient's right to suicide. Have them present their views to the class, and then write a brief assessment of the discussion. Compare your assessment with others in the class. Are there differences? Does the listener's own bias account for some of the differences? To what extent does this exercise reveal barriers to communications?

   Then select two more opponents to discuss a different issue. Listeners should merely summarize the side of the argument they least agree with. Compare summaries. Are the differences fewer or greater than in the first part of the exercise? Why? To what extent does the tendency to evaluate interfere with the listening process? In what business situations might this tendency hinder effective communications? What are the possible remedies?

4. Singly or in a group, through research or visits, compare the process of communicating in a fairly small company (up to 100 employees) and a large one. Consider the upward flow, downward flow, and lateral flow. Try to draw some conclusions about the different communications needs in a large organization as opposed to a small one.

CHAPTER **2**

Strategies in Planning for Writing and Speaking

The Importance of Planning

Planning can help you avoid many of the risks of interference in communication. In the business world, where the results of casual mistakes may be more dire than in the everyday world of family and friends, it makes sense to give forethought to what you are communicating. Planning is especially important if you are writing. In ordinary conversations you can afford to be spontaneous, since the instant feedback of the person you are talking to allows you to correct any mistakes immediately. An angry or skeptical look, or even a raised eyebrow, will point the way to changes. With formal oral presentations, you need to prepare carefully, but at least the audience's reaction helps you gauge the impact of what you are saying.

Writing does not have that kind of instant feedback. Since correction is more difficult once a message has been delivered, it's important to try to avoid misinterpretations beforehand. Careful attention to planning, as well as careful attention to editing, is your best insurance against misunderstanding. Rather than dashing off the first thing that comes to mind, think of writing as a three-stage process in which planning, drafting, and editing have equal time.

Although much of the advice on planning in this chapter and on drafting and editing in following chapters is directed at writing, it can apply as well to formal speech. Chapter 10 will focus specifically on formal oral presentations.

A Problem-Solving Approach

It's useful to think of business communication as presenting a problem for which there may be no one right answer. As a communicator, you will often have to choose from a variety of options. To decide wisely, consider the context of your communication, as outlined in Figure 2-1. Ease your way into the task by asking the most basic questions first: What is the reason for communicating? Who is the receiver? What is his or her environment?

Considering the Reason and Desired Result

Business communication usually has one of two general purposes: to inform or to persuade. But in devising an initial strategy you need to be more specific about your reason or reasons for communicating. Failure to do so has resulted in many failed exchanges — the sales agent who describes the features of the product but forgets to ask for the order; the customer service clerk who sends a requested refund but annoys a customer in the process; the job applicant who, in listing qualifications, inadvertently supplies ready-made reasons for being turned down. In figuring out exactly why you are communicating, remember that you may have more than one purpose, in which case you need to distinguish the primary reason from the secondary ones. Here are some of the most common reasons why people in business communicate with others. Some are action-oriented, geared to a specific business objective, while others have more to do with getting a general response from the receiver:

— to ask for or give information;
— to explain (whether a new company policy or a drop in revenue);
— to issue instructions;
— to advise or recommend;
— to create a record;
— to persuade (whether in a sales pitch or job application);
— to thank or congratulate;
— to foster an atmosphere of goodwill;
— to improve the company's image;
— to create a good impression of oneself.

In considering the reasons, it's useful to go beyond what you want to do, and to focus also on the result you want from the receiver. Unless your writing is a matter of pure record-keeping, you will usually want the receiver to do something — to act, decide, or approve — or simply to think in a certain way. Before you begin, try completing this sentence: "As a result of this communication, the receiver will . . ." and list all the results you want.

As you will see later, determining specific reasons and desired results will help you decide how to focus and organize your message. It will help avoid wasting your time and your reader's on unimportant details or irrelevancies. Anticipating receiver response will help you to word your message so that it creates the impression you want and doesn't foster misunderstanding.

Assessing the Receiver in Context

Socrates' prescription for understanding is first to "Know yourself." For business communication, that wise dictum might be amended to read, "Know your audience." The most frequent and serious of all mistakes in business correspondence comes from an incorrect or inadequate assessment of the person receiving it. Too often people communicate as if to the thin air or to some faceless machine, or else they assume that the receiver will think the same way they do. As a result they produce letters or reports that are writer-based rather than reader-based, and speeches that miss their mark with the audience.[1] Don't fall into this communications trap: spend time assessing your receiver. And since people don't exist in isolation, consider also the receiver's environment, or context, which may infuence the receiver's response.

1. **How will the receiver benefit?** In a routine memo, the benefit may simply be that the reader will be better informed, but in correspondence in which you are making suggestions, you need to figure out specifically what benefit there is to following your proposal. By pointing out the benefit, such as increased savings, higher profits, or improved company morale, you have a better chance of interesting the receiver in what you are saying — and of getting results.

2. **What is the receiver's position and responsibility?** Is he or she your superior, your subordinate, or on the same level as you? Considering the receiver's position may help you decide the level of formality to use. Determining the area of responsibility will help you to decide the kind of detail to include.

   Suppose you have an idea for a new product and want to sound out others in the company about its feasibility. Clearly you would want to have a different emphasis and a different set of questions for the marketing manager than for the plant manager or the controller. Where one person would be most concerned with potential markets and sales, another might be concerned with production problems or costs. In the same way, if you are composing application letters, you should stress different aspects of your qualifications, depending upon the different responsibilities of the people you are writing to.

3. **What is the receiver's knowledge?** Considering this question will help prevent you from being either condescending or confusing. Most business people have a specialized understanding of certain aspects of their business. If you give them information that they already know, you may annoy them. It would be condescending for a surveyor to write to a lawyer, "A survey by a registered surveyor has legal authority," or for a boss to send a memo to a new secretary saying, "I require my letters to be properly spaced and free of typographical errors." (The boss should speak to a new employee anyway, rather than send a memo.)

   On the other hand, you don't want to assume too much about a person's knowledge, giving information the receiver will not likely understand or issuing

---

[1] Linda Flower discusses these terms in detail in *Problem-Solving Strategies for Writing*, 3rd ed. (San Diego: Harcourt Brace Jovanovich) 1989.

instructions the receiver will have difficulty following. Technical experts often make the mistake of giving highly specialized information to managers who are confused by it and, as a result, often annoyed. By thinking about the receiver's field and level of knowledge before you begin, you will be better able to decide the kind of technical or specialized information you should include.

4. **What interests and concerns the receiver?** I'm not suggesting here that you play psychoanalyst and try to dig deeply into the psyche of the receiver. What I do recommend is that you use your practical understanding of human nature and of the particular reader to establish what will arouse interest or concern. How will the receiver likely react to your information or suggestions? Is he or she known as a stickler for details or impatient with them? Impressed by creativity or nervous about quick change? Will an older employee feel threatened by the ideas of a young "upstart"? What specific objections will the receiver likely raise?

5. **What is your experience with the receiver?** If you have dealt with the receiver before, you can benefit by establishing in your mind what was positive or negative in the relationship. You can try to avoid potential areas of friction and repeat what worked. Occasionally, you might even decide to send correspondence elsewhere.

    A junior employee in an auditing firm learnt this lesson early in her career. She had a manager who was repeatedly critical of her inattention to details. When she wrote a memo to him, presenting an imaginative idea for saving time on a large auditing account, he dismissed the concept with the comment that she was just trying to avoid detailed work again. Some time later, she presented the idea to a different manager who accepted it with high praise. The moral is that past experience can colour thinking and influence the reception of a message.

    Past experience may also be company experience. If you are trying to collect money owed, for example, you should see if the creditor has often been delinquent with payments and what the response has been to previous appeals. Similarly, if you are writing a promotional letter to customers, you should find out how they reacted to earlier promotions.

6. **What is the receiver's environment?** From industry to industry, expectations vary about what is acceptable behaviour with customers or suppliers. Although you aren't bound by these expectations, you should be aware of them.

    You should also be aware of any expectations based on a different cultural background. In an increasingly multicultural society, and with growing international trade, understanding the receiver's cultural environment will reduce the chance of friction in communication. Although one cannot become an instant expert on other cultures, being aware that there are cultural differences will at least help you avoid the arrogance of assuming that others will or should react as you do.

    The political and economic climate can also shape communication needs. Political concern about pollution, based on widespread public concern, might affect a report to a boss on the purchase of new machinery. An economic downturn, or the threat of one, might shape a sales letter to a customer or an internal proposal for an expensive acquisition.

Understanding the broader environment of the receiver can in many instances make a dramatic difference to the effectiveness of communication.

7. **Will the correspondence reach secondary readers?**   In some cases, a secondary reader can assume major importance. For example a performance evaluation may become a lawyer's weapon in a lawsuit for wrongful dismissal. An internal report on a chemical spill might somehow find its way into a press exposé of pollution. "Be prepared" is the best motto. Consider who *might* read the communication as well as who will *read* it.

It may seem that this detailed list of questions is too elaborate to bother with. In fact, getting a precise fix on the context of the communications task is really not very time consuming. With a routine letter or memo to a familiar associate you will gauge your receiver quickly.

Even if the task is more problematic, you will soon discover that the few minutes spent considering these preliminary aspects will prevent false starts and discarded drafts. Your analysis will help you create receiver-based communication that gets results.

FIG. 2-1   Basic Communication Process

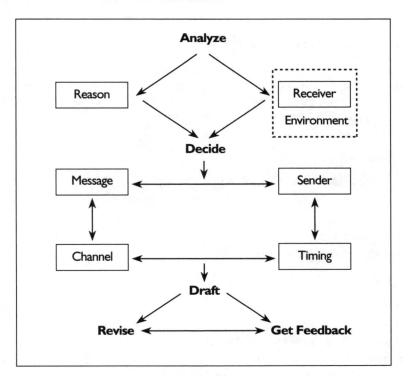

Choosing the Sender

You may not always be the best person to carry out the communication, even if you are responsible for handling the issue. You need to decide whether you are the person most likely to get the desired results from your particular reader. A superior may have more influence. An associate with different experience may have more credibility. You may decide in some instances to have someone else write or speak or, more often, draft correspondence that will go out under another person's signature.

Consider Timing

Sometimes it's a good idea to delay a while. You may be in a hurry to get results, but the receiver may be immersed in other matters. For example, a president worried about giving an important report to the Board may not be instantly responsive to your latest marketing idea. Employees in the midst of a layoff process may not react favourably to a motivational memo.

With some tasks, you may even decide to create a sequence of correspondence over a set period of time. The process of collecting delinquent bills usually follows such a sequence.

Whatever the communication, timing can affect its chance of success.

Picking the Channel and Media

There are no hard and fast rules about which channel of communication to choose. Whether you should speak or whether you should write depends on the context. Decisions about communicating, either individually or to a group, may depend on the personalities of the people involved. Nevertheless, it's possible to establish some guidelines, based on common sense.

You write when:

— you or the reader wants a record of the communication;
— you don't need an answer but are simply supplying information;
— the receiver is preoccupied with other pressing matters;
— the information is complicated or detailed;
— costs of telephoning are excessive.

You talk when:

— you want to encourage discussion;
— you need a quick response;
— you want to foster a personal relationship;
— you want to build group rapport;
— you are dealing with a personal or sensitive matter.

Aside from whether you write or speak, the particular medium you choose can affect the reception of your message. The term *medium* overlaps the term *channel* but usually has a more specific meaning, referring to the vehicle or mechanism by which you choose to communicate, whether a meeting, the telephone, a memo, or sophisticated technology. When McLuhan said, "The medium is the message," he may have overstated the case, but no doubt the choice of medium influences how messages are interpreted.

One way of attacking the problem of choice is to think about the "richness" of the medium, that is, the number of different ways a message can be inferred or reinforced. For example, a telephone is a richer medium than a newsletter, because the receiver can listen to the tone as well as the words, and can question the sender. Similary television is richer than radio, because it permits seeing as well as hearing. Lengel and Daft have suggested that the more non-routine the information, the richer the medium you should use.[2] As Figure 2-2 shows, a memo will work well for a routine message, but for news about plant layoffs, a face-to-face meeting would be better.

FIG. 2-2   Choosing the Best Medium*

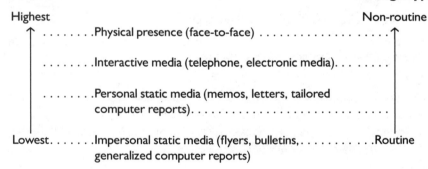

Media Richness   **Message Type**

Highest   Non-routine

. . . . .Physical presence (face-to-face) . . . .

. . . . .Interactive media (telephone, electronic media). . . . .

. . . . .Personal static media (memos, letters, tailored
                 computer reports). . . . .

Lowest. . . . . . .Impersonal static media (flyers, bulletins, ...Routine
                 generalized computer reports)

Adapted from Lengel & Daft.

The Effect of the Electronic Office

Rapid changes in technology mean that what is a good choice for communicating one year may be surpassed by a new type of medium the next. Generally the advances have not only increased the ease of communicating but also reduced the cost. Although a list of communications media would be out of date almost as soon as it was printed, it is wise to keep informed. We all to a certain extent resist changes in our habits, but exploiting the possibilities of new technology can increase our effectiveness as communicators. Here are some of the advantages and potential pitfalls of the three communications developments that have recently had the greatest impact on offices.

---

[2] R. Lengel and R. Daft, "The Selection of Communication Media as an Executive Skill, The Academy of Management" *Executive* (2:3, 1988), pp. 225-232.

1. **Electronic mail**. The term **E-mail** usually refers to internal mail sent from computer to computer by linked networks. Its benefits are many:

    — Transmission is instant.
    — Responses can go back and forth quickly, reducing the need for meetings.
    — It is easy to send the same message to many people.
    — It can substantially cut the costs of internal mail.
    — It avoids "telephone tag."
    — Messages can be sent any time, without regard to the problems and costs of differing time zones.

    E-mail also has some disadvantages:

    — Receivers must each have a computer — not always cost-effective in an organization.
    — Receivers may have to wade through a lot of "junk mail," since it's so easy to send messages everywhere.
    — Reading off a screen is more difficult and slower than reading print. Long messages that go beyond a single screen (still less than a page) pose particular difficulty.
    — Receivers may forget to access their mail.

2. **Voice mail**. Sometimes called "voice processing," voice-mail is a telephone answering system in which the caller leaves a message in a "mail-box," rather than having to speak directly to the receiver. Its advantages are that:

    — the same message can be routed to several people at once;
    — receivers do not need a computer, but only a touch-tone phone;
    — it reduces the time and effort needed to send brief informational messages;
    — the tone of voice can provide added information.

    As with E-mail, the receiver may forget to review the messages, and the sender will never know. Voice-mail has other disadvantages:

    — Listening to a message is much slower than reading it.
    — Callers are more likely to be unfocused or unclear if the message is long. Many people ramble or do not enunciate clearly.

3. **Facsimile machine**. FAX transmission allows exact copies of text as well as pictures to be sent in a few seconds from one machine to another anywhere in the world — via telephone lines or satellite. The quality of duplication has improved greatly in the last few years, and will likely continue to get better. A FAX copy of a document is as legally binding as the original.

    The time advantage of sending something by FAX rather than through the mail is obvious, but FAX transmission is also replacing the older Telex transmission, which can only send words. It is costlier than the mail, but since saved time usually means saved money, the increase in FAX use has been dramatic and will no doubt continue.

The trend in communication technology is for machines to be interconnected, so that, for example, a person can compose text on a word processor and send it by FAX directly from the computer without having to print it out first. Whatever the new developments, however, one thing is certain: technology cannot make a muddled message clearer or an annoying one more pleasing. You will always need to consider carefully *what* you send along with how you send it.

Considering the Proper Tone

Although tone is one of the subtler aspects of communication, an inappropriate tone can certainly cause problems. Tone is the emotion or attitude that is conveyed by our voice or language. In everyday conversations with people we know well, we probably unthinkingly use a variety of tones, and our friends are probably not upset if we're occasionally sarcastic or irritable. But with business colleagues we do not know as well, we need to be more careful — especially in a letter, where lack of instant feedback rules out quick correction. Here are some guidelines for setting the proper tone.

Be Courteous

The fundamental rule of business communication is to adopt a courteous tone. Your letters, memos, and reports can quite properly have other characteristics, such as enthusiasm or pride, but courtesy is the foundation. Even if you are angry for good reasons, you will be more effective if you don't make discourteous remarks. What does courtesy mean? A number of synonyms come to mind — consideration, politeness, tact — but perhaps the common feature of them all is sensitivity to the feelings of the other person.

Consider the following memo, sent by the manager of a restaurant to the employees:

> This is to tell you that you shouldn't talk to other employees about non-business matters while you are working. Surely you realize that a lot of trivial chattering is inappropriate business behaviour.

> If you want to keep your job, keep your unimportant conversations to the times when you are on a break. Pay attention to customers when you are working and the restaurant will be more profitable.

If you were one of the employees, what effect would this memo have had on you? Would you have reacted differently to a more courteous version?

Benjamin Franklin knew the importance of courtesy. Renowned as an international diplomat, he once said, "You catch more bees with a drop of honey than with a pint of gall." In businesses where you will be dealing with people you don't know well, it can be hard to undo the damage of impolite, belittling, or sarcastic comments. When you are working with people of different ages, personalities, and backgrounds, you will avoid offending anyone if you treat everyone with courtesy.

Choose the Right Level of Formality

Although courtesy is the basis for a pleasing tone, you also need to decide the appropriate level of formality, or register. A moderately informal tone is usually best for business correspondence as well as business presentations, but not always. Occasionally a very informal tone can work well. Consider this notice, written by an employee in a large company. At his suggestion, management had recently provided employees with an exercise room and changing areas, but the maintenance department was now complaining that the mess in the men's changing room added to their workload. Recognizing that the people using the facility were mostly young employees like himself, he posted this message on the changing room door:

> Guys, this locker-room is the pits! We're in danger of either breaking an ankle on the trash or of having our lungs corroded from the fumes of all the stale jock junk. Seriously, the maintenance department is hitting the ceiling, and if we don't pick up our socks, I won't be surprised if management does a number on us and closes the place. So don't trash it — stash it or take it home and wash it!

The informal, slangy tone of the notice is appropriate because the writer is appealing to associates of the same age and position in a social rather than business context. He wants to be a "buddy" rather than an authority, and is in no danger of being misunderstood.

The trouble with slang is that it is usually short-lived; slang words come in and out of fashion quickly. Twenty years ago no one would have used the phrase "do a number," and in twenty years from now, it may be forgotten. Another problem with slang is that it is often limited in its use to a certain age or cultural group. What is common among twenty-year-olds may be misunderstood by sixty-year-olds. Moreover, the slang of Vancouver may be different from the slang of Montreal or St. John's. For most business writing, therefore, you should try to stay away from slang.

At the other extreme from slang is very formal language. Consultants, lawyers, and government officials often attempt a formal style when they are producing large or important documents that will be read by a number of people. They think that formality gives an air of authority to what they are saying. For the same reason, public speakers may have a formal style on solemn or important occasions such as a funeral, a graduation, or public dedication ceremony.

Unfortunately, most writers who try to be formal in their language seem merely pompous. A great many formal reports are burdened with wordy, cumbersome prose. In short, they're deadly to read. A guide for most business writing, therefore, is to avoid the extremes of formal and informal language. Choose a middle level, one that is moderately informal. For letters, memos, and internal reports (reports sent to people inside your organization), be conversational. Choose the kind of language you would use if you were talking to an associate. Here are some tips in creating a conversational writing style:

1. **Stay away from old-fashioned words and archaic legalisms.** In wrongly thinking that formality is the essence of good business writing, and that old legal documents are the model to copy, one businessman regularly begins his letters,

"Your favour of the 28th received and contents duly noted, and in reply to same would state . . . " Nowadays such an opening is silly as well as stuffy. Although some lawyers, unfortunately, continue to use cumbersome and unnecessary phrases, business writers should stay away from words like *heretofore, aforementioned,* and expressions like *duly noted, the undersigned,* and *in reply to same.* A good rule of thumb is to avoid opening and closing statements beginning with words ending in *ing* ("referring to your letter"; "trusting you will agree").

2. **Use personal pronouns.** Bureaucratic writing is often boring because it is impersonal; we don't know which person is behind the idea or action described. The writer may say "it could be argued" or "a decision was made" rather than "you could argue" or "we decided." Similarly, students sometimes scrupulously avoid putting an *I* in any academic essays. If this is your habit, you will have to change it, except for certain kinds of formal reporting. In your everyday business correspondence, use personal pronouns freely. Refer to *I, me, you,* and *we,* as you would in conversation. Personal pronouns emphasize that communication is between people rather than faceless automatons:

   x   A discussion of sales figures for the appliance division will take place on Monday.

   ✓   We will discuss the sales figures for your division on Monday.

You is the most important pronoun of all. As you will see in Chapter 6, it focuses attention on the reader rather than the writer, heightening the reader's interest.

In trying to avoid personal pronouns, many writers slip into the habit of using expletives — *it is* or *there is* beginnings. Occasionally these are efficient phrases, but more often they add clutter and dullness. See if you can eliminate them.

   x   It is hoped that all supervisors can attend the meeting.

   ✓   I hope you can join us at the meeting.

   x   There are two ways to recover the costs.

   ✓   You can recover the costs two ways.

3. **Use contractions.**   Just as you use contractions in speaking, except on the most formal occasions, so it's appropriate to use them in business writing when you want to establish an informal rapport. In your letters and memos particularly, consider writing *can't* rather than *cannot, it's* rather than *it is, I'm* rather than *I am,* and *we're* rather than *we are.* This advice holds only if you feel natural with these contractions. If the occasion is more formal than the usual business communication, or if your writing seems peppered with apostrophes, use contractions more sparingly. In any case, if you write in a way that is as natural to you as possible, you are likely to put your reader at ease.

When You Need to Be Formal

Some businesses or institutions may require you to write more formally at times; say, when you are writing a report for another company or when you are preparing a formal policy paper. Depending on the custom, you may have to disregard some of the guidelines for informal writing. Specifically, you may have to

— avoid contractions, since these give a chatty quality;
— avoid individual names, since the focus is more likely to be on policies or procedures — on the requirements themselves — than on the individuals who work with them;
— avoid first-person pronouns. The custom of writing *I*-free reports is being followed less and less, however, since it leads to passive, convoluted sentences. The chapter on formal report writing discusses the problem and suggests alternatives.

Figure 2-3 compares a formal tone with a moderately informal and a very informal one.

FIG. 2-3   Characteristics of Different Levels of Formality

Formal Tone	Moderately Informal Tone	Very Informal Tone
solemn	conversational	chatty, familiar
can use archaic or legalistic phrases	avoids archaic and legalistic phrases	can use slang
avoids individual names	uses individual names	uses individual names
avoids personal pronouns	uses personal pronouns	uses personal pronouns
avoids contractions	uses contractions	uses contractions
sentences are often complex	sentences tend to be shorter	point form or sentence fragments are acceptable

EXERCISES

● Section A

1. The following advertisement appeared in the program for plays performed at the Shakespearian Festival at Stratford, Ontario. Think about the context and characterize the type of person likely to predominate in the audience. Then consider whether the tone, diction, and message are appropriate for the intended reader.

2. Compare two advertisements for different brands of the same kind of product (for example, cars, liquor, shampoo, perfume, soap). Analyze the intended reader, the message, and the tone of the ad as well as the effectiveness of its words and images in creating its appeal.

3. Assume that you want to start your own small business and are looking for some start-up money. You plan to create a written proposal. Think of two different types of people you might approach and do a receiver analysis for each, based on the questions suggested in this chapter. (You might, for example, approach a bank manager, wealthy friend, venture capitalist, or a relative.) What are the implications for the way you would write each proposal?

4. Which communications channel and medium would you choose in the following situations? Discuss the advantages of your choices.

   a) You have an idea for a new promotion but are not sure how it fits into the marketing manager's plans.

   b) You want department heads to know of modifications in procedures for firing unsatisfactory employees.

   c) You are the recent replacement for an autocratic manager in a department where morale is low. You want the employees to know about your priorities.

   d) You suspect an employee of padding his expense account.

    e) You want to know if managers in five different departments can attend a budget meeting on Friday at 9 o'clock.

    f) As Assistant to the President, you have received a favourable offer to buy a warehouse your company has for sale. Either the President or Chief Financial Officer needs to sign the offer-to-purchase document, but they are attending a convention at a large hotel in another city.

    g) You want to tighten the lax expense-allowance system in a department you've been put in charge of. Most of the employees have been there for years.

    h) Your plant manager is preparing for a visit from head office executives, and you need to give him recent sales figures.

    i) Two new stenographers have produced sloppy letters; they will be let go if they do not improve.

    j) You discover racist jokes on the washroom wall, and suspect that one or two of the employees working for you are responsible.

    k) Someone in the office complains to you, the office manager, that the calendar of nude pinups on an employee's office wall is offensive.

    l) As manager of the sales department, you want to congratulate all employees in the department, since the department collectively surpassed sales targets for the month by fifty percent.

5. Revise the following sentences so that the tone is courteous and conversational:

    a) There will be considerable cause for concern if the billings are loused up by the accounting department with respect to our most important client.

    b) Although I hate to disturb anyone who is sleeping, it would be a pleasure to have our order filled by your department on time for a change.

    c) If the ladies in the steno pool want a quick payment for their overtime typing work, they should come to my lair on the fourth floor before Friday.

    d) With respect to your letter of August 9, please be advised that you neglected to send the camera, which prevents us from assessing your allegations of poor performance.

    e) Mr. Miller, that customer's complaints are off the wall — but let's touch base about how to stroke him so that he doesn't take off with his business.

    f) Pursuant to my previous memo of the 28th, the new instructions for the photocopying machines should henceforth be duly distributed not only to supervisors in the marketing and sales departments but to all personnel using the aforesaid machines.

    g) Since I'm busy with important matters, instead of our usual weekly meeting, just let me know if your department will have the page proofs ready on time for a change.

6. Revise this impersonal memo from a senior human resources manager so that is has more personal pronouns. What is the effect of the revision?

    It is important to note a change in the dental plan for all Tricorp employees. As of July 1, there is an opportunity to recover 50% of the cost of orthodontal work. Details are set out in the attached form. The eligibility extends not just to employees but to their spouses and dependents.

    This improvement in benefits reflects the company's continued interest in the well-being of its workforce.

7. Fill in the blanks with words or phrases close in meaning to those provided, according to level of formality in each column.

Formal	Moderately Informal	Slang
_____	dead	bit the dust
domicile	_____	pad
_____	sick	under the weather
regurgitate	vomit	_____
converse	_____	rap
disorganized individual	messy person	_____
reprimand	_____	give the gears
_____	help	give a hand
tiresome	boring	_____
purloin	steal	_____
_____	crazy	nuts
intoxicated	drunk	_____
_____	fire	sack
give an affirmative response	say yes	_____
wealthy	rich	_____
sycophant	flatterer	_____

Notice how dated slang often seems and how moderately informal words are usually the plainest and most familiar.

8. Here is an example of a formal invitation to be sent to business clients. Change it to a moderately informal invitation for a pre-reception lunch on the same day for members of the firm.

John H. Charlesworth, FCA,
Senior Partner,
requests the honour of your presence
at a reception
to celebrate the fiftieth anniversary
of Holden & Gunn
on Thursday, June twentieth
at six o'clock
in the Empire Room, Regency Hotel.

R.S.V.P.
Mrs. Grace Philips
924-3289

 Section B

1. The External Relations Committee of your college has agreed to help raise funds for the blind people in the community by undertaking a charity car-wash on Saturday and Sunday afternoon. Despite some publicity, so far few students have volunteered to help.

Three members of the committee each draft a letter to be slipped into the student lockers along with a sign-up sheet. If you were the head of the committee which one would you pick? Analyze the three letters and give specific reasons for selecting one and rejecting the others. Take into account the intended receiver and reason for writing, as well as the tone and wording of the letters.

a) People have to take responsibility in this world. Taking part in the college's charity car-wash this weekend is the way to show that you are a responsible member of society. It should be brought to your attention that volunteer work is not something you get paid for but something you contribute to others. Having a lot of studying or essays to do is really no excuse for not helping those who are less fortunate, such as the blind in the community. Become a responsible member of society and join the college charity car-wash! Sign up today! Give to the blind!

b) After all the trouble the Executive External Relations Committee has taken to organize the charity car-wash for this weekend, it's indeed depressing that so few students have volunteered to help. The car-wash is the most important function of the Committee this year and it can make an inestimable contribution to the handicapped in the area. We have put in a lot of hours to arrange it, so get off your duff and help! The participation rate in this college is the pits. Do something about it and volunteer! We need more bodies! We need you!

c) The charity car-wash is our college's way of helping the blind people in the area. By giving just a few hours of your time on Saturday or Sunday afternoon this weekend, you can support the college and support the blind. We need more volunteers to fulfill our commitment to raise funds. Please help! Join the car-wash team. Give a few hours and have the satisfaction of helping others in this community. We need you — and so do they!

2. Joy MacArthur works in the promotion department of a Calgary toy manufacturing company trying to establish itself in western Canada. Before joining the company, she had staged a skating show in the city with the proceeds going to the local Society for Handicapped Children. Since the show had a sell-out audience of 4200 and netted $22 000 for the charity, the Society asked if she would produce the show again in April. Joy thinks she needs a week off work to do the job properly. Her supervisor suggests that she send a memo to the general manager, Philip Donaghue, asking the company to donate a week of her time to the show. Although Joy doesn't know him well, she does know that Donaghue has a marketing background and a good eye for business opportunities.

a) Create a point-form assessment of the reason for writing the memo and the intended reader.

b) Based on your assessment, evaluate the following draft of the memo:

10 January 1992

To: P. Donaghue, General Manager
From: J. MacArthur, Promotion Department
Subject: Company Donation to Skating Show

Last year I produced a successful skating show in Calgary, which wowed the crowd.

You may be interested to know it made big dollars for charity: $22 000 to be exact.

I've been asked to produce another show in April for the same charity — the Society for Handicapped Children. Since I would have to work like a dog to do the show properly, I would like to have a week's paid leave. Obviously it is a worthwhile cause and will benefit disabled children. I'm sure you realize that business has a responsibility to contribute to society as well as make a profit.

Please let me know your decision as soon as possible.

c) Rewrite the memo, following the strategies discussed in this chapter.

CHAPTER **3**

Writing Clearly

Since business writing is practical, an effective business style is not fancy but functional. It's simple and straightforward. Some writers deliberately stuff their writing with high-flown terminology and elaborate phrases, thinking that such a style will make them seem more intelligent or sophisticated. Don't make this mistake. Complicated writing is often confusing, and may make you seem confused. On the other hand, if your writing is lucid, you will seem a lucid thinker. It follows that if you really want to impress your most discerning associates, you will begin by making your writing clear.

Choosing Clear Wording

In selecting words, it's worth remembering the difference between the dictionary meaning of a word (its **denotation**) and the associative meanings or range of suggestions it calls up (its **connotations**). The words listed as synonyms in a thesaurus do not always mean the same thing. Some words have positive or negative associations, while others are more neutral. For example, the adjective *strong-minded* is grouped in a thesaurus with *strong-willed, hardy, firm, resolute, dogged, determined*. But what executive wouldn't prefer being called "strong-minded," "resolute," or "firm," to "dogged"? Take care, therefore, that the subtle shadings of the words you choose give the message you want.

Beyond this general prescription, here are some specific guidelines for producing clear wording.

Use Everyday, Plain Words

Through the centuries, English speakers have adopted and adapted a great many words from other languages, especially French and Latin. Yet the most common words in the English language are usually the oldest. The words children first learn are derived from the same Anglo-Saxon stock used since before A.D. 1000. Whether we recognize the reason or not, we usually choose these words for our conversations, since they seem most natural. Plain English words are also generally short — another good reason to use them.

By contrast, a lot of foreign derivatives, even if they have been in our vocabulary for years, still seem less natural. Nevertheless, while a string of them will make your writing seem artificial or pretentious, they can be effective when used sparingly.

French derivatives, for example, may give an aura of class. Every copywriter knows that you sell a fine wine by its bouquet rather than its smell, and a perfume by its fragrance. Every ad for upper level real estate seems to mention residences with foyers rather than houses with front halls. Even if you consider yourself a plain "meat and potatoes" kind of person, you surely would feel inelegant at a restaurant if you asked for pig rather than pork (from *porc*) or cow rather than beef (*boeuf*). The point is that in business writing you may choose French-based words or expressions for a particular effect, but you will generally avoid a lot of them if you don't want to seem phony. Notice the natural, direct quality of the words in the second column, compared with those in the first:

French Derivatives	Plain English
request	ask
desire	want
assist	help
endeavour	try
dine	eat
pursue	follow
commence	begin

You should also avoid a lot of Latinate words. Even if you have never taken Latin, you will recognize Latinate words by the attached prefixes (such as *pro, anti, ante, sub, super, ad, ab, ex, con, pre*) or suffixes (*ism, ent, ate, ite, ise* or *ize, tion*). Such attachments are useful in science, since they add precision to the description of structures and processes. (Think of common scientific verbs like *evaporate, crystallize, react, ingest, absorb*, and *liquefy*; or noun forms like *condensation, magnetism*, and *coagulation*.) Even in a formal but non-scientific context, the occasional Latinate word can add a feeling of scholarly dignity.

The trouble comes with too much: writing that is full of Latinate words is dense and difficult to understand. Business people who want to appear scientific often mistakenly fill their writing with unnecessary Latinisms, and nearly kill their meaning (to say nothing of their readers). Unfortunately, the Latinate disease is spreading, but you should try not to catch it.

1. **Be wary of newly-formed *ize* words** (or *ise* words, if using British rather than American spelling); for example, *incrementalize, utilize, prioritize, sensitize, finalize, operationalize, optionalize.* Although words like *maximize* and *minimize* have taken such firm root in our vocabulary that they are unlikely to be weeded out, it's a good idea to use plainer substitutes when you can.

Latinism	Plain English
finalize	finish or complete
operationalize	start
maximize	increase
optionalize	allow choice
prioritize	rank
utilize	use

2. **Avoid lengthy nouns that end in *ion* and are formed from verbs,** especially when the verb has an *ize* ending. Notice how the wording in the three columns becomes progressively more complex — and weaker — through the use of Latinisms:

Plain	Latinate Verb	Noun Form
order	systematize	systematization
toughen	desensitize	desensitization
start	operationalize	operationalization
make aware	familiarize	familiarization

Be Specific

To keep readers from second-guessing you, be as exact in your words as you can. You can often replace vague, "all-purpose" verbs like *involve, concern,* and *affect* with ones that are not as open to interpretation. In addition, use specific names, dates, times, and amounts to increase the clarity of a message. Admittedly, when you are referring to a group, it may be impractical to list each member or item. When you have a choice, however, be specific rather than general:

   x We are concerned about the environmental factors that affect two provinces.

   ✔ We are worried about (or, we are studying) the acid rain which threatens the lakes of Ontario and Quebec.

   x Management is concerned that your costing expert be involved in the planning process for the renovation.

   ✔ Hugh Willis wants your costing expert, Sheila Moore, to do estimates for the renovation.

   x Since you were involved in the report, I'd be interested in knowing about it sometime.

✔ Since you prepared the report, please call me next week to discuss it.

✗ Aitlin had a significant rise in sales recently.

✔ Aitlin's sales increased ten percent in the last six months.

Remember also that the pronoun *this* or *it* must refer to a specific noun. Writers often use one or the other in a vague way, so that it is unclear what exactly the reference is. Here is an example:

> We completed the project this week, by working until late Friday night, and by bringing in an extra typist. *This* pleased our client.

What does *this* refer to? Revising the phrase to *this completion* or *this extra work* makes the meaning clearer.

Avoid Jargon

Most areas of knowledge have a terminology which helps experts communicate with each other. The special terms allow them to say quickly and precisely what they mean, without having to resort each time to definitions or explanations. Scientists in particular rely upon technical terms, as a doctor does when describing a patient's medical condition to a colleague. The difficulty comes when people unnecessarily use jargon — complicated or unfamiliar terms — perhaps in an attempt to appear scientific or sophisticated. Rather than clarifying an issue, they obscure it. The teacher who wrote the following bit of jargon may not have been trying to appear sophisticated, but certainly was obscuring the message:

> Harry often exhibits overtly aggressive tendencies in interactive situations with his peer group, especially in extra-curricular activities.

What the teacher could have said was:

> Harry often fights with his classmates, especially outside the classroom.

People in business sometimes make the mistake of cluttering their writing with jargon to demonstrate their "insider knowledge." Instead of following this approach, remember that the brightest minds are those that can simplify a complicated issue, not complicate a simple one. The guideline is straightforward: use specialized terms if they are a kind of short form, making communication easier. Avoid jargon when plain English will do.

Writing Clear Sentences

Writing clear sentences is not only a matter of choosing plain, clear wording; it also entails using correct grammar and punctuation. What "correct" means is sometimes open to dispute. Acceptable grammar and punctuation are really conventions or customary practices; the way educated people speak and write over a period of years and a wide area becomes known as "standard" English. Although the standard gradually changes and will continue to change, following a standard is useful in business writing. It enables people from a variety of areas and backgrounds to understand one another readily. Most of the rules of grammar and punctuation are a way of making sense — of communicating efficiently.

Chapters 12 and 13 explain the important rules of grammar and punctuation, providing examples and exercises. If your knowledge of the rules is scant or rusty, refer to them. You can also take advantage of your ears and eyes:

1. **Listen to what you say.**   Practise reading your work out loud in a firm voice. Listen carefully. Children learn the language not by rules but by ear; writers also need to use their ears. If something doesn't "sound right" to you, chances are it won't to your reader. If you find yourself stumbling over a sentence, try reconstructing it in a simpler way. If you have to catch your breath several times in the middle, the sentence is probably too long. Break it up. Reading out loud, although it takes more time than a silent skim, will make you a better critic.

2. **Do a spot check.**   Eyes are a second line of defence against sentence errors. Try to remember the kinds of mistakes you made in the past and check especially for them. If you learn to spot your mistakes when you are editing, you will soon find that you make fewer of them.

Creating Clear Paragraphs

Paragraphs are difficult to define because they have so many shapes and sizes. They are needed, however, to help the reader follow the development and shift of ideas. These guidelines for paragraphing will help you maintain a sense of clarity and order in your writing:

1. **Create a new paragraph for a change in idea or topic.**   Paragraphs develop and frame ideas. By creating a new paragraph, you signal to a reader that you have finished developing one idea or an aspect of it and are switching to another. Of course, it is possible to outline several ideas in a single paragraph — for example, if you are briefly stating the reasons for some action. If you discuss an idea at any length in a paragraph, however, you should create a new paragraph when you move on to another idea.

2. **Make the first sentence the main point.**   The human mind prefers order to disorder, and always struggles to make sense out of an array of facts. By immediately providing that order in the key point or generalization, the reader (or listener) can more readily fit together the particulars that follow. The assimilation of information is easier.

Read the following paragraph. Notice that the main idea is at the end. Although this indirect order is perfectly reasonable, the busy or impatient reader will more readily catch the drift of the paragraph if the last sentence becomes the first one.

> From 1975 to 1990 in Baytown, the percentage of our citizens over 65 years doubled, and demographic analysis suggests that this trend will continue. Many seniors live lonely, isolated lives. Over a third are on small pensions and living below the poverty line. Our municipal government should assume more responsibility for identifying the particular needs of our seniors and coordinating services to them. We need a Coordinator of Seniors' Services for Baytown to help improve the quality of life of our older people.

Admittedly, not all paragraphs in good prose have a beginning key point or topic sentence; nor does every topic sentence have to appear at the beginning. In creating a persuasive argument, for example, you may want to lead indirectly to the key idea, by starting with particular facts and later pulling them together with a general statement. Yet for most of your business writing, begin each paragraph with the main point. Do a quick check on the sequence of paragraph beginnings in your writing. If you get a clear idea of the line of your thinking, your writing will likely seem well-ordered and logical to other readers.

3. **Vary paragraph lengths.**   The trend in business writing is to short paragraphs. They look less dense than long ones and are more inviting to read. Follow this trend and avoid long paragraphs. When you see a chain of long paragraphs (over eight or ten lines), try splitting some at an appropriate spot. On the other hand, a string of one-sentence or two-sentence paragraphs can make your writing seem choppy and undeveloped. Clearly, a single-sentence paragraph can effectively begin a letter or call attention to an idea, and short paragraphs are appropriate for news releases and brief correspondence. However, for reports or other complex discussions, the ideas need more development if they are to be accepted. Typical ways to develop an idea in a paragraph are by

— illustrating the idea;
— classifying the parts;
— revealing cause or effect;
— giving a solution to a problem;
— comparing or contrasting with another idea.

Of course, you may want to take more than a paragraph for any of these methods of expansion, but at the least, see that your paragraphs go beyond a simple point to a discussion of that point. If readers have commented that you need to explain your ideas more fully, the list provides good ways to do so.

Good writing in business usually comprises a range of paragraph lengths, from short (two or three sentences) to moderately long (seven or eight sentences), with most paragraphs somewhere in between. In considering your own paragraphs, try for variety; it's as much the spice of writing as of life.

4. **Keep the focus.**   Some paragraphs may not seem focused, even though the sentences are all on topic. The reason may be that they are constantly shifting the grammatical subject. Notice the difference in these two paragraphs (the grammatical subjects are in italics in each):

Poor:
Business *analysts* have noted the different ways managers operate. Sometimes all the *decisions* are made by a manager, and *employees* are given orders or procedures to follow. The *success* of this kind of manager is not long-term, since leaders are not developed as potential successors. The opposite *type* is the manager who avoids making decisions, tending to delay by forming committees and requesting endless studies. *Managers* of this sort are also not effective. *Employees* find themselves between these extremes with managers who encourage their participation in planning. *Responsibility* for making the final decision remains in the bosses' hands. *These* are effective managers.

Better:
As business analysts have noted, modern *managers* have different ways of operating. *Some* tend to make all the decisions, giving employees orders and procedures to follow. In the long term *they* are ineffective, since they do not develop leaders who can succeed them. Other *managers* avoid making decisions, tending to form committees and request endless studies. *They* are also ineffective. In between these extremes are *managers* who encourage employees to participate in planning, but who take final responsibility for decisions. These *managers* are effective.

The second paragraph is clearer and easier to read because it is better focused; more of the grammatical subjects are the same — managers.

You may wonder: If the grammatical subject is always the same, how can a paragraph not be boring? Here are two tips, both followed in the second paragraph above:

- Use stand-in words. These are **pronouns** and **synonyms** of the subject.
- Put something in front of the subject. Although the grammatical subject is most often at the beginning, it can also come later in a sentence. Putting a word, phrase, or clause in front of the subject ("As business analysts have noted," "in the long term," "in between these two extremes") makes the subject less noticeable.

5. **Link the ideas.**   Some words and phrases have a linking function, signalling to the reader the relationship between sentences and parts of a sentence. They act as both glue to the logic and guide to the transitions between ideas. By correct use of

the common linking words and phrases listed below you will help make your paragraphs more clear and coherent.

Link	Logical Relation
and again as well further in addition likewise moreover similarly	addition to previous idea
as a result of because since owing to	explanation of previous idea
although but yet by contrast despite even so however in spite of nevertheless on the other hand rather	change from previous idea
accordingly consequently for this reason hence so therefore thus	summary or conclusion

Numerical signals, such as *first, second, third*, are also useful linking words.

A Final Tip: Finish Writing Before You Revise

If you are constantly worried about correctness when you sit down to write, you may freeze at the switch and have difficulty getting started. A solution is to forget about grammar, spelling, or any kind of mistake and simply get your ideas down on the page. Many experienced writers find that working straight through the first draft is the best way to begin. Only after they've finished writing do they start revising and editing. This method will help you to avoid writer's block. You will have to leave a lot of time for editing and revision, however. Even if you revise as you go, you need to spend time editing. Clearly, the most effective writer is not the one who can bang out the first draft quickest but the one who edits best.

A useful order for editing is to "start big and finish small." That means to begin with the organization and development of ideas at the paragraph level. Then move to sentence style and word choice as it affects the flow and vitality of your writing. Finally, check the mechanics of grammar, punctuation, and spelling, as well as the graphical elements — typeface, headings, and illustrations. By starting with the big picture rather than the details, you will better address the reader's first question, which is "Do the ideas make sense?"

EXERCISES

● Section A

1. Choose plain English words or phrases for these more elaborate ones:

proceed	signification
indisposed	accumulate
humorous	materialize
conceptualize	construct
edifice	equivalent
inalterable	expedite
facilitate	reimburse
sufficient	transmit
attempt	approximately
operationalize	equitable
beneficial	domicile
occasion	inform
remuneration	

2. The meaning of a word depends in part on its associations for the receiver. The same word therefore may not have exactly the same connotations for everyone.

   Reorder the following groups of adjectives so that the words with the most positive connotations come first and those with the most negative come last:

   a) eccentric, strange, weird, unusual, individualistic

   b) strong, determined, domineering, confident, aggressive, tough

   c) subdued, meek, shy, reserved, retiring, unaggressive

   d) rash, daring, venturesome, devil-may-care, headstrong, incautious

   e) cunning, shrewd, artful, wily, astute, sharp, sly

   f) sensitive, warmhearted, sentimental, softhearted, impressionable, perceptive, thin-skinned

g) firm, steadfast, stubborn, inflexible, fixed, unbudging

h) curious, inquisitive, inquiring, prying, nosy, thirsty for knowledge

i) courteous, polite, refined, soft-spoken, obsequious, ingratiating

j) talkative, fluent, verbose, eloquent, chatty, glib, long-winded

3. Consider the following paragraph. Where is the most important idea? Could it be placed in a different postion?
   Ensure that the sequence of sentences allows a busy reader to easily get the point of the paragraph.

   > Our research has discovered that the Apex plants have outdated manufacturing processes. Senior management, which is highly centralized, autocratic, and secretive, has walled itself off from operations' employees, while allowing little local decision-making. Not surprisingly, the employees are not highly motivated and the company has not been as productive or profitable as the competition. It makes little sense to invest in Apex until its processes and management have changed.

4. Pick three or four paragraphs you have written for this course or another one — paragraphs you think are not clearly written. Analyze them carefully and list the reasons for the lack of clarity, using this chapter as a guide. Then revise the paragraphs. (Include the original when you hand your exercise in.)

5. Revise the following sentences, replacing many of the Latinisms, unnecessary noun phrases, and jargon with plain English:

   a) It is incumbent upon our sales representatives to make overtures of a positive nature to prospective clients prior to the finalization of their respective sales forecasts.

   b) In accordance with managerial policy, any intensification of effort on the part of employees leading to a maximization of production will be met with commensurate compensation.

   c) It is the decision of supervisory personnel that, with respect to employees, attendance charts will be maintained on a monthly basis.

   d) It should be noted that greater utilization of the company manual, which provides an outline of factory hazards, will have as a consequence an improvement in our safety record.

   e) We would be obliged if you would give an indication of the parameters of the delivery problem, so that we can interface with suppliers about this strategic matter, in the interest of effectuating an improvement.

   f) At this point in time we do not have plans under consideration for the termination of employees, but the bottom line is that in this period of decreased economic activity, the profitability factor must have top priority.

   g) All employees should endeavour to familiarize themselves with the new fire regulations so that personnel can be mobilized with due haste should there be an occurrence of fire in the vicinity of our offices.

6. Rearrange the following sentences so that something is in front of the subject:

   a) We cannot afford to hire a new secretary this month.

   b) I finished the report last Friday and sent it to be photocopied.

   c) She is very good at selling, despite her quiet manner.

d) We should be able to complete the assessment by June 30 at the latest, and possibly even earlier.

e) I plan to stick with my quote, whether or not it is underbid by competitors.

f) I was selected, along with three other supervisors, for the special project team.

● Section B

1. The following response to a report was written by a highly trained business manager. In groups of three,

a) record the time it takes to read the paragraph and understand its message;

b) underline all the words with prefixes and suffixes, except those suffixes showing tense (*ing* and *ed*);

c) rewrite the paragraph in plain English. Exchange your group's revision with another group's and compare the time it takes to read and understand the revision with the time it took to do the same with the original.

> While the initial study committee has made a skillful and in-depth analysis of the alternative resource mixes as they relate to the proposal in question, the optimal functions as selected by the committee's thematic projections would suggest a nonaffirmative response if the executive office were forced to make an immediate decision. In view of the paramount importance of the multifaceted aspects for the proposal, it is my recommendation that a special task force be created with the assigned responsibility of appropriately developing sound administrative options to the proposed implementation decision. Reliable and tested administrative procedures would enhance the practicality of the proposal and add to the incremental viability factors essential for the type of creative innovation that functions within established guidelines.

2. Write three or four paragraphs, intended for employees, which explain why plain English is needed in business correspondence and tell how to achieve it. Remember to practise what you preach.

3. From any publication, pick two or three paragraphs in which the wording is murky and difficult to understand. Try revising them. (You may want to look at business, legal, educational, or sociological articles — or government publications.)

4. The following paragraph has blank spaces where linking words or phrases would be useful.

a) Read the paragraph aloud as it now is.

b) Fill in the blanks with appropriate logical connectors.

c) Read the paragraph aloud again and note the difference in coherence.

d) Not all the blanks need to be filled. Consider which ones benefit most from logical connectors — those signalling added information, those providing explanation, or those signalling a change.

> We need more entrepreneurs, _____ they are the great job-creators in our economy. _____ many people who say they would like to start their own business are really dreamers. They have an urge to open a restaurant, an antique shop, or a travel agency, or even to produce some new household product _____ they are unlikely to act. _____ many of those who do try to get going

haven't really determined the unique service or benefit they would provide in order to compete successfully. To be an entrepreneur isn't easy. _____ , you need an idea that will sell. _____ , you need expertise in the area. _____ , you need to work long and hard for little initial return. If you have doubts about your idea, you will probably have difficulty selling it to customers or clients. _____ you will probably have difficulty raising the necessary capital. _____ if you are confident of the idea, and have the competence, discipline and drive to carry you through the rough beginnings, you will probably succeed.

5. The following paragraph is well focused, but it is boring because so many sentences start the same way. Revise it by substituting pronouns or synonyms for the subject, or by putting something in front of the subject.

> The Excalibur photocopier has many advantages. The photocopier is fast, producing a page in half the time of our present one. The photocopier can print in colour, unlike our present one. The photocopier is reliable as well, and has a six-month warranty on parts and service. The photocopier produces high quality reproduction so that much of the work we now send elsewhere could be done here. The photocopier will therefore have paid for itself in a year. The Excalibur photocopier is, in my opinion, the best buy for our needs.

CHAPTER 4

Writing with Impact

Readers infer writers' personalities from their writing style. A ponderous, boring writing style suggests, rightly or wrongly, a ponderous, boring person. Conversely, a lively style suggests a lively person. If you, like most people in business, want to create an impression that you are energetic and forceful, then you should try to develop an energetic, forceful style. Such a style is especially suited to management, where vigour and decisive action are virtues. In any business, you will clearly make more of an impact if you write with impact. To do so, you need to be concise and forceful in your wording and to structure sentences so that important ideas stand out.

Being Concise

Cut Out Clutter

Just as removing deadwood in a forest makes the remaining trees stronger, so getting rid of dead or useless words makes sentences more vigorous. Wordiness weakens. Thin out common cluttering phrases, such as the following, or omit them altogether:

Cluttering Phrases	Alternatives
at this point in time	now
due to the fact that	because
with regard to	about
it is possible that	maybe
it is probable that	probably
as a matter of fact	actually

for the purpose of	for
in the near future	soon
consensus of opinion	consensus
in the eventuality that	if
when all is said and done	(omit)
in all likelihood	likely
on a daily basis, on a regular basis	daily, regularly
in view of the fact that	since, because
be of the opinion that	think, believe
until such time as	until

Avoid Chains of *Which, Who, That* Clauses

A string of clauses beginning with *which*, *who*, or *that* can make a sentence seem cluttered. In many cases these clauses can be reduced, often to a single word:

    x The offices that are damaged will be renovated by two carpenters who are unemployed.

    ✔ The damaged offices will be renovated by two unemployed carpenters.

    x The two proposals, which were outlined earlier, will increase staff in the departments which have employees who are overworked.

    ✔ The two proposals, outlined earlier, will increase staff in the departments with overworked employees.

    x The files that are located in his office can be destroyed.

    ✔ The files in his office can be destroyed.

Use Adjectives and Adverbs Sparingly

The shotgun approach — spraying modifiers in the hope one will hit the mark — rarely works. One well-chosen adjective or adverb is more effective than several closely related ones:

    x He proposed an extraordinarily daring and bold strategy.

    ✔ He proposed a daring strategy.

    x Her campaign was imaginative, original, and creative and thus was highly acclaimed.

    ✔ Her innovative campaign was highly acclaimed.

Qualifying or intensifying adverbs should also be used sparingly. Strange as it may seem, *very* or *extremely* in front of an adjective is usually less forceful than a precise adjective by itself. "She is an imaginative person" packs as much wallop as "She is a very imaginative person" — and it avoids the risk of sounding gushy. Qualifiers such as *rather* and *quite* are also often unnecessary. Why say "rather costly" when you mean "costly" or "quite effective" when you mean "effective"?

Be ruthless with redundant adverbs. *Very unique,* or *completely finished* makes as much, or as little, sense as *rather bankrupt* or *quite dead.*

Being Forceful

Use Active Verbs

Verbs are the most energetic of words. Writers known for a forceful style usually have only a light sprinkling of adjectives and adverbs, but a variety of strong, specific verbs. The relative energy of the four main types of words can be charted:

strongest ←————————————————————————————→ **weakest**

verb   noun   adjective   adverb

However, an active verb has more energy than a passive verb, as the terms themselves suggest. With an active verb, the subject *does* something as an active agent:

> The engineer **discovered** that the casing was faulty.
>
> We **decided** to sell our shares.
>
> I **expect** an upturn in the bond market.

With passive sentences, the grammatical subject does not act but is acted upon. Sometimes a human agent is missing or buried in a modifying clause. It's not always clear who does what:

> The faulty casing **was discovered.** (Agent missing.)
>
> The faulty casing **was discovered** by the engineer. (Agent in modifying phrase.)
>
> It **was decided** that the shares would be sold. (Agent missing.)
>
> An upturn in the bond market **is expected** by us. (Agent in modifying clause.)

If your writing seems flat, it's probably filled with passive verbs. Try replacing most of them. Use active verbs to create "whodunnit" sentences, in which the subject **has done**, **is doing**, or **will do** something.

Passive verbs *are* appropriate in four instances:

- When the focus is on someone as the victim or unwilling recipient of an action:
  > The workers were let go when the plant was shut down.

- When you want to emphasize the thing acted on rather than the person acting:
  > The unsafe machine must be replaced.

- When you want to avoid an awkward shift of focus in a sentence or paragraph:
  > When fumes seeped into the cafeteria, they were first noticed by the cashier.

- When you want to avoid placing blame or seeming accusatory:

    The bill hasn't been paid.

Unless one of these exceptions applies, use active verbs.

Choose Verbs over Noun Phrases

Nouns, although stronger than adjectives and adverbs, are still less dynamic than verbs. Writing that is heavy with noun phrases can be a burden on the reader. As shown earlier, nouns ending in *ion* are especially troublesome. Try replacing noun phrases with verbs for a more energetic style:

    x Since they had an expectation of higher profits, management made a decision in favour of increased remuneration for the workers.

    ✓ Since they expected higher profits, management decided to pay the workers more.

As well, avoid clusters of nouns used as adjectives. In this instance a reordering, even if it adds a word, will make understanding easier.

    x employee benefits payroll deduction forms

    ✓ payroll deduction forms for employee benefits

    x plant energy conservation project

    ✓ project to conserve plant energy

Make People the Subject

Remember the "personality principle": we relate more to other people than to objects or abstractions. Newspaper editors know that human interest stories attract attention. Readers turn to a story about a particular laid-off worker before reading a statistical analysis of unemployment. A picture of a starving child has more impact than any abstract discussion of food shortages. Similarly, if you refer to individuals, your business writing will be more interesting:

    x We met two supervisors last night.

    ✓ We met Susan Arthurs and Harry Jones last night.

    or

    ✓ We met the supervisors, Susan Arthurs and Harry Jones, last night.

For greater stylistic impact, try to make people the grammatical subject, so that it's clear *who* has been doing what.

    x It was discovered that staggered hours were unacceptable to our supervisory staff.

    ✓ We discovered that our supervisors did not want staggered hours.

Business writers trying to be objective sometimes begin a sentence with an impersonal "it is" or "there is." Although these phrases, called expletives, can be useful, they more often contribute to lifeless prose. Where it's easy to do so, avoid them.

> x   It is necessary for her arrange new financing.
>
> ✓   She needs to arrange new financing.
>
> x   There are several remaining options for increasing office space.
>
> ✓   Several options remain for increasing office space.

Avoid Clichés

Clichés are truths so well-worn they are threadbare. Originally, many of them were colourful metaphors or similes, but through overuse they have lost their power. How does one determine what has become a cliché? A good rule of thumb is that if someone can supply the ending to a phrase, the phrase is a cliché. Apply the test to this passage:

> At this point in _____ , when inflation again threatens to rear its _____
> _____ , it goes without _____ that government spending should be
> curbed. In point of _____ , the nation as a whole should tighten its
> _____ . Of course, this is easier said _____ _____ . It stands to
> _____ , however, that those in the government corridors of _____ should
> lead the _____ . If they take drastic _____ to nip spending _____
> _____ _____ , then slowly but _____ our economic health will be
> _____ . With all due _____ , those economists in their ivory _____
> who encourage government deficits must beat a hasty _____ . Otherwise,
> without a question of _____ , inflation will again increase by leaps _____
> _____ . There is no time like the _____ . Government must strike while
> the iron _____ _____ to restore the faith of Canadians in a land of
> _____ . If our leaders do not act, we will all suffer for generations to
> _____ .

If a politician were to give this speech, we'd pity the listeners.

As well as being tiresome, some clichés are redundant. Sadly, many of these redundancies find their way into business writing:

mutual agreement	advance planning
end result	serious concern
future prospects	genuine opportunity
serious crisis	

Use Concrete Details and Examples

In business, we often need to discuss complex concepts such as economics, profitability, inflation, solvency, management, leadership, responsibility, and security. These are abstract terms, because we cannot discover them through any of the senses. We understand them only through intellect. By contrast, what is concrete we can see, hear, touch, or smell. For example, I cannot grasp ''insolvency'' through the senses, but I can see or touch an empty wallet or empty till.

Our reason allows us to generalize — to think abstractly. But since concrete words are more sensuous and need little intellectual effort to be understood, they make reading easier and more vivid than a string of abstractions would do. To explain moral concepts, Jesus used parables — stories about individual people. Similarly, ancient philosophers often used analogies — comparisons with familiar situations — to make complex ideas more accessible.

What is the guide for business writers? Use concrete details wherever you can. If you have a choice between an abstract word and a more concrete one, choose the concrete. When you do need to use a lot of abstractions, balance the mix through examples, analogies, or illustrations. This is one instance when a few words added to your writing will improve it.

Make Important Ideas Stand Out

One good way to make writing forceful is to emphasize important ideas and de-emphasize unimportant ones. You can achieve this kind of weighting in several ways.

1. **Place key words in strategic positions.**   The most emphatic parts of a sentence are the beginning and the end. Writers often naturally put a key idea at the beginning of a sentence, since this is the usual order of speech. It's less natural, but often more effective, to put a key word or phrase at the end. Notice the difference in impact between the following two sentences:

   > x   The hydro contract will be a money-maker, despite our early concerns.
   >
   > ✔ The hydro contract, despite our early concerns, will be a money-maker.

   In the first sentence, the key word, ''money-maker,'' is buried in the middle. The second sentence ends with more force.

   When a word or phrase is taken out of its usual place and put at the beginning it becomes more noticeable. When put at the end, it gets even more emphasis, especially if set off by a comma or dash. Compare these three sentences:

   > She usually gets along with the manager.
   >
   > Usually she gets along with the manager.
   >
   > She gets along with the manager — usually.

2. **Subordinate unimportant facts — or those you want to hide.**   Put a fact you want to stress in an independent or main clause, and put one you don't in a subordinate clause.

   > ✔ Although the advertising cost more than we anticipated, it brought many new clients.

If you put both facts in independent clauses, they will have equal stress, as in this sentence:

> The advertising cost more than we anticipated, but it brought many new clients. (Two independent clauses are joined by a coordinating conjunction.)

It's generally a mistake to put a "negative" fact in the main clause and a "positive" one in a subordinate clause, unless you want to stress the negative.

> x Although the advertising brought many clients, it cost more than we anticipated.

3. **Underline or boldface occasionally.**   Underlining or boldfacing key words is the simplest trick of all. Used sparingly, it can be an effective way of stressing information. Don't underline constantly as a substitute for other less intrusive ways of creating emphasis.

4. **Use contrast.**   Just as a jeweller emphasizes the sparkle in gems by placing them on dark velvet, so you can highlight your points through contrast. Read this unadorned sentence:

> We won this contract through hard work.

Now consider the impact of this contrast:

> We won this contract not through luck but through hard work.

Similarly, compare the force of these two sentences:

> The machine keeps breaking down because of faulty operators.
> The machine keeps breaking down, not because of faulty parts, but because of faulty operators.

5. **Use repetition.**   The rhythm created by repeating a key word or phrase can build the drama of a sentence. Because of the emotional force of this device, it should be reserved for special events or issues:

> To reach our profit target, we analyzed the product, we analyzed the market, and we analyzed the competition, but most of all we analyzed our own method of managing.

6. **Vary sentence length.**   Short sentences are emphatic. Long sentences, which meander gently, winding their way to a conclusion, are more reflective. In earlier days, when reading was largely confined to the leisure classes, readers were accustomed to extended sentences that would weary the typical reader today. The average sentence length two hundred years ago was about fifty words. Responding to the need to transfer information quickly and easily, good journalists and good business writers now favour shorter sentences. Their average sentence length is between twenty-one and twenty-five words.

A block of long sentences may put your reader to sleep. On the other hand, if every sentence is short, your writing may seem immature, like the staccato prose of a child's reader: "Look at Jane. See her jump." The moral? Check for variety when you are editing a passage, and break up blocks of long sentences. For special emphasis use a very short sentence, occasionally even a sentence fragment. Like this.

EXERCISES

● Section A

1. In each of the following sentences, decide which of the two independent clauses should have the main emphasis, and change the other clause to a subordinate one. For extra emphasis, try putting the main clause last.
   a) The safety inspector came, and we stopped work.
   b) I have worked outdoors, but I have no experience as a forest ranger.
   c) He didn't have anywhere to stay, and I invited him home.
   d) The costings are accurate and they are later than anticipated.
   e) She is disciplined and hard-working, and I think we should hire her.
   f) He will welcome your opinions and he must decide himself.
   g) I got a raise and I will take you out to dinner.
   h) The report was badly organized and difficult to read and it did not please Mr. James.
   i) In reports prepared for me, I expect careful work but I am not a nit-picker.
   j) You will learn a lot and you may get a lot of pressure working for Ann Hall.

2. Vary the position of the italicized word in each sentence to give it more emphasis. (In some sentences you may have to alter the wording slightly.)
   a) John found that firing incompetent employees was the most *distasteful* of all the jobs he had to do.
   b) In the end, he convinced the workers by his *actions* not by his words.
   c) Most members of our team respect Mary's *ability*, whether or not they like her sharp tongue.
   d) When the firm was small, our work seemed more *stimulating*, because we were always doing a variety of tasks.
   e) Mr. Marks is clever, but he is a pompous *bore* in his speeches, I think.

3. Reduce the relative clauses beginning with *which*, *who*, or *that* in these sentences:
   a) The boy whom we saw yesterday is one of the applicants for the job which was advertised on Saturday.
   b) The project that is most important this week is the proposal for the government contract that Seymour hopes to get.
   c) I hope that the errors that we made in the report will not have repercussions that will be serious.

d) That huge woman, who wore a leopard skin coat and large hat which matched, drove a red sports car which had a convertible top.

e) I'm sure that the problem, which is complicated, will finally have a solution that is simple.

4. In the following sentences, put active verbs in place of the nouns ending in *ion*, or any other nouns.

a) Jones made a suggestion favouring the acquisition of a new coffee machine.

b) There is a recommendation from the investigator favouring the continuation of payments to the Centre.

c) Our hope is that the introduction of fitness programs by the company will bring about an improvement in employee health and a reduction in absenteeism.

d) It is the boss's expectation that, when we have an increase in the sales staff, we will have an increase in earnings.

e) Now that I've made an arrangement for the installation of new carpets in the office, I have an inclination to get the walls painted.

f) Despite the engineer's plans for the inspection of the building, his delay in the introduction of changes allowed a continuation in the deterioration.

g) After an investigation of options, it is our intention to make a quick decision about the method of organization for the seminar.

h) We have no indication that the lawyers have yet made an allocation of the proceeds realized from their settlement of the lawsuit.

i) Although we asked for clarification and elaboration of the data by the controller, we made no attempt at verification.

5. Use simpler or more energetic substitutes for the phrases in italics:

a) *It is our understanding* that the packaging division *maintains approximately* ten checking accounts; *it is recommended* that these be consolidated *at an early date*.

b) *Subsequent* to our investigation, a report will be provided *for the purpose* of outlining procedures for *the procurement* of new equipment.

c) *It is our opinion* that *in order to achieve a reduction* of overdue accounts you should require a deposit *in the amount of* 20% *prior to* delivery.

d) *In view of the fact* that the control checks *were not performed in accordance with* the *aforementioned* guidelines *on a regular basis*, our decision must be *held in abeyance*.

e) *There are possibilities* for our delaying the contract *until such time as* we can *arrange a better allocation of* resources.

f) *As per our discussion* last week, *it is likely that* we will *make a submission of* budgets *on a quarterly basis*.

● Section B

1. Make the following sentences more forceful. Get rid of clichés and clutter (some of it jargon), and use personal subjects and precise, active verbs.

a) It is to be hoped that our sales figures for the month of February will show a consistently steady improvement.

b) Considerable concern existed on the part of the directors that our expenditures would be in excess of revenue and that the end result would be bankruptcy.

c) June Briant was quite involved in the planning of our campaign and her contribution has been recognized by us as a factor in its success.

d) Due to the fact that permission has been granted by head office for employees to have an extra day of holiday over Christmas, Christmas parties for all departments should be completely restricted to hours not normally part of the working day.

e) The problem of employee dissatisfaction has been increased by the unwillingness on the part of the supervisor to make an investigation of the complaints made by employees with regard to ventilation.

f) If an expansion of the plant is to be made in the near future, the inclusion of day-care facilities should be a matter for immediate and serious consideration by management at the planning meeting which will be held in January.

g) At this point in time, there is a decision to be made by Jim about hiring a full-time accountant, in view of the fact that the work of the accountant who is part-time entails a considerable number of overtime hours.

h) An announcement was made in the speech of the president that the end result of management's introduction of robots in the factory, which is scheduled for this year, will not be the termination of employees.

i) It is anticipated that the full total of the damage which was caused by the fire can only be assessed by engineers who are specially trained, but we have made a very rough guess of approximately $220 000.

j) If it is the immediate priority of the manager to effect an increase in sales, then it stands to reason that an interface session with key employees should be instituted on a regular basis to discuss the parameters of the sales effort.

k) There is a valid reason why the aforementioned trespasser, who was discovered by the security guard in the vicinity of the computers prior to the fire, was not submitted to a rigorous police interrogation using tried and true methods.

2. Jake Hardy has written this draft of a letter to a longtime friend and business associate, Martin Field. Hardy is replying to an invitation to a lunch celebrating Field's promotion to Marketing Manager at Warren Enterprises. In groups of three, discuss the weaknesses in wording and style. Improve the letter.

Dear Martin

Regarding your new job at Warren Enterprises, it's indeed a pleasure to learn that you are now Marketing Manager. In this day and age of cut-throat competition, it's extremely gratifying when a man of very great talent and tried-and-true ability gets his just deserts so to speak.

It's a genuine disappointment that I cannot be present at your celebration party which will be held on Monday, the twelfth of July, due to the fact that I will be otherwise engaged at a meeting. The meeting, which has been scheduled since last month, is with a wealthy investor, who is from New York and who is coming here for the purpose of making an investment in a business. When all is said and done, it's to be hoped that the final result is worth the expenditure of effort on my part at this point in time.

Let me repeat my regret at the impossibility of my presence on that occasion of joyous celebration. In my absence please extend my sincere best wishes to your better half.

3. The following sentences contain abstractions or generalized statements. In a sentence or two, help to clarify each or make it more vivid by adding a concrete illustration or example.

   a) Pensioners suffer when inflation is high.

   b) Many Canadian entrepreneurs have already penetrated the American market.

   c) A country's deficit cannot keep increasing without causing severe problems.

   d) The media have too much influence on the political process.

   e) Expanding public transit makes more economic sense than expanding the road system.

   f) We need more pollution controls to protect a deteriorating environment.

4. As a way of fostering community relations and of providing work experience for its art students, Metro College held some Saturday morning art classes for young children in the area. Below is the release form the parents were asked to sign before enrolling their children. Revise it, keeping in mind that the parents have varied cultural and educational backgrounds.

   ### Release Form for Children's Art Classes

   In consideration of the aforementioned child being permitted to participate in the aforementioned program, I, as parent/guardian of the said child, do hereby release and forever discharge and agree to save harmless and indemnify in full Metro College and all of their respective agents, officials, servants, and representatives, from and against any and all kinds of actions, causes of actions, claims, liabilities, costs and expenses and demands, in respect of death, injury, loss or damage, occurring just prior to, during or subsequently to any part of the aforementioned program and whether on the premises of the Metro College or otherwise, to the person or property of the said child, howsoever caused, and arising out of the said child being permitted to attend or in any way take part in the program as a participant.

   (Signature of parent/guardian)   date

   By submitting this application, I acknowledge having read, understood and agreed to the waiver release indemnification.

5. A manager drafted this short message to his workers as part of a New Year's issue of the company newsletter. Try to improve it by getting rid of the clichés and clutter and making some of the points more concrete. You may have to add some details.

   Times are changing and things aren't what they used to be. No longer are North Americans on top of the world with regard to business. The challenge from foreign parts is not to be taken lightly. Indeed, in the near future it may pose a grave threat to the livelihoods of countless people.

   At this point in time, we must all bear in mind that profits are earned. Nobody owes us a living. Life is not a bowl of cherries. When all is said and done, if we're going to become number one in our own business, we've got to keep our nose to the grindstone. Needless to say, I'm not pointing a finger at individuals, but have as my intention to spur us all on to greater effort as a team on a regular basis. I'm of the opinion that those of us in the seat of power and those who are not must join hands in an all-out attempt to become top of the heap in our business. As we face the New Year let us respond to this challenge. Victory is within our grasp!

CHAPTER 5

Letters and Memos: Giving Routine and Good News

New electronic equipment gives us new choices about the the medium for communicating. Yet the mainstay of business correspondence remains the memo or letter, however it is sent.

Normally, letters go to people outside the writer's organization and memos go to insiders. Although the formats differ, the principles of organizing are the same. For simplicity, the discussion here will refer mainly to letters, but the advice applies equally to memos. Since "time is money" in any business, it pays to be able to write both efficiently.

Different cultures have different conventions for letter-writing, in layout, phrasing, and punctuation. As international trade expands, don't make the mistake of assuming that the way you are used to seeing business letters is the only acceptable way to write them elsewhere, even in countries where the language is English. Although the advice in this chapter applies to North American custom, when communicating with others be prepared to be flexible in your attitude and sometimes in your approach.

Letter Format

In all cultures, appearance counts. Just as people's looks often influence how they are judged, so the look of your letter will influence its reception. The quality of the paper, the typescript, and the layout can all help to make a good-looking letter. For most business letters you should use good quality paper in white or ivory. The typescript can vary from letter to letter but should be consistent within each.

The layout is probably the most important aspect of appearance. Don't crowd the message. It's better to use two pages rather than squeeze information on one page. Remember to frame a letter with white, by

— centering the message;
— leaving 2.5 cm (1 in.) margins at the top and right hand side and 4 cm (1½ in.) margins at the bottom and left-hand side. The lines within each paragraph are always single-spaced.

A business letter has a standard order:

1. **Company letterhead**   If the paper has no letterhead, first type the company name (if there is one) and the address, including the full name of the province and the postal code.

2. **Date**   Use numerals rather than words for the day ("21" rather than "twenty-one"), but you may put the day before or after the month:

    June 18, 1992 *or* 18 June 1992.

    You may also use a fully numerical date, but this can be confusing, since the order varies. Americans usually follow a month-day-year order (06 18 92). The accepted international method, however, is to move from large to small — from year to month to day (92 06 18). If you think a numerical date might confuse the reader, stick with spelling the month.

3. **Reader's name, title and company, and the full company mailing address**   If you don't know all the exact details, including correct spelling of the reader's name, call the company's switchboard operator or receptionist, who usually has a complete listing of employees.

4. **The salutation**   "Dear _____" is standard. Wherever possible, use the person's name and courtesy title (Dr., Professor, or whatever). This personal approach will help to establish a rapport. The computer has made it easier to use names even on form letters. Many firms with mass mailings for sales or requests for donations follow this personal route. If you can, do the same with all your business letters.

    What if you are addressing a group, or if you can't determine the reader's name, sex, or preferred form of address? Here are some options:

    • When you don't know the name, you have a choice. You may still use the traditional "Dear Sir or Madam," although this salutation seems increasingly old-fashioned. You may also give the person's title or status: "Dear Personnel Manager" or "Dear Customer."
    • When addressing a group, you may begin with "Sales Representatives" or "Health Care colleagues" or "Members" or any other common identifier. In each case, omit "Dear."
    • For a person whose sex is unknown, you may simply use the first initial: "Dear L. Jonas." Although less common, you can also use M. to cover both sexes.

- For a woman whose marital status or preferred form of address is unknown, use Ms.
- A way out of all these difficulties is to follow the recent practice of replacing the salutation with a subject line (see below). Sometimes the elimination of the salutation is accompanied by an elimination of the the complimentary close, producing what is called American Simplified Style. The disadvantage is that the letter will seem less personal.

5. **Subject line** A simple underlined heading, such as *Retirement Party for Jan Weims*, although optional, can quickly provide to a busy reader the focus of the letter. It can either replace the salutation or be put below or above it.

   Make the subject line as specific as possible. Instead of a vague reference, such as *Benefits*, say something like *Changes to Dental Insurance Plan*.

6. **Attention line** Occasionally the phrase "Attention Ms. X" replaces the salutation. An attention line is useful when you are dealing with a particular department of a company — for example, when you are writing to an order desk. An attention line will put the letter in the hands of the appropriate person but indicates that others can also deal with it.

7. **Body** The body should be placed in the middle of the page. To achieve this balance, vary spacing between the parts — namely between the letterhead, date and reader's name. Leave extra lines at the top (after the letterhead and the date), and again at the bottom (after the body of the letter).

   Since the body is the key part of the letter, the method of selecting and organizing the content will be discussed more fully later.

8. **Complimentary close** The simple ending, "Sincerely," or "Yours sincerely," is becoming the standard form, acceptable for most purposes. Professional firms that want to be more formal sometimes use "Yours truly," or "Yours very truly." On the other hand, writers who know their reader well may prefer the less formal "Cordially" or "Regards."

   Follow the close with your signature. Type out your name in full four lines underneath the close, unless it is already part of the letterhead. If you are writing to someone who doesn't know your position, add your title below your name. With someone you write to frequently, you may choose to sign only your first name, even though your full name may be typed below.

Other Notations

1. **Reference initials** often appear at the bottom left of the page — Sometimes the sender's initials in capitals, followed by a colon and the typist's initials in lower case:

   MP:jc.

Other times just the typist's initials appear. If you are the typist, you can simply omit this notation altogether. You can also omit it if you want your letter to be more informal.

2. **Indicate enclosures** that are to go with your letter by putting a notation below the reference initials:

   Enclosures: 2

3. **Indicate copies** by typing "c" for photocopies, followed by a colon and then the initials and last name of the readers:

   c: A. Smith
      R. Hadji

4. **Page headings** are useful if the letter continues over one page. At the top of additional pages put the reader's name and the page number (begin with page two). Some organizations also include the date. The paper of any page after the first is always plain — without a letterhead.

Layout Variations

Although you may occasionally see other layouts, there are three common styles:

1. **Traditional style**   The date, close, and signature begin at the centre of the page. Each paragraph is indented five spaces. In the past, the indentation at the left was the only signal for a new paragraph, but recently writers have tended also to leave a line blank between paragraphs, to increase visual variety and ease of reading. In other words, the traditional style has been modified to incorporate the central feature of a block style — paragraphs are blocked off by space between them.

2. **Full-block style**   Every line begins at the margin, including the date, close, and signature. A new paragraph is formed by leaving an extra line rather than by indentation at the margin. This arrangement is easiest for the typist, but the left-side emphasis can look lopsided, and the lack of indentation makes the text slightly harder to read.

3. **Modified block style**   Each line in the body begins at the margin, but the date, close and signature begin at the centre. This layout produces a more balanced look than the full block style.

Punctuation Options

Within the body of a letter or memo, always use standard punctuation. With the other parts of a letter you have options. Although the custom of your organization may determine your choice, the trend is to less punctuation. Here are the two most popular approaches, as illustrated in Figures 5.1 and 5.2:

Open Punctuation

- For the date and reader information, use punctuation only between the parts of a line (Oakville, Ontario) but not at the end of a line.
- The salutation and complimentary close have no punctuation at the end.

FIG. 5-1 Full-Block Style of Letter Layout (Open Punctuation)

SIGNET
32 Maple Street
Sudbury, Ontario P4E 2K1

92 02 24

Dr Hollis Deeks
22 Princess Street
Brandon, Manitoba
R5A 6D2

Dear Dr Deeks

Re: xxxxxxxxxxxxxxxxxxx

xxxxxxxxxxxxxxxxxxxxxxxxxxxxxxxxxxxxxxxxxxxxxxxxxxxx
xxxxxxxxxxxxxxxxxxxxxxxxxxxxxxxxxxxxxxxxxxxxxxxxxxxx
xxxxxxxxxxxxxxxxxxxxxxxxxxxxxxxxxxxxxxxxxxxxxxxxxxxx
xxxxxxxxxxxxxxxxxxxxxxxxxxxxxxxxxxxxxxxxxxxxxxxxxxxx
xxxxxxxxxxxxxxxxxxxxxxxxxxxxxxxxxxxxxxxxxxxxxxxxxxxx

xxxxxxxxxxxxxxxxxxxxxxxxxxxxxxxxxxxxxxxxxxxxxxxxxxxx
xxxxxxxxxxxxxxxxxxxxxxxxxxxxxxxxxxxxxxxxxxxxxxxxxxxx
xxxxxxxxxxxxxxxxxxxxxxxxxxxxxxxxxxxxxxxxxxxxxxxxxxxx

xxxxxxxxxxxxxxxxxxxxxxxxxxxxxxxxxxxxxxxxxxxxxxxxxxxx

Sincerely

Hugh Moore
Controller

HM:tb
Enclosure

Mixed Punctuation

- The date and reader information, as above, have punctuation only between parts of a line.

FIG. 5-2   Modified Block Style of Letter Layout (Mixed Punctuation)

Alison Construction Company

29 Bay Street
Halifax, Nova Scotia B4C 1F5

May 4, 1992

Mrs. Geraldine Scott
22 Cherry Lane
Fredericton, New Brunswick
EB7 2F8

Dear Mrs. Scott:

xxxxxxxxxxxxxxxxxxxxxxxxxxxxxxxxxxxxxxxxxxxxxxxxxx

xxxxxxxxxxxxxxxxxxxxxxxxxxxxxxxxxxxxxxxxxxxxxxxxxx
xxxxxxxxxxxxxxxxxxxxxxxxxxxxxxxxxxxxxxxxxxxxxxxxxx
xxxxxxxxxxxxxxxxxxxxxxxxxxxxxxxxxxxx

xxxxxxxxxxxxxxxxxxxxxxxxxxxxxxxxxxxxxxxxxxxxxxxxxx
xxxxxxxxxxxxxxxxxxxxxxxxxxxxxxxxxxxxxxxxxxxxxxxxxx
xxxxxxxxxxxxxxxxxxxxxxxxxxxxxxxxxxx

xxxxxxxxxxxxxxxxxxxxxxxxxxxxxxxxxxxxxxxxxxxxxxxxxx

Sincerely,

Jim Alison

Jim Alison

- The salutation ends with a colon (*Dear Dr. Fortier:*). If the letter is personal rather than related to business, use a comma instead.
- The complimentary close ends with a comma (*Sincerely,*).

Memo Format

Memos are the most common form of business writing, since most correspondence is within a company rather than between companies. Many businesses have specially printed memo paper for ease and uniformity in sending messages. If you don't have such memo paper, you have some choices for format. Here is a typical one:

— At the top left side of the page, put on a separate line each of the following headings:

> *Date:* xxxxx
> *To:* xxxxxxxxxxx
> *From:* xxxxxxxxxxxxxx
> *Subject:* xxxxxxxxxxxxxxxxxxxxxxxxxxxxxxxxxxxxxxxxxxxxx

Memos have no salutation, complimentary close, or signature, although some writers add their initials or name at the bottom or after the typed name.

FIG. 5-3   Example of a Memo

BEAVER CORPORATION

December 11, 1992

To: R.W. Woods, S. Fenner
From: J. Stanley
Subject: Meeting of Safety Committee

Our meeting is rescheduled for this Thursday at 2 p.m. in my office.

We'll be discussing the consultant's report. Sue Hill has a copy if you need one. Please read it before the meeting.

Although memos are often written informally to familiar associates, don't be misled into thinking they don't much matter. Since they often convey important information or ask for something to be done, they need to be as precise as a letter. Like any form of correspondence, they can have a big impact — for good or ill. Make your memos work for you.

Guidelines for All Letters and Memos

1. **Keep to one topic.**   Do not, for instance, give a sales report and a staffing request in the same memo. Rather, for each separate topic send a separate memo or letter. The reasons are practical: the reader will remember more easily information relating to one topic, and the correspondence can be categorized for filing more easily.

   An exception to this rule is correspondence supplying miscellaneous routine information. A department head, for example, might be asked to supply the boss with a monthly report containing different categories of information, but even in this case, the overall subject is really departmental performance.

2. **Be brief.**   The well-known KISS formula for business writing — "Keep It Simple, Stupid!" should be amended to "Keep it Short and Simple." Procter and Gamble, the successful soap-selling empire, insists on one-page memos, and spends considerable time training new recruits to do them well. Even if the reader of your letter or memo is not as insistent on brevity, there is a subtle psychological barrier to turning a page. The moral is obvious: keep to one page if you can. If you cannot, at least be as brief as possible.

3. **Make sure the information is complete.**   This advice might seem a tall order if a one-page memo or letter is the goal. How can one be complete and brief at the same time? It may take a little practice. To be complete means to include all the information needed for a letter to achieve its purpose. If you are placing an order, you obviously will need to include all the details that will permit the reader to fill it. If the supplier has to telephone or write to you about some aspect you have forgotten, your letter was incomplete.

   Incompleteness is often a result of vagueness. If you write to a plant manager, saying, "Mr. Biggs wants to meet some employees on his next visit," you likely will get a quick call asking who exactly he wants to meet, why, and when he is planning to visit. The information would have been more complete if you had said, "During his June visit, Mr. Biggs wants to meet the shift supervisors and the employees on the safety committee to discuss the safety program. I'll let you know when he decides the date." Remember that to be brief doesn't mean to omit details, but to sift out those that don't matter.

Complete information means not just the facts, but also some indication of *why* the information matters. You are trying to keep the reader from merely shrugging and saying "So what?" In other words, if you want people to turn off their computer monitors at night or to come to a meeting, give the reason as well as the request. If you are announcing a new policy, show how it affects the reader.

4. **Keep the focus "you-centred."**   Since correspondence is between people, not machines (even if you use machines to write or send it), make it personal and centred on the reader. *You* and *your* are useful reminders to a reader that you are aware of the individual. Try to use these pronouns throughout the correspondence, and especially in the opening and closing sentences. Instead of saying, "I received the report today," say

> "Your report arrived today"
>
> *or*
>
> "Thank you for your report."

Even when you are not using the pronoun *you* or the reader's name, keep the message focused on the *reader's* interest rather than the writer's.

   x We require a signed contract before starting on the project.

   ✓ Your project will begin as soon as you sign the contract.

Using the reader's name in the body of the letter is useful occasionally to emphasize the personal touch, but don't overdo it. Once is enough in a letter, and make sure you use the reader's name only in connection with something positive.

   x Mrs. Brown, your account is overdrawn.

   ✓ Mrs. Brown, we're extending your line of credit by $500.00.

5. **Be positive.**   Naturally you don't want to make the reader feel irritated or defensive. By substituting positive for negative phrases, you can help maintain a friendly, courteous tone. Avoid words that have an accusing tone and those suggesting a loss or fault rather than benefit.

   x You neglected to give us the name of your bank, so we cannot deposit the money there yet.

   ✓ As soon as you send us the name of your bank, we can deposit the money there directly.

   x We are not responsible for administering the project after June 30.

   ✓ We will be responsible for administering the project until June 30.

Similarly, avoid negative words and phrases, such as

blame, error, mistake, fault, careless;
you failed to;
you disregarded;
surely you don't;
you claim (or allege).

A Note on Word Processors

The computer with its word-processing function is changing the way companies handle both internal and external correspondence. It is quickly replacing the typewriter — and the typist — that business writers have long relied on.

A word processor allows you to

— personalize form letters cheaply and quickly;
— make major and minor changes more easily;
— store information (old correspondence or other records) in less space and retrieve it quickly.

Developers of computer software — the programs that run on computers — have spent millions of dollars developing word processing packages that are easy to use. The features may vary from program to program, from Wordstar to Wordperfect, Microsoft, Multi-Mate, Display Writer, or any other. Yet they are all user-friendly. Even if you think of yourself as a computer dunce and can hardly type, your efforts learning to use a word processor will be repaid by time saved in revising and editing. In more and more businesses, managers are discovering the benefits of drafting and editing their own work on a word processor, rather than relying on busy or scarce typists.

Inexpensive, short courses are available in many places to help you master the word processor. Libraries and bookstores stock paperback guides for every level from beginner to advanced specialist. If you plan to learn on your own, with a software manual as your guide, here are a few tips:

1. **First learn only what you need to know to accomplish your task.** You will get frustrated if you try to learn everything at once. Start by learning the basic commands that will allow you to put words on the screen. Once you have discovered how easy it is to input information, then try the commands for correcting mistakes by deleting letters or inserting words. Next, move to other editing commands that will let you quickly insert, delete, copy, or move whole blocks of text.

   The point is to bother only with what's needed to do your present writing job efficiently. Become comfortable with these commands, and you will find you are using your word processor more and more. Gradually increase your repertoire as you need to, for such tasks as creating columns or addressing form letters through a mail-merge process.

2. **Regularly save what you have written.** One of the few really discouraging moments for computer users comes when a long passage of work is lost — irretrievably wiped out. You can avoid this discouragement by using the "save" command at regular intervals — say, every twenty minutes. Remember that you can lose work not only by pressing the wrong keys or by quitting before saving; you can lose it also if the power goes off, or if some other technological breakdown occurs.

   When your work is important — for example, if you've worked long and hard on the draft of a report — make an extra copy on a separate disk.

3. **Use a spell-check as a proofreading aid.** Most of the recent word-processing packages have a capacity to check spelling. This, of course, is a real boon to poor spellers. A spell-check will also catch most typographical errors — a benefit to poor typists. However, don't depend on it to catch all of them, since it cannot spot actual words that are wrongly used. For example, it will let pass *there* when you meant *their*, *accept* when you meant *except*, and *pat* instead of *part*. Nonetheless, using a word processor can cut a proofreading job in half by spotting most of the slips that a writer, who knows what's *supposed* to be on the page, may miss.

Structuring Correspondence:
The Direct Approach

Size up your reader: will he or she be receptive to what you have to say? If so, the primary rule is, "Get to the point quickly." The first sentence in a routine or good-news letter should contain the key information. You don't have to be a psychologist to realize that when people are eager for information or curious about something, they become impatient with unimportant preliminaries. A business letter can lose the reader's interest by a flat opening. As a general rule, emphasize the opening news by keeping it in a separate paragraph.

This organizational approach is variously called the "direct approach," the "top-down approach," or the "pyramid approach." Journalists use it to report the news, since people read what is at the beginning of news stories but often don't continue to the end, especially if they have to turn a page. And since the end of a news story contains the least important points, editors feel free to trim off the bottom to fit a given space, without fear of distorting the story.

The basic pattern of a routine or good-news letter is easy to follow if you remember the "put it up front" principle:

1. Put the most important points first.
2. Give supporting details.
3. End with a goodwill statement.

A goodwill statement is really a final cordial touch — a sentence which expresses appreciation, offers extra help, or looks to future relationships. Such a finishing touch will strengthen the personal, courteous tone of a business letter. In a routine or good-news letter, rather than putting such a goodwill statement at the top, as beginning writers tend to do, put it at the bottom.

Poor:

Thank you for your order. We at Laurentian Packaging are happy to do business with small companies such as yours and look forward to future orders. The corrugated cartons you ordered on April 4 were in stock in the Aries line, which has a reinforced bottom. The shipment of 1500 should arrive in Brandon on April 15. We followed your request and shipped them by train. They were sent this morning.

Thank you again for your business.

Better:

The 1500 corrugated cartons you ordered were shipped by train this morning. You should receive them in Brandon on April 14. They are in the new Aries line, which has a reinforced bottom.

At Laurentian Packaging we are happy to do business with developing companies such as yours and will promptly fill any of your future your packaging needs.

Often the first sentence of a letter or memo is weakened by an unneeded opening phrase. Here are some "throat clearers" that will never be missed:

This letter is to tell you that . . .

I would like to inform you that . . .

With regard to your memo . . .

Pursuant to your letter of May 20 . . .

Avoid this kind of clutter. Instead, start right in with the main point. On rare occasions, as a legal technicality, it may be useful to refer to the date of previous correspondence, but most of the time it's not. You needn't fear that you will seem too abrupt, as the example above illustrates.

A Caution about Directness

Before using the direct approach, remember that directness is a western, and especially a North American, value. In other cultures, such as the Japanese, to be direct is often to be rude. Even among European nations, differing degrees of directness are appropriate. For example, Germans are usually more direct than the French. Within Asian cultures, Hong Kong Chinese, exposed to western ways, are used to being more direct than people in the rest of mainland China. The Japanese habitually favour an indirect approach, even for routine requests. When communicating with people from other cultures, therefore, first find out what level of directness or indirectness is customary.

For most business correspondence in North America, however, the direct approach is the best approach. Many different kinds of letter and memo fall into this category.

Probably the most common are routine requests, routine responses to requests, and instructions. Although written less often, letters of thanks and congratulations can also be an important part of the job for managers who deal with a lot of people.

Routine Requests

Placing an order, asking for information or credit, and making a routine claim are all situations which call for the direct approach. In each case,

— make sure the request is explicit rather than merely implied;
— supply all the details needed for the receiver to fill the request. In making an application for personal credit, for example, give details of your employment and your banking arrangements;
— if the request has several parts, itemize them, using a list format. If there are many items, group them into categories.

Placing an Order

Most large companies either place orders by phone or have standard order forms. If you have to create your own order letter, the key is to make the details specific, complete, and easy to follow:

1. Begin with a statement indicating you are placing an order.
2. When you need a number of items, arrange the details in columns, which can be headed *Quantity*, *Model* (or *Stock No.*), *Description*, *Unit Price* and *Total Price* (or whatever is appropriate). The combined total price can easily be tallied by adding up the right-hand column.
3. Give specific advice about the method of shipment and address, the method of payment, and the delivery date.
4. End with a courtesy close, although you may choose to omit this if you are regularly sending orders to the same company.

Requesting Information

When you want information from someone who will receive no direct benefit from supplying it — such as details of company policies or procedures — make sure the request is as brief as possible. A rambling list which seems to ask for the moon may end up getting nothing.

The following request for information about a prospective employee is vague about the requirements of the job. It's also unselective and repetitive.

> I am considering employing Arthur Seaburg in my company. I understand that he has worked for you in the past. Can you please give me information about his educational background, job responsibilities, work habits, ability to get on with others, organizational ability, health, initiative, reliability, and experience. He has named you as a source for a reference and we would appreciate it very much if you could supply the above information.

FIG. 5-4   Example of Letter Placing an Order

The Callaway Group

45 Princess Street
Kingston, Ontario

March 10, 1992

Ms. Jane Roberts
Sales Manager
Hogan Office Furniture
12 Queen Street East
Toronto, Ontario M4W 1Z2

Dear Ms. Roberts:

Please send the following office furniture, as listed in your recent brochure:

Quantity	Model	Description	Unit Price	Total Price
2	# 342	secretary's chair, brown	$ 75.00	$150.00
3	# 390	arm chair, beige	$105.00	$315.00
5	# 12	wastebasket, black	$ 18.00	$ 90.00
		Subtotal		$555.00
		Tax		$ 44.40
		TOTAL		$598.40

Please charge the items to our account and ship them by truck no later than June 30th. We appreciate your record of prompt service.

Sincerely,

May Scott

May Scott

Better:

Could you please give me some information about Arthur Seaburg, who has applied for a job as a management trainee in our bottling company. He has worked in your office for the last two summers.

— Does he work well with people?

— Has he given evidence of organizational ability and initiative?

— Is he honest and reliable?

We would be grateful for any other information which would help us determine his suitability for the management trainee position.

Of course, your remarks will remain confidential.

Note how the improved version is more direct in its organization. It omits the request for facts which should be obtained from the applicant himself — facts such as educational background and health. It also helps the reader by stating the type of job in question. The vertical list highlights for the reader the specific information needed.

Making a Routine Claim

It might seem that the direct approach is an odd approach to use for routine claims, since a claim can hardly be good news for the receiver. Yet successful businesses want customers to be satisfied and most are interested in resolving reasonable complaints or difficulties. A letter that lets them know simply and directly about the difficulty gives them a chance to rectify it and keep the customer's goodwill.

1. **Don't beat about the bush.**   State right at the beginning the nature of your claim and the reason for it. You may also want to give some urgency to your claim by relating the consequences of the problem; for example, a loss of sales, or a business activity which has had to be curtailed.

2. **Be explicit about what you expect the company to do.**   Don't exaggerate or indulge in emotional outbursts. A reasonable request which sticks to the facts is more likely to draw a prompt, favourable response than one which makes accusations. An angry reader often resists settling claims.

    How would you react to this letter?

    I had always wanted an electric typewriter, and finally I spent a lot of money and got one. I bought your brand because friends had told me it was a good one. Now I realize that it is totally unreliable. I have had it only eight months and the return key doesn't work. I want it fixed immediately. The warranty covers the repair but it doesn't cover the nuisance.

    How do you expect people to buy your products if they don't work? I for one don't plan to buy them any more.

Wouldn't you react better to this version?

    Please fix the return key on this typewriter. As you can see from the enclosed bill, it is only eight months old and still under warranty.

Since this breakdown has prevented me from my usual practice of completing work at home on the weekends, I would appreciate it if you would fix and return it to me promptly.

Routine or Good-News Replies

Use the direct approach when responding with favourable or neutral information. If you have to temper the information with some facts that are not favourable, make sure you don't undermine your effort by being unnecessarily negative.

The following letter should be a good-news one, since it gives the customer a benefit he is not entitled to under the warranty. Yet the accusing tone and negative wording are likely to annoy the reader. Moreover, since it doesn't use the direct approach, the positive message loses its impact.

Instructions were supplied with your new automatic coffee-maker warning that the base should not be immersed in water. Our repair people tell us that the mechanism in your machine had rust spots, which indicated that you had got it wet. Since misuse is ordinarily not covered by warranty, we should charge you for the repairs. Nevertheless we like to keep our customers satisfied, and therefore are replacing the damaged parts free of charge. You should remember in future, however, not to get water in the mechanism.

Your coffee maker was shipped this morning by parcel post.

The next reply is likely to produce a satisfied customer, even though he or she has to pay for part of the repair cost.

Your repaired automatic coffee-maker was shipped to you this morning by parcel post. It's in tip-top shape.

We have enclosed with the coffee-maker a copy of the instructions, which show how to clean it without immersing the base. Rust spots on the interior mechanism were the cause of your problem, a condition ordinarily not covered by the warranty. We want to keep you a satisfied customer, however, and are therefore not billing you for the labour, but only for the new parts.

Remember to keep the mechanism dry and your coffee-maker should give you years of convenience — and good coffee.

Thank-You Letters and Letters of Congratulations

A note of appreciation can strengthen business relationships as well as personal ones. It needn't be lengthy, as long as it is genuine. This proviso is the key: you need to show that your thanks or congratulations are not an empty formality. If people have done things that benefit you, let them know precisely how. Give one or two details that show why you are grateful. If you are congratulating someone on an appointment or award, give a reason why you think it is deserved, or comment on how that person has benefitted the company or community.

The following thank-you letter is perfunctory because it lacks concrete detail; it seems almost a form letter.

> Thank you for letting the class visit your plant. It was a very interesting experience for us and we appreciate your assistance.
>
> Thank you again.

On the other hand, the next letter does not seem genuine because it exaggerates. It is too effusive — almost gushy — and therefore has the mark of insincerity, despite its claim.

> We want to express our sincere appreciation for our visit to your plant. It was the most exciting moment in the course, and the illustration of robotics was awesome. All of us in the class were really impressed by your unique talent as a manager. We are indeed grateful for your kindness in giving us this special treat.

Now for a letter that is direct, concrete, and sincere in its thanks. Notice how paring down the superlatives improves the effect.

> We appreciated the visit to your plant last week to see robotics in action.
>
> The visit was a highlight of our course on technological innovation, since it gave us a practical illustration of the theory we are studying. We were also impressed by the methods you had used to introduce the robots.
>
> Thank you for the opportunity of seeing how to manage technological change effectively.

EXERCISES

Note: In some of the exercises in this chapter, and in following chapters, you may wish to supply added information as needed, such as names or specific details about the item discussed. Unless the instructions for writing exercises specify writing a complete letter or memo, you need write only the body.

● Section A

1. List the weaknesses in the following memo:

May 13, 1992

> *to* R. Fletcher
> *from* A. Dunn
>
> Regarding the proposal for a touring promotional show sent to me on Tuesday, I read it yesterday. When you have corrected the problems I have found in it, I will gladly give it my support at the next divisional meeting, since it has merit. The

financing section is sound, except that you failed to include the cost of gas. You should have estimated a cost per kilometre along with your leasing figures. I also think your marketing section lacks enough detail. Ruth, you should have added more facts.

Other than these problems, the proposal looks fine. By the way, when you do the estimates for the London office renovations, include a breakdown of costs for the Waterloo and Hamilton renovations. They will help us to make comparisons.

Sincerely,
Allan

2. Using a word processor if possible,
    a) change the traditional style of the following letter, with its closed punctuation, to a full-block style with open punctuation;
    b) change the letter to a memo. Add or delete as needed.

Assume that both your letter and memo are on stationery with a letterhead at the top.

January 10, 1992

Mr. Kenneth W. Smith,
Manager, Human Resources, Simex Limited,
P.O. Box 25,
Sudbury, Ontario

Dear Ken:

Please add my name to the list for the March seminar on interviewing techniques at the Skyway Hotel.

If others from the company are planning to attend and need transportation, I will be taking my car and can pick up those people who live in my area. Ask them to get in touch with me.

Thanks for letting me know about the seminar.

Sincerely,
Jerry Dutka

3. Consider the order of this memo. How would you reorder it? Would you make any other changes?

To: A.C. Biggar, Administrative Manager
From: K. Pivniki

Salaries

Last week Ann Timmins and I met to discuss employee salaries. As you know, you had asked us to review salaries among all support staff in our division and to recommend to you a correction for any inequities.

Ann and I reviewed salaries with the help of the benefits group's new computer program for assessing employee compensation. You had asked us to comment on the effectiveness of the program for company-wide application.

We found only one area where the salary range for support staff is inequitable. The library assistants are underpaid by comparison with other staff. We therefore recommend that the salary range for library assistants be increased by $2000.

We also found that the computer program was a practical and efficient tool. You can be confident of using it for the whole the company.

I hope this meets your satisfaction. If not, please call me.

4. As the administrative manager at Apex Food Services Ltd., you want information about Smith Microwave Ovens. You need ten, and hope you can get a discount for purchasing in quantity. You want to find out about the different models and their features, and about the kind of guarantee the supplier offers. Write a complete letter of inquiry to Select Equipment Co. The address is 12 Queen Street, Hawkesbury, Ontario, K1B 1L2.

5. Three weeks ago, you ordered some stationery from Harding Bros. for your new office in Burnaby, British Columbia. The order arrived minus a carton of twenty printed pads for telephone messages (catalogue no. 20-A). The pads are listed on invoice no. 3047, and you have been charged $20. You want the missing pads sent by parcel express. Write a complete letter to the order desk clerk at Harding Bros., 300 Centennial Drive, Vancouver, B.C., V3C 1A2.

6. Last Thursday, Alice Chiu, personnel director at Northern Bank, was the guest speaker at your Business Club's monthly lunch. The subject of her talk was "Employee Training Programs: Challenges for the Nineties." Since it was your turn to write a letter of thanks on behalf of the club, you quickly wrote the draft below. You now realize it is unsatisfactory in its organization, tone, and wording. Discuss the problems in class and then rewrite the body of the letter.

> Dear Ms. Chiu:
>
> The speech that you delivered last week was something I had looked forward to for a long time, since I work in the personnel field. It was indeed an honour to have someone of your stature come to talk to us on such an interesting subject. Thank you again for your time and effort on our behalf.

7. On November 10, you phoned the Confederation Hotel to make tentative arrangements for the annual Sales Awards Lunch of your company, Goody Toys. Subject to your later confirmation, you reserved the Dominion Room for Friday, January 10 for a three-hour period starting at 12 noon. You also arranged for a buffet lunch for thirty people at a cost of $12 each. The cost is to include ten bottles of wine. You now realize that you will also need a lectern, an overhead projector, and a screen.

In a letter to the manager of the hotel, John Stubbs, confirm the arrangements and ask for the additional equipment.

8. You have just learned that Helen Thomas, the energetic assistant buyer for National Fashion Stores, has been promoted to chief buyer. She is now in a position to make the important buying decisions. As the sales manager of Elegance Manufacturing, you have dealt with Ms. Thomas before in selling your line of women's sportswear. You get along well with her and think that, since she is efficient, she will be good at her new job. Write a letter of congratulations.

Section B

1. After assessing its weaknesses, revise the memo in question 1 of Section A, adding or deleting as needed. If possible, use a word processor to do the revision.

2. Make these sentences more reader-centred:
   a) As consultants we have many years of managerial experience.
   b) It is the organization's policy to require partial payment before beginning the second stage of a large project like this one.
   c) On May 10, we will deliver the complete report.
   d) Our research engineers have tested the product for ten years to make sure it is safe.
   e) A subsidy is available from our office for companies hiring student trainees.
   f) We are in receipt of your brochure.
   g) Assistance with the new computers is available from three specially trained administrative assistants.
   h) The office desk can be had with a variety of optional attachments, according to individual preference.

3. Where possible, eliminate negative words or phrases, and create a more positive approach.
   a) You claim that we did not send a refund, but our records show it was sent by registered mail on July 12.
   b) Since the office will be closed on Friday, don't forget to pick up your parking permits before 5 o'clock on Thursday.
   c) The accounting department has informed me that 25% of you have neglected to submit your expense reports for last month.
   d) You incorrectly assume that we will be reducing our part-time sales staff.
   e) We do not assume responsibility for damages to cars left anywhere but in our underground parking garage.

4. Short letters of thanks or congratulations can be effective rapport-builders with friends, associates, and clients. Think of someone you know to whom you could write such a letter. Take five minutes in class to draft the letter. Exchange drafts with a partner and assess your partner's letter according to three criteria:
   — Is it personal?
   — Is it concrete?
   — Is it sincere?

5. You are heading up a fund-raising drive to furnish a new children's wing in your local community hospital. You want to send a letter of thanks to all contributors. The drive has reached its target of $100 000, and the children's wing will have its new acquisitions (furniture, toys, and play equipment) by spring. Compose the letter.

6. Eight months ago you bought an Almond radio at Biltmore Sound Store for $149. The tuning dial became stiff after three months; Biltmore sent it to Almond and had it fixed free of charge under the six month's warranty. Now, two months after the warranty has expired, the dial suddenly does not work at all. You want it repaired free, since it first had difficulties during the warranty period and may not have been fixed properly, or may have a defective part.
   a) Write a letter to Almond, which will accompany the radio when it is sent for repairs.
   b) Change roles. As head of customer service at Almond, you have agreed to the request. Write a letter which will inform the customer of your decision, and increase customer goodwill toward Almond.

7. You are in charge of customer relations at Northway's Resort Hotel. The hotel specializes in vacation packages for families. It advertises free tennis, swimming, and wind-surfing.

   The Miller family (parents and two children) came for a week in July and paid a bill of $1500. However, Mr. Miller has written asking for a partial refund, since the tennis courts were being repaired and were out of play for four of the seven days. He says the family's main reason for choosing Northway's was the tennis facility.

   You think Mr. Miller's claim is a fair one and decide to send a $300 refund. Write the accompanying letter.

8. Your job as assistant to the Registrar is to give a short welcoming letter or talk (2-3 minutes) to a group of new students. You also want to give them information about two of the following:

   a) places to eat and drink on or near the campus;

   b) sports facilities and activities;

   c) campus social activities.

   Write the letter or present your talk to the class.

CHAPTER 6

Refusals or Giving Bad News

It's always harder to say no than yes, and harder still to say no in writing. Nobody likes sending a letter which causes disappointment or anger. Even though the receivers of bad news are unlikely to follow those ancient Greeks who killed the messenger, they may still resent the writer. In business there's no easy escape; from time to time you will have to refuse a request, turn down an idea or a person, or send a written reprimand or negative evaluation. The challenge is to send a message which gives the unpleasant facts but doesn't create hostility between you and the receiver.

Structural Options

You have two choices for structuring bad news. As in so many other instances, let your decision be guided by the context, especially the reader.

The Direct Approach

If you know the reader well, or the reader is impatient for a response to a query, you may be better to stick with a direct approach. You should probably also stick to it if the bad news is expected or not very important. For example, the direct approach would be appropriate for letting a colleague know that a routine report will be completed later than scheduled, or for telling a boss the details of a known problem.

The direct order for bad news is similar to that for good news, except that it tries to soften the message by giving the reader a helpful alternative.

1. State the bad news simply and directly.
2. Give the reasons.
3. Give an alternative, if possible.
4. Close with a goodwill statement. Don't refer back to the bad news. You don't want to keep reminding the reader of the source of any displeasure.

Here's an example:

Dear Mr. Moore:

The quotation you wanted has escaped our detection.

In looking through our record of corporate speeches on free trade with respect to agriculture, we haven't come across anything similar to the remarks you mentioned. When I asked Mr. Lockhart, he had no recollection of anyone in the company having made that type of analogy.

You may have better luck by conducting a trace of *Globe & Mail* stories and articles on the subject. You might try speaking to someone in the Metro Reference Library, where I think they have a substantial clipping collection.

We hope your search is soon successful.

The Indirect Approach

If you don't know the reader well, or if the bad news is unexpected or could cause a negative emotional reaction, consider the advantages of the indirect approach. It has this order:

1. Begin with a neutral or pleasant opening statement, related to the subject. This is the buffer that gets the letter started on an agreeable note.
2. Give reasons or circumstances leading to the bad news.
3. State the bad news in as positive terms as possible. Occasionally, if you have paved the way clearly, you may be able to imply the bad news, without actually stating it.
    Suppose, for example, you want to turn down a request to develop a new trade show in Vancouver. You could imply a refusal by saying: "We have decided to concentrate our efforts on establishing ourselves in the American market for the next three years and not to develop new shows in Canada during this period." If you do merely imply a refusal, be careful that the reader knows clearly that the answer is "no."
4. Give a helpful suggestion or alternative, if one exists.
5. Close with a goodwill statement.

Think of human nature. People usually react better to bad news if they are prepared for it. Unpleasant facts will encounter less resistance if they seem to follow logically from an explanation. By contrast, reasons *after* the bad news are more likely to be interpreted as excuses. Since the indirect approach is the path of least resistance, you will find it most appropriate for your trickiest writing tasks — when you are faced with angering or upsetting a reader.

When using the indirect approach remember these tips:

1. **Don't mislead the reader** with an opening that's too positive. You don't want a build-up to lead to a let-down.

2. **Do keep the reasons or explanation as short as possible.** The reader shouldn't have to wade through a lot of detail to get to the key information.

3. **Do make sure the reader is clear about the bad news,** especially if you don't state it but only imply it. A misinterpreted message is a failed message.

4. **Do avoid negative words and phrasing,** if there are positive ways to give the message. (See page 66 for a list of undesirable negatives.)

5. **Don't end with a statement that's artificially up-beat** when you know the receiver will be deeply disappointed by the communication. You may seem like a Pollyanna — someone who is relentlessly cheery even in inappropriate circumstances. It's often possible to look forward to future business or service, an approach that is both positive and sincere.

Here is a letter which uses the indirect approach to turning down a request for funding. Notice how the writer creates a reasonable and helpful atmosphere.

> Every year in February our Donations Committee meets to discuss deserving appeals for funding, such as your request for support of the Montrose Revue.
>
> Your proposal arrived in March, after we had already made our selections for this year. Our budget for charities is now fully committed and we are therefore unable to help you at this time. If you plan to make the show an annual event, we will certainly add your proposal to the list for consideration next year. Please let us know before January 31.
>
> In the meantime, I wish you every success with this year's revue and congratulate you on your initiative.

If the following letter had been sent instead, its harsh negativism would likely have created antagonism towards the writer or the writer's firm. The blunt refusal in the opening sentence would have made the reader less receptive to the explanation.

> We regret that we are unable to give financial support to your proposal. We have many requests for funds and have already committed our budget for charitable giving for this year. Unfortunately we have to reject many ventures such as yours, since we have only so much to distribute.
>
> We wish you success with your venture.

The final goodwill statement at the end rings false, since the tone of the rest of the letter is so writer-centred and impersonal. It has the mark of a form letter — and a poorly constructed one.

Turning Down a Job Applicant

Most companies these days have far more applicants for jobs than they can possibly hire. Some are inundated every spring with application letters from students. A few companies have a quick solution: they answer only those applicants they want to interview. This approach is both discourteous and unwise. A company that treats job applicants badly is fostering a poor public image. Besides, an applicant who one year is turned down may another year be an important prospective customer or client.

Personalize as Much as Possible

If you are in charge of responding to job applicants and you haven't the resources or time to give individual answers to a flood of applications, then devise one or several form letters. In this era of word processors, it is relatively easy to partially personalize letters; at the least, you should use the applicant's name. If you have taken more of the applicant's time by having an interview or requesting references, then you should write a personal letter. Whichever route you follow, try to avoid rejecting the person as a person. Focus more on the reasons for the company's selection.

Compare the order, tone, and wording of the following two letters. Both of them could be form letters, but the second has a more reasonable and reader-centred tone, as well as an indirect structure.

Poor:

We are sorry that we must refuse you employment at Wisharts. We had many applicants seeking employment with us this year, no doubt because of Wisharts' growing success and reputation. Obviously we could accept only a few for the accounting department, and after careful consideration of all applicants, we have decided not to offer you a position.

We wish you success with other employers.

Better:

Thank you for taking the time to apply for an accounting position at Wisharts.

Since we received over a hundred applications for the three positions available, we have had to disappoint many well-qualified candidates. We based our initial selection for interviews not only on academic background but on work experience. The applicants finally chosen for the positions had at least three years of relevant work. Although we cannot offer you a position at this time, our decision is no reflection on your potential to do well in accounting.

We appreciate your interest in Wisharts and wish you success in your accounting career. If in future an appropriate opening comes up, we would be happy to consider another application from you.

Be Truthful

If you would never consider the applicant for a job, do not suggest that you would. By falsely raising hopes, you will only produce more bitterness down the line. The last sentence in the preceding letter could easily have been omitted for an applicant who is unlikely to be considered seriously. A good substitute would be to suggest other employment routes. On the other hand, if the applicant is someone you might employ another time, it's a good idea to say somewhere that the rejection is only for the job or jobs available at that time.

Turning Down an Invitation

Business people are often invited to join organizations, give speeches or sit on boards or committees. If you must refuse such an invitation, at least do it graciously:

— show that you appreciate the invitation;
— acknowledge the importance of the organization or event;
— give specific reasons why you cannot accept;
— suggest an alternative, if you can, or leave the door open for another time.

Remember that the more concrete you are, the more you will appear to have taken the invitation seriously. If you keep to generalities, your refusal will run the risk of offending. You may not always be able to give as specific an alternative as the following letter-writer, but at least you should try to soften the refusal with some positive remarks.

> I have always admired the work that the John Howard Society does in helping prisoners and am honoured to be asked to speak at your annual dinner. On checking my calendar, I realize that unfortunately I will be in Alberta that week attending the Bar Association convention.
>
> If you would like someone else to talk on prisoner rehabilitation in business, you may want to try Henry Albright, Director of Personnel for Consolidated Industries, who had considerable success in hiring former prisoners when he was plant manager in Kingston. He is an experienced speaker.
>
> I'm sorry that I won't be with you on April 9, but I'll continue to look with interest on the work of the John Howard Society.

Turning Down a Claim

Some claims are more reasonable than others and some people are more honest. Yet no matter how outrageous you think a claim is, or how skeptical you are of the details, you should respond with courtesy and tact. Customers are not always right, but they're always prospective customers. Of course, if someone is a persistent pest and you don't want the business, be as frank as you like, as long as you are not rude.

Most people who take the trouble to make a claim believe they have a strong case. They want satisfaction, or at least expect an explanation. You must present the refusal in such a way that, even if they are not happy with your answer, they at least know the exact reasons for it and do not doubt your honesty. The do's and don't's of refusing claims are an extension of the basic guideline for all business writing: put yourself in the reader's shoes. Consider the claimant's position and respond in a way that will make sense to the claimant. Specifically,

1. **Do begin with a statement you can both agree on.** You might try an opening such as, "You are right to expect top quality form from New Wave products." Or, "Your clear and straightforward statement of your problem with the photocopier deserves a clear and straightforward answer."

2. **Do review the facts.** Be objective and unemotional in your tone so that your subsequent refusal seems a logical conclusion to the review. Don't be long-winded, but provide enough detail that the reason for refusal is obvious.

3. **Don't accuse or lecture the claimant.** A claim-rejection letter is one instance where passive verbs may be more effective than active ones. Instead of saying, "You dented the gear-box," soften the tone with "the gear-box was dented." Avoid phrases such as

   — you failed (neglected, disregarded);
   — you claim (insinuate, imply);
   — contrary to what you say;
   — we take issue with.

4. **Don't belittle the claimant.** Avoid phrases such as "Surely you must know," "It should be obvious," and "If you had read the instructions."

5. **Don't use company policy as an excuse.** Other people couldn't care less about company policy. They want a reasonable explanation — just as young people want more than a "Because I said so" answer from a parent or teacher.

6. **Don't offer elaborate apologies for refusing.** A simple "I'm sorry" will do, if the circumstances warrant an apology. Many times an apology is not needed, and it is better to avoid one.

7. **Don't pass the buck,** saying it's not your responsibility or your department's responsibility. If it truly isn't your job to respond, give the claim to someone whose job it is.

8. **Do close in a friendly, positive way.** You have some options for closing, depending on the circumstances:
   a) After refusing the claim, you might offer a counterproposal, which shows that you are trying to be helpful even if you can't do exactly what the claimant

wants. You might, for example, offer to repair a part even if you can't replace the whole. Or you might suggest a substitute for the product or service — or even some information about where to get help with the difficulty. (This last approach is not passing the buck if the solution lies outside your company's responsibility.)

b) You might indicate that, if the claimant has additional information available, you'd be happy to review the case. This, of course, would be useful when the claimant has not included a sales slip or invoice, or has omitted some important evidence. Naturally you would not want to use this closing indiscriminately, inviting every claimant to try again.

c) Often you can end with a remark pointing out the benefits for the claimant of using another of your products or services. You need to be tactful here, so that your letter does not seem like a sales pitch rather than a response to a claim.

Whatever close you use, be positive. Don't suggest that the reader may be dissatisfied ("I'm afraid you may be unhappy with this decision"). Neither should you plead with the claimant ("Please try to understand our position" or "I trust you will agree with this explanation"). By doing so you imply that the claimant may not understand or agree — a negative way to end. If you have responded to the claim in a reasonable, helpful, and courteous way, you should let the case rest.

Now for two examples of claim refusals which work:

1. One of our aims at Domestic Appliances is to provide homemakers like you with time-saving kitchen equipment at a reasonable price. The inexpensive hand blender you bought two years ago has proven to be one of our most popular products. I'm sorry it has not given the satisfaction to you it has to so many others.

   When you bought the blender, the description on the package and in the instructions stated that it was for easy blending of liquids and other soft food. It was not designed for puréeing meats or tough substances, as you have realized.

   We have checked your blender and found it in good working order. It will continue to give you excellent results with liquids and soft food. We stand by our money-back guarantee of our products, but since the blender has now had two years' use and is working as it should, we are unable to give a refund.

   For puréeing meats, may I suggest our Blendomix. This heavy-duty blender will save you time and do a superb job on tough foods. I'm enclosing a discount slip which will allow you 10% off the regular price of the Blendomix at any of our retail outlets.

   We are pleased to have you as a customer and are confident that our products will give you many years of reliable service.

2. I can appreciate your need for a reliable lawn mower, especially with your large lawn.

   Our repair department has done a careful check on your Turfmaster to see what was causing the problem. The blade cover was pressing on the blade, preventing it from turning properly. A dent on the cover indicates that something was dropped on it. Since our one-year warranty does not cover damage to the machine, we must charge you for the new blade cover. When we replaced the cover, however, we also cleaned and oiled your machine — free of charge. With proper care, your Turfmaster should give you many years of efficient, easy grass-cutting.

For added convenience with a large property, have you considered using our Turfmaster Lawntrimmer? It's available on the early spring special at most large hardware and department stores.

Refusing Credit

Granting credit to a person is easy. A direct letter of acceptance is usually all that is needed. Refusing credit is more difficult. In fact, it is a more sensitive task than refusing a claim because it is a more personal matter. The most frequent reasons for not granting credit are the character or financial position of the applicant — both sensitive areas. It is a letter-writing challenge to produce a tactful refusal that retains the goodwill of the person refused.

The general tactics are the same as for other "bad-news" letters:

1. **Begin with a "buffer"** — a neutral or positive statement related to the credit application. Try to tie it into the explanation that follows. For example, if the refusal has to do with the relatively few assets (against liabilities) of the applicant's new business, you might start with, "Your application for credit in purchasing Remor parts indicates that your new business is nicely underway. We are interested in helping new businesses keep on a sound financial footing." This opening could then easily connect to a second-paragraph explanation of why credit at this time would not be a sound financial decision.

   If you must send a refusal in a form letter, because of the numbers you have to deal with, you may have to stick with the trite "Thank you for your application for credit" kind of opening. But even here, try to be a bit more specific, by including the name of your company or the help you can give to the applicant; for example: "We are grateful for your interest in having an account with Harcraft Stores and want to help you obtain quality building supplies."

2. **Explain the circumstances leading to the refusal.** One good approach is to state the conditions under which you grant credit. Your refusal to someone who does not meet these conditions then seems to follow logically. For example, you might say, "One of the conditions of granting credit is that a person has been employed for at least a year" or, "We find that credit works best with companies that have a strong assets-to-liabilities ratio."

3. **Refuse tactfully.** In some cases, such as when the reasons relate to character rather than finances, it may be better to refuse by implication rather than by explicit statement. If applicants have been dishonest or have left a trail of bad debts, they know it. A hint that you know is all they really need.

4. **Finish with a positive, friendly statement.** No one likes to be turned down, but you will leave a better impression if you can point to a more positive relationship. You might suggest a future credit acceptance, point out the benefits of cash buying, or indicate some other way in which you could be of help. A form letter precludes giving the close an individualized touch, but at least try to show that you care about the specific customer.

Poor:

We regret to inform you that your application for credit has been denied. Our review of your financial situation indicates that you do not meet the conditions we require to grant credit to small businesses. Unfortunately we cannot bend our requirements because of the past problems we have had with poor credit risks.

Better:

We appreciate the interest you have shown in our merchandise through your application for credit.

As a manager, you will understand that to run our own company effectively we have had to establish certain conditions for granting credit. One is that the assets of a small business should be at least twice its liabilities. At the rate your business is growing, it will soon meet this condition. When it does, we will be pleased to review your application again.

In the meantime you can enjoy our 5 percent discount for cash sales. We will look forward to giving you prompt, efficient service.

Writing a Performance Review

In recent years, legal decisions and union contracts have led to formal procedures for preventing wrongful or arbitrary dismissal from a job. As part of these procedures more and more companies are requiring managers to write annual performance reviews for employees. Since these reviews may be used in a grievance case or court action to justify a later dismissal, transfer, or denial of promotion, they must be taken seriously. Some companies are creating their own performance-review forms, with specific categories for the employee's superior to fill in. Often the employees themselves fill in a part.

If you have to devise your own written review, you cannot afford to give a thoughtless "you do a wonderful job" kind of evaluation to a mediocre or poorly performing employee. Nor can you afford to let personal prejudices get in the way of sound judgment and objective comment. Remember also that written evaluations work best when accompanied by an interview with an employee. The written assessment then becomes a focus for the discussion.

Although performance reviews can be seen as either good news or bad news, a favourable written evaluation is easier to do than an an unfavourable one. In either case, however, an annual review is not a substitute for the regular informal feedback that all employees want.

Writing a Review of Good Performance

As you would with other "good-news" writing, follow the direct organizational approach.

* Be specific in pointing out the accomplishments and good qualities of the employee — you may even choose to categorize the comments according to the requirements of the employee's job.
* Consider leaving a section at the end for specific objectives for the next year. Where possible, these should be left as tentative objectives to be worked out cooperatively in a discussion with the employee.

Reviewing Poor Performance

An unfavourable evaluation is harder to do. You need to consider carefully what results you want from the assessment:

Do you want the employee to improve?   In most cases this is the goal. An indirect approach, therefore, works well.

* Begin with an account of the positive features of the employee. Even with poor performance there is usually a positive aspect, such as being on time or courtesy with other employees.
* Move to the negative aspects, but keep criticism as constructive as possible. Remember that the goal in most cases is not to provide grounds for getting rid of someone but to bring about change. Try to phrase your remarks so that they seem more like suggestions for improvement than an attack. Focus on the behaviour not the person — for example, on the record of lateness rather than on a person's laziness or lack of interest. It's human nature to become defensive when attacked.

    For employees who are generally effective but have a few weaknesses, suggest how certain actions or behaviour could improve a good record or performance. For the person who is impatient with others in the office, for example, you could say, "If you show the same patience with with co-workers as you do with clients, you will get more cooperation from them."

* Don't exaggerate or use emotionally loaded words. Rather be objective, fair and specific — keep to the facts. Instead of saying, "You are forever creating scenes with the accounting clerks and making their life miserable," say something like, "We have had three complaints from the accounting clerks that you had unnecessarily berated them in public." Make sure it is clear why a certain area needs change. Instead of saying "Your files are a complete mess," say "The disorder in your files makes it difficult for anyone else to find what is needed quickly." Focus on only one or two desired changes. Since people cannot improve a number of weaknesses at the same time, be clear about which are the most important areas to improve.
* End with some specific objectives for improvement. Indicate the time in which you expect changes to be made. Where possible, give quantifiable targets.

Do you want to record grounds for dismissing an employee?   Usually this will be the case only after previous reviews have failed to bring the desired improvement, or if the employee is so unsuitable there is little to dispute. This is no time for subtle hints. Use the direct approach:

- State the problem at the start. Make sure that description of the weaknesses is obvious and unequivocal.
- Review the record of previous suggestions or warnings.
- Give the date at which further action will be taken if the employee does not make specific changes. Let the employee know the consequences of not making the changes.

Discuss as well as write.   Whatever results you want from the evaluation, talk to the employee. While an interview is a useful accompaniment to any review, with a "bad-news" review it is essential.

Oral Discussions About Performance

A formal review that includes discussion as well as written comment can be an opportunity rather than a headache. If properly conducted it can help to:

- discover barriers to improved performance, whether inability, lack of training, or an organizational barrier;
- clear up any misundertandings, and allow the employee to explain actions and goals;
- determine the employee's potential for development, and readiness to take further responsibility.
- encourage employee collaboration in finding solutions to problems;
- assure that a problem employee understands the consequences of behaviour;
- assess future training needs;
- work out short- and long-term individual goals.

Since the review should reflect the whole year's work and not just the few weeks preceding it, plan for the interview and review notes from the previous year as well as any other documents that record employee achievement or problems. The employee should be aware in advance of the purpose of the discussion and be encouraged to prepare for it also.

As a result of the interview, employees should know not only how their performance ranks in relation to employer expectations, but what their objectives should be for the next year. They should feel they have had a chance to express their own views and plans for the future and be left with the sense that they have been treated with consideration.

As the person reviewing, therefore, you should make sure you spend a part of the interview listening carefully and encouraging the employee to participate in the discussion.

Except in the case of employees who have not responded to earlier reprimands or warning, you should try to structure the interview so that the employee feels that the discussion has strengthened the relationship rather rather than diminished it. For most employees, this sequence works well:

1. **Opening**

   — Begin by establishing rapport and helping the employee to relax.

   — Review the purpose and format of the interview.

2. **Performance discussion**

   — Discuss overall performance.

   — Discuss specific achievements.

   — Focus on the specific improvement needed, and how best to achieve it.

   — Agree on objectives and time frame.

3. **Closing**

   — Summarize the discussion.

   — Finish with a note of optimism.

Although it's useful to plan questions that will help to move the interview through desired areas, don't be so hidebound by your agenda that you fail to uncover the employee's questions and concerns. Remember that the employee is a human being who most often wants to do well, rather than an automaton hired to perform tasks. Willing cooperation or collaboration is a better goal than compliance.

EXERCISES

● Section A

1. For the last two years, you have been helping young children learn to play hockey. The president of the local hockey association, Arthur Hughes, has written you a letter, asking you to coach the peewee team this year. As a third-year university student, you have already decided you will need to work harder at your studies to raise your marks. You haven't the time to do the coaching job this year. However, your roommate has mentioned an interest in coaching the team and is a good hockey player.

   Write two letters to Mr. Hughes, declining the job. Use the direct approach in one and the indirect approach in the other. You may add details if needed. In pairs or small groups, evaluate each other's letters. Which approach is easiest to write? From the reader's perspective, which seems best?

2. Revise the following sentences, making them more positive and less accusing or demeaning to the reader:

   a) Since you did not include the bill, we cannot give you a refund.

   b) Surely you don't think we can act on a complaint two years after the purchase?

   c) We suspect that you dropped the typewriter and bent the carriage.

   d) You haven't survived in business the required six months, and therefore we cannot give you credit.

   e) It's too risky for us to give someone like you credit since, frankly, your credit rating leaves much to be desired.

   f) Mr. Elliot, you haven't supplied a full and honest explanation, and we need the explanation if you want us to replace the machine.

   g) The basis of your complaint is a misreading of Section 2 of our policy statement.

   h) Any good entrepreneur would know, Mr. Taylor, that a sound financial footing is necessary for a business to prosper.

   i) Your failure to follow the operating instructions caused the breakdown of the machine.

3. List the weaknesses in the following letter, which turns down an application for credit.

   > We are sorry that we cannot grant your application for credit. Our company policy is to extend credit only to those people who have been employed for a year. You fail to meet this requirement.

   > We trust you will understand our position and are sorry we cannot oblige you at this time. In any case, we hope you will continue to shop at our store on a cash basis.

4. List the strengths in the following refusal for credit:

   > We appreciate your continued interest in using Harwood Building products in your construction business, as shown by your application for credit.

   > In this tough economy, one of the ways we keep ourselves on a sound financial footing is to require a business to be operating for two years before we grant credit. Although your references confirm your good reputation, your business hasn't yet reached this position. Your record of growth suggests that you soon will, and we look forward to reviewing your application again at that time.

   > In the meantime, we promise you prompt and reliable service with your cash orders and enclose a flyer about our spring discounts for cash sales.

5. In front of the class and with a partner, take turns role-playing for one or more of the following "bad-news" assignments. Alternatively, work in groups of three with the third person being the observer and commentator afterwards. (These assignments may also be adapted for written responses.)

   a) You are in charge of a student entertainment show in which a big-name musical group will be performing. On the day of the show, you discover that through a miscalculation you have sold twenty-five more tickets than there are seats in the auditorium. Fire regulations prevent you adding more seats or using standing room. You hope that some "no-shows" will take care of the problem, but ten minutes before the show begins nine angry ticket-holders appear, having found nowhere to sit.

Your task is to
— give the bad news that you can't find room;
— give a refund and tickets to attend another performance later in the week;
— try to assuage their anger and get them to leave peacefully.
(Have your partner play an angry ticket-holder.)

b) After interviewing four people for a summer exterior-painting business owned by Paul Purdy, you have hired the people the company needs. You chose those who either had painting experience or had done a lot of physical work. The fourth applicant had neither. Now you must let that applicant, Sharon Brown, know your decision. Sharon will realize that the three you hired were male and may suspect that sexism was behind your decision.

c) You are the assistant manager at a hotel, and two parents have just stormed into your office because they were not allowed to take their children to the hotel's evening floor show. Hotel regulations do not permit children under sixteen to attend, for a variety of reasons, including the area's drinking laws. The parents say families should be able to sit in a special area where drinking is not allowed. Although you think the idea has some merit, you cannot make the decision yourself, and therefore cannot give permission for the children to attend this evening's performance. (The hotel also offers free movies for families with children in the Green Room; tonight's show is *Never Cry Wolf.*)

Your task is to refuse the parent's request and retain goodwill.

● Section B

1. An out-of-town friend has asked you to see his son, Paul Dubois, a young college graduate who wants a job in sales. As the sales director of Lancer Foods, you agree to talk to Paul about his plans, knowing that a junior sales position will soon become available.

During the interview, it becomes clear that, although Paul has a pleasant, outgoing personality, he has no sales experience. More important, he has no record of work or other experience to indicate that he is hard-working and reliable.

Since Paul is going home the next day, you promise to write to him within two weeks. When you discuss the job opening with your personnel manager, you find that other applicants are more qualified.

Write a letter of refusal to Paul. (He will probably show it to his father.)

2. A neighbour and owner of Tastee-Treats Franchises, Herbert Carter, has applied for credit in buying kitchen equipment from your Company, ABC Industries. As credit manager of ABC, you discover that Carter has a record of late payment of his bills; his business appears to be financially shaky.

Write a letter to Carter, refusing credit. You don't want to arouse animosity or create friction in the neighbourhood.

3. Bill McIntyre, the head of a local boys' softball league, has written to you, the owner of the Donut Dunk, asking you to sponsor one of the teams for $300. Your promotional budget is already allocated for this year. Since you already sponsor a girls' softball team, you are not likely to sponsor another team in the next few years.

Write a letter of refusal to McIntyre. You will be including with it 100 coupons for a free donut, to be distributed to the boys in the league.

4. Your company has recently instituted a policy of written performance reviews. Managers are to write a memo to each employee in which the employee's work for the year is evaluated. They are to discuss the evaluation in a personal interview. You have two employees scheduled for a formal review.

Walter Pitts   Last year you hired Walter as a new bookkeeper. Although still in his twenties, Walter has had several previous jobs as a bookkeeper. He has always been courteous and pleasant, but he has made repeated mistakes which have been costly to the company in time spent trying to sort out the errors. Despite discussions and attempts to help him, his work continues to be sloppy. You think Walter is lazy. He doesn't seem to give much effort to checking his work. In addition, he is frequently late getting to work—four times last month. If his performance does not improve, you will probably have to replace him.

Claire Lecour   Claire is a five-year employee who was formerly a succesful sales representative for your publishing company, and has recently been promoted to district sales manager. You have heard grumbling from those who work for her that she is disorganized and inefficient, although easy to get along with. The sales figures in her area have increased by only 2% as compared to the 10% average increase for the rest of the company. You are not sure of the exact cause of the problem, but think management training in delegating and planning may help. You value Claire's past contribution to the company and think she can succeed in this job.

a) Write the performance review, which you plan to discuss later with the employee.

b) In groups of three, take turns in an interview being the the employee, employer, and observer-commentator. Although you may have to compress the interview into a shorter time-frame than it would take normally, at least work into part of the discussion an area needing improvement.

7

Persuasive Writing

You would probably be surprised if you stopped to count the number of times during the day when you are trying to influence others to do something, or others are trying to influence you. A typical student might ask a friend to lend some lecture notes, pick up an extra coffee at the cafeteria, get tickets for the hockey game, or go on a date. The same student working in an office might ask a fellow worker to handle a difficult customer, check over a letter or report, or help straighten out a bookkeeping mix-up. These are small favours, unlikely to need much persuasion or meet much resistance. When you want people to do things they have no interest in doing or don't want to do, you need greater powers of persuasion. In business writing, a persuasive letter or memo is one which requires special strategies. It must appeal to a reader or readers in such a way that they make up their minds to act.

Persuasion is not an easy job. There is no one, sure-fire way of doing it. Psychologists, politicians, marketers, and advertisers have spent millions researching the subject. Although they still can't tell what will always work, they have discovered some approaches that work better than others.[1]

In planning persuasive communication, you have three basic influences to consider: your own credibility, the motivation of the receiver, and the structure and content of the message itself.

---

[1] Annette Shelby has compiled a useful summary of relevant research in "The Theoretical Bases of Persuasion: A Critical Introduction," *Journal of Business Communication*, 23: 1 (Winter, 1986), 5-29.

Credibility of the Persuader

To persuade successfully, you should first consider how credible you are. Here are some contributors to credibility:

1. **Position power** If you are the boss or hold an important position, you clearly have built-in credibility since the position itself confers a certain clout or authority. However using the credibility of your position to persuade is different from coercion—using your position to enforce your point of view. In most cases you will want to use the former power.

2. **Expertise** People will often heed the suggestions of a subordinate who has specialized knowledge that they don't possess. What special knowledge do you have?

3. **Trust** Are you considered trustworthy and fair-minded, especially on the subject under discussion? If you are perceived to have a hidden agenda or a vested interest in what you are advocating, your credibility will be diminished.

4. **Similarity** People are more apt to believe someone they perceive to be like them, rather than someone who is not. What do you have in common with the receiver? What bonds of similarity can you point to — home town, background, clubs, special interests?

If your credibility is low, consider getting the support of someone who is more credible than you are to strengthen your case. In business this might be a respected senior executive or an acknowledged expert in the field.

Motivation of the Receiver

It's a truism that to get people to do something they must want to do it. Remember the old saying: "A man convinced against his will is of the same opinion still." It's true for both sexes. But how do you get a person to want to act? What is it that provides motivation? There are no definite answers to these questions, but Abraham Maslow, the well-known organizational behaviourist, provides one useful guide.[2] He suggests that there is a hierarchy of needs that individuals strive to fulfill. Only when they have satisfied basic or "deficiency" needs do they move on to higher ones.

Figure 7-1 indicates the five different levels of needs.

Maslow's ranking of the needs is disputable. Poverty-stricken artists are often less concerned with food and security than with self-fulfillment. However, his insistence that people react according to individual needs is undoubtedly correct. Even with business managers at the same level and in the same type of job, one manager may be concerned about costs, another about prestige, and another about group harmony.

---

[2] Abraham H. Maslow, "A Theory of Human Motivation" in *Motivation and Personality*, 2nd ed. (New York: Harper & Row, 1970).

FIG. 7-1   Maslow's Hierarchy of Needs

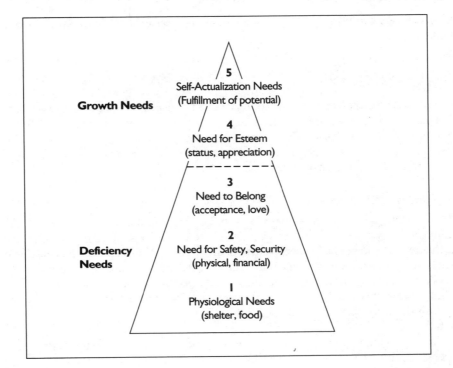

When planning persuasive communication, therefore, spend some time determining the precise need of your receiver. In sales training this step is often referred to as "qualifying" the potential customer, finding out through questions and discussion the need the customer wants filled so that the later sales pitch can work to satisfy it. In your persuasive communication, you should similarly tailor your message to the receiver's perceived need.

The research findings of Wheeless, Barraclough, and Stewart[3] complement Maslow's hierarchy of needs and suggest these strategies for persuasion:

- To persuade someone motivated by survival and safety needs, preview the consequences of following or not following the advice. Advertisements for insurance or road safety often take this approach.

- To persuade someone with a need to belong, stress group identity. Most beer and soft drink advertisements are examples of this strategy.

- To persuade someone with a desire for self-fulfillment, stress values and social obligations. Fund-raising drives for the arts often exemplify this approach.

---

[3] Lawrence R. Wheeless, Robert Barraclough and Robert Stewart, "Compliance-Gaining and Power in Persuasion" in *Communication Yearbook 7* (Beverley Hills, CA: Sage Publications, 1983), 105-45.

Message Options

Your message can be shaped by appeals based on reason, emotion, authority, and evidence.

Appeal to Reason

Managers try to act on reason. They often reach their decisions after analysis, whether they use techniques learnt in business courses or the judgment of experience. When you want to influence people in business, therefore, it's appropriate to present your case in a reasonable way and to appeal to the receiver's desire to be reasonable. Logic — or even the appearance of logic — is convincing.

Handling Opposition

When you are talking to the converted — that is, suggesting something that fits into the receiver's viewpoint — you can get a quick response by reinforcing only one side of the case. If you are facing someone with an opposing point of view, however, you will seem more balanced and fair-minded by giving a two-sided argument.

The psychologist Carl Rogers maintains that people are more likely to change a point of view when they don't feel threatened. The most effective approach with opposition, therefore, is to demonstrate not a combative attitude but understanding.[4]

For written arguments, a practical application of this strategy is first to describe the opposite point of view in a non-evaluative way. When you have shown that you appreciate the reader's position, you will then have the reader more willing to listen to yours. With a Rogerian argument you are less concerned about "winning" than about gaining support.

You can structure such an argument two ways, as Figure 7-2 shows:

1. **Begin with a concession statement.** In a paragraph or two summarize the opposing position clearly and objectively. Then proceed to your side of the case, showing how it overrides the preceding argument. For example, if you want to support the advantages of North American free trade, you would begin with the reasons others give for not supporting the concept.

2. **Use a zig-zag structure.** Begin with one of the opposing points, then counter it. Move to the next opposing point, and counter it. And so on. As a supporter of free trade, you could use this structure to present and counter three popular arguments against free trade.

---

[4] Rogers first proposed this approach in "Communication: Its Blocking and Its Facilitation," a paper delivered at Northwestern University on October 11, 1951.

FIG. 7-2   A Rogerian Approach to Argument

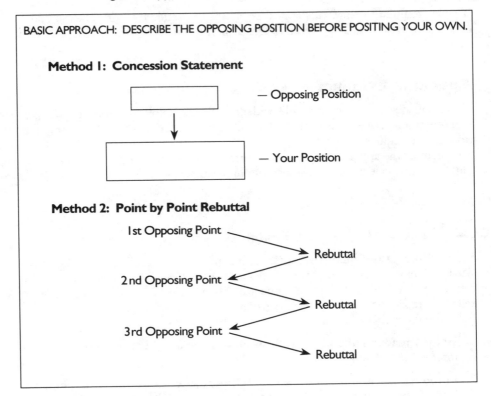

BASIC APPROACH: DESCRIBE THE OPPOSING POSITION BEFORE POSITING YOUR OWN.

Method 1: Concession Statement

— Opposing Position

— Your Position

Method 2: Point by Point Rebuttal

1st Opposing Point

Rebuttal

2nd Opposing Point

Rebuttal

3rd Opposing Point

Rebuttal

Appeal to Emotion

Even with "hard-nosed" decision-makers, reason will not win the day in all circumstances. Sometimes it takes an added appeal to move people — an appeal to emotion.

Take cigarettes, for example. Most smokers are convinced — that is, they rationally agree — that cigarettes are bad for the health and smoking is a silly habit. But are they persuaded to stop smoking? Obviously not.

Advertisers know that no matter how objective we try to be in our judgments, emotion has a way of creeping in. Advertising copy often capitalizes on this fact by appealing to one or more basic emotions — pride; fear; envy; or the desire to be loved, happy, or respected. The promotion of consumer products, whether liquor, cars, or deodorant soap, usually has a strong emotional appeal. In other kinds of persuasive business correspondence, the play on emotion is usually subordinate to reason and more subtle.

An emotional appeal does not work with someone who is strongly opposed. Nor is its effect very longlasting. It is most useful as a way of tipping the balance for someone who already has good rational arguments. When you choose to play on emotions, be moderate in your appeal.

Appeal to Authority

If your credibility is low, this appeal is especially useful. By using the testimony or support of someone the receiver trusts or respects, you can bolster your own case.

Appeal to Evidence

Using statistics and other verifiable evidence will also help gain support when personal credibility is low. Supplying new proof is always more persuasive, however, than trotting out old, familiar evidence.

Of course, the appeals described above are not mutually exclusive. You can combine more than one in any persuasive communication.

Basic Patterns for Persuasion

For most persuasive letters, the reader is more likely to be indifferent than hostile to what you have to say. Yet since indifference is an obstacle — a form of passive resistance — you will need to overcome it if you are going to persuade the reader to read on, let alone to adopt your suggestion. The basic order for a persuasive letter helps overcome this resistance:

1. **Get the reader's attention.** This opening attention-getter should be brief — at most a short paragraph of three sentences.

2. **Introduce the proposal or product and persuade the reader of the benefit**. Build interest by showing how the proposal or product fills a specific need. Anticipate any objections and answer them.

3. **Indicate the action the reader must take.** Link the act to the benefit.

As with other kinds of business correspondence, persuasive writing must be you-centred if it is to work. Even though the subject of the communication may be a product or another organization's needs, the appeal must be directed at the reader.

Persuasive writing has many different uses, but it nearly always works best if it takes an indirect approach. Many writers mistakenly state the request straight off, thinking it will save the reader's time. Admittedly a routine or straightforward request to a receptive reader can and often should be direct. A request requiring persuasive power, however, needs reader preparation.

The most common kinds of persuasive writing in business are requests for volunteer help, sales letters, and collection letters. Each follows the basic persuasive pattern, although some, such as the sales letter, modify it considerably.

Requests for Volunteer Help

Volunteer work has been called the glue that holds a community together. As active members of society, business people are often asked to give unpaid help to an organization or cause, or ask others to do so. Written pleas for donations or time, requests to give speeches or lectures at no charge, invitations to serve on the boards or committees of charities, calls for help in political campaigns — these are all forms of persuasive communication.

A request for unpaid help can often appeal to the social conscience, to a sense of obligation to the community or a desire to make a contribution. The good feeling and self-respect that come from doing valuable service can be reason enough for responding favourably. The writer's job is to make clear that the service is valuable.

Readers may also be moved by other indirect benefits to themselves or their businesses — the chance to meet potential customers, to promote their own interests or viewpoints, to obtain a position of leadership, or simply to have another outlet from their workaday jobs. Whatever appeal or appeals you use — and often you can use more than one — be sure to give the reader good reasons for accepting, rather than suggest reasons for refusing. The letter below provides an easy out for the reader. It also mistakenly states the request directly:

> I have been authorized to ask you to join the Concerned Citizens Committee, which is planning a fund-raising fair for the handicapped in our city. We hope to raise enough money to provide a bus for the handicapped. The handicapped vitally need our support and we think our efforts will be improved by having people with business experience involved.
>
> We know you are a busy man, Mr. Kraft, but hope that you will find the time to join our committee. Please let me know your answer as soon as possible.

By contrast, this next letter uses the indirect order for persuasion, and is more concrete in outlining the request and the benefits. It tries to make the reader want to accept, and suggests a specific action for the reader to follow.

> Many a handicapped person in Rosemount sits at home day after day, depressed and lonely because it is difficult to get out. The Concerned Citizens Committee wants to correct this sad situation by providing a specially equipped bus for the handicapped.
>
> To raise money for the bus, we are planning a spring fair. Will you join our committee of community leaders and help to make the fair a success? Your experience in business would be a great asset in organizing the event. We plan to meet for only two hours every other Tuesday evening until the May event.
>
> Can you drop me a note or telephone me (923-5150) within the next week to say that you will join us? When the handicapped of Rosemount can get out and around on their bus, they will be grateful to you.

Sales Letters

Since sales letters bring in millions of dollars, a great deal of money has been spent researching how to do them. Sales letters tend to be longer than other kinds of letters, because they include a lot of specific facts. The concrete details about a product are what heighten a buyer's desire to have it. But sales letters clearly do not just ramble on; every part is carefully crafted. Good ones have a flow and vitality which hold the reader's attention from beginning to end.

Many sales letters are form letters, sent out in the hundreds or thousands to people who haven't asked for them. Unsolicited sales letters require more skill than any other kind of letter, because they must stir uninterested readers to action. Professional writers are well paid to keep us from throwing out "junk mail." Even though the percentage of returns is small, unsolicited letters are effective sales weapons. So, of course, are solicited letters. Written after a request for information, they are an easier task, because they are responding to a demonstrated interest. Nevertheless, they still must meet the challenge of turning an interest into a sale.

Whether they are composed individually or as a form letter, all sales letters need careful planning. You should attempt to write one only after you have done some serious thinking about the product and the market. (Although you may be selling an idea or a service rather than a product, for simplicity I will refer to products.) At the least you should have answers for the following questions:

- How does the product work and what are its materials?
- What are its outstanding features that make it different from its competitors?
- What is the price and how does it compare with the price of other, similar products?
- What kind of warranty and service arrangements does it have?
- What is the profile of the intended buyer? Here's where marketing research helps. Try to find out as much as you can about the target market. Consider, for example, age, sex, income, area and type of residence as well as lifestyle. From this information you will be better able to figure out the buyer's perceived need.
- What will be the benefits to the intended buyer of having the product? Will it improve appearance, for example, or give more comfort, safety, or status?

After you have analyzed the product and market, determine what will be the central **selling point.** There may be several outstanding features to choose from, and you will probably want to mention all these features in the sales letter, but one central selling point should dominate. This point becomes the theme of your sales letter — the focus that holds all the other details together.

Sales Letter Sequence

A sales letter follows the indirect order of other persuasive letters, but the formula is more precise. Its sequence can be remembered by the acronym AIDA: *attention, introduction, desire, action.*

FIG. 7-3   Example of a Sales Letter

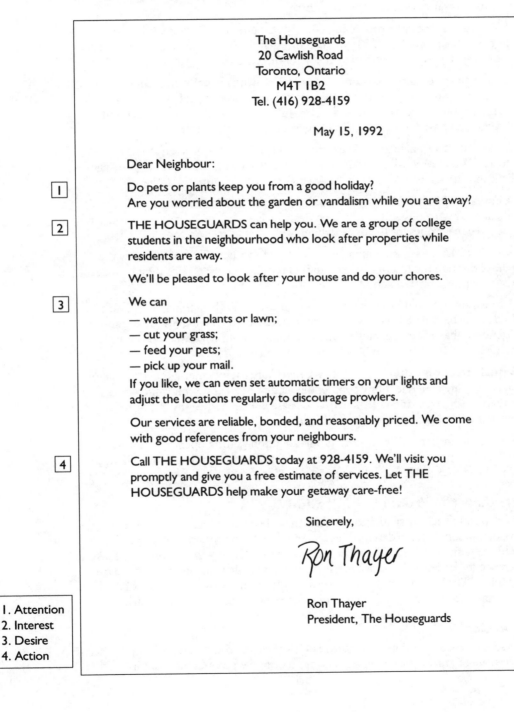

The Houseguards
20 Cawlish Road
Toronto, Ontario
M4T 1B2
Tel. (416) 928-4159

May 15, 1992

Dear Neighbour:

1

Do pets or plants keep you from a good holiday?
Are you worried about the garden or vandalism while you are away?

2

THE HOUSEGUARDS can help you. We are a group of college students in the neighbourhood who look after properties while residents are away.

We'll be pleased to look after your house and do your chores.

3

We can
— water your plants or lawn;
— cut your grass;
— feed your pets;
— pick up your mail.
If you like, we can even set automatic timers on your lights and adjust the locations regularly to discourage prowlers.

Our services are reliable, bonded, and reasonably priced. We come with good references from your neighbours.

4

Call THE HOUSEGUARDS today at 928-4159. We'll visit you promptly and give you a free estimate of services. Let THE HOUSEGUARDS help make your getaway care-free!

Sincerely,

Ron Thayer

Ron Thayer
President, The Houseguards

1. Attention
2. Interest
3. Desire
4. Action

Capture Attention

There are several ways to do it, among them:

- **A startling or thought-provoking fact**   "One out of every four adults will develop a back problem"; "If you had invested in Fairview Estates ten years ago, your property would now be worth at least three times what you paid for it."

- **A stimulus to the imagination**   A description with concrete, sensuous details works well, especially with a product that has romantic appeal, such as a sailboat: "Picture yourself at the tiller on a sunny July day, sailing over the crystal waters of Georgian Bay." Remember that "sensuous" refers to all the senses.

- **An anecdote or narrative**   Many products can be introduced effectively by a story: "When Mrs. Miller bought her Nulite sewing machine twenty years ago, little did she know it would still be sewing her grandchildren's clothes."

- **A bargain**   Few people can resist finding out the details of a bargain. Many will be caught by the possibility of a good deal, such as the come-on, "Now you can get three magazines for the price of one."

- **An offer**   Like a bargain, an offer presents a direct benefit, and can draw the reader through the rest of the letter to find out the details: "Here's a way to cut your shopping time in half."

- **A question**   "Would you like to cut your heating bills by a third?" "Should Canadians be worried about our environment?" If you use a question to capture attention, make sure the reader will not want to answer negatively. If the answer is a quick "no," the reader will not bother to read on.

- **Visual attention-getters**   Pictures are especially useful for emotional appeals, since they are concrete. For example, the picture of an appealing child who suffers from some childhood handicap or disease is an effective way to begin a request for funds to combat the problem.

A word of caution: Make sure that any attention-getting opener is related to the central selling point of the product. It's no help having a catchy beginning if it doesn't lead into the sales pitch that follows.

Introduce the Product or Proposal

This step in the AIDA sequence has sometimes been called "Interest." Clearly, the introduction should try to develop interest. Linking the introduction of the product to a specific benefit will help. Think of the question, "How will the product make a difference to the reader?" Introduce it in such a way that the benefit is inseparable. Example: "The Vogageurs' Business Travellers Insurance Plan will rid you of the high cost — and accompanying anxieties — of sickness or injury in foreign countries."

Build Desire

This step extends the effort to stir the reader's interest. You are stepping up the sales pitch, trying to make the reader not just appreciate the product but want it.

Details sell, and the more concrete the better. Showing the product in action, however, has more effect than an inert description. Try to describe the product as if the reader were actually using it. Instead of saying, "This comfortable Reilly chair has a cushioned leather seat. It can swivel as well as recline," you might describe the chair as if the reader were in it:

> Sink into the soft leather of the cushioned seat. Lie back and catch forty winks. Or swivel around to watch your favourite T.V. program. Either way, you'll feel comfortable and relaxed in a Reilly chair.

Remember that the more sensuous your descriptive detail — the more the reader has a sense of seeing, touching, hearing, or smelling — the more the product will come alive, whether it is a camera or a can-opener. Don't pile on the adjectives, however. A few, chosen to convey the central selling point, are better than a lot. If your central selling point is luxury, you are better to repeat the word *luxury* or *luxurious* than to spray the text with a range of less appropriate adjectives.

In building desire, you can appeal to emotion or to logic, but you are trying to move the reader to ask, "And how can I get this?" Beyond concrete description, you can offer additional evidence or incentives, such as:

- **Overwhelming statistics**   "Over 100 000 students have enjoyed the benefits of our scholarship plan in the last five years"; "Independent research shows that cars with Rust-Away last an average of two years longer."

- **Testimonials**   The credibility of the person doing the persuading can affect reader reaction. For this reason many sales letters use testimonials from people who are generally considered trustworthy, such as doctors and scientists. Even though their credentials are not scientific, sports and entertainment celebrities are often hired to endorse products. Buyers assume that since they are experts in one area they are believable in another — questionable logic perhaps, but often effective.

- **A deal, freebie, or savings**   When a deal or bargain is not the central selling point, offering one can often be a useful additional incentive to buy. The offer of a free bonus or a home-trial with a money-back guarantee can sometimes tip the balance of reader desire. Even if you are selling an idea or service rather than a product, you could show how it would save money.

Show the Action Needed to Get the Product

Here's where you ask for the order. It's crucial at this point to include all the information the reader needs. Do it concisely, however. A brief paragraph of one or two sentences will make it seem simple for the reader to act.

- **Stress promptness**   The longer readers delay, the less likely they are to order. Say something like "Send in your order today" or "We'll mail you the prospectus as soon as we hear from you." Keep the directions simple. A self-addressed envelope or enclosed order form is helpful. If you welcome telephone orders, be sure to include the telephone number along with the address.

- **Be positive but avoid super-hype**   Speak confidently. Instead of a phrase like "I hope . . . ," give direct instructions which assume that the prospect will act. On the other hand, don't harangue your reader with a lot of "Act now! Don't delay getting this fabulous bargain!" exclamations. Although sales letters for some products habitually seem to shout, many readers are turned off by this tactic. A calm but positive tone is usually a better bet than supercharged hyperbole.

A Note About Price

If cost-saving is the central selling point, you should emphasize it from the beginning. If it is an added feature, you could include it in the interest section. If price is not a selling point at all, discuss it at the end of the sales pitch, just before you give the details on how to buy. One way of de-emphasizing the cost is to link it with benefits. You can make it the subordinate part of a sentence in which the main part mentions the reward: "For only $12.99 you can have 24 issues — two years of entertaining reading."

If you simply want to use the sales letter as a chance to get in the door, you may want to eliminate the mention of price altogether. The action step you want in that case will be a request for a brochure of an appointment. This approach is often used when the price of getting something will initially seem high. The disadvantage is that the reader has a potential objection that remains unaddressed, but that trade-off may be better than the risk of losing a prospect because of high price.

Collection Letters

If you are in a business that has many transactions with customers or clients, you will likely be faced with the problem of unpaid bills.

Although chasing money is distasteful to many people, it's a job that cannot be ignored, or done in a half-hearted way, if the business is to stay profitable. Successful bill-collecting is a matter of three P's: promptness, patience, and perseverance. It requires promptness in going after the debtor at regular intervals, patience in remaining courteous, and perseverance in not letting the debtor off the hook.

The collection process usually takes the form of a series of letters making increasingly insistent demands on the reader to pay the bill. If you are in a company with a lot of debtors, it is probably best to design a series of form letters which can be personalized, depending on the resources available to do the job. Word processors will allow you to insert or delete to fit the customer. As with any other form of customer or client correspondence, the more individualized the letter, the more likely it is to be effective.

The collection series usually consists of three to five letters sent over a period of one to four months after payment is first due. Whether all or some of the letters are sent depends largely on the character and record of the debtor. In deciding what kind of letter will be most effective, therefore, the first step is to assess the debtor: is he or she is a good credit risk or a poor one?

A good credit risk

— usually pays on time; or
— sometimes forgets but pays promptly when reminded; or
— makes arrangements to pay in installments, when he or she cannot pay immediately.

A poor credit risk

— has a record of unpaid bills elsewhere; or
— is habitually late in paying; or
— pays only when threatened with legal action.

By trying to figure out in advance the type of person you are dealing with and the likely reason for the unpaid bill, you can adapt the letter to the situtation, increasing the chance of recovery and decreasing the likelihood of hard feelings.

General Guidelines

Three guidelines apply to all good collection letters: be polite, stick to the facts and follow through with what you say.

Be Polite

When the other side in a dispute is clearly at fault, it's easy to be hostile. A good collection letter remains polite, even when it is severe and stringent in its demands. Remember that the aim of most collection efforts is not to impose some penalty but to get the debtor to pay. If the customer or client is someone whose business you want to retain, it's doubly important to keep the relationship as free from animosity as possible. Here is the kind of language to avoid, and some alternatives to it:

   x If you were dissatisfied, you should have returned the saw in the ten-day trial period.

   ✔ Our ten-day trial allowed you to test the saw and return it for a full refund within that period, if you wished.

   x Since you have failed to pay your bill, you are being charged interest at a rate of 18% per year.

   ✔ Until the bill is paid, interest will be charged at a rate of 18% per year. (This is an instance where the passive verb works better than the active, since it is less accusatory.)

Stick to the Facts

Give precise dates for when you expect payment and give exact figures of the amount owing. Don't exaggerate or indulge in emotional overkill:

   x You are forever forgetting to pay your bills.

   x Clearly nobody can rely on you.

Follow Through with What You Say

Be honest about your intentions and then stick to your guns. If you say that you will be willing to negotiate terms for payment, be sure that you will do so. If you threaten to take legal action by a certain date, when the times comes, act immediately. If your threats are seen as idle ones, they will be disregarded.

Collection Letter Sequence

The most common sequence of letters in a collection series is a reminder, followed when necessary by an inquiry, a positive appeal, a negative appeal, and an ultimatum.

Reminder

This is usually the first letter sent, unless the debtor has a record of late payment. Many people, especially individual consumers, will simply have forgotten or been too busy doing other things. A reminder is enough to get quick payment. Even for habitually late payers, a reminder can serve notice that interest charges are building:

> This is a reminder that $540.00 remaining payment for your new carpets was due on April 30th. To avoid a build-up of interest charges, please slip your payment promptly in the enclosed envelope.
>
> At Pricefields we look forward to serving you again.

For reminder notices, some businesses simply send a copy of the original invoice with a stamp or sticker saying "Reminder," "Overdue," or "Second Notice" in a conspicuous spot.

Inquiry

The purpose here is to obtain immediate payment or, alternatively, to get an explanation that will allow you to work out a plan for future payment. This approach works well for customers who fully intend to pay but who have a temporary cash shortage. By asking for the reason for non-payment (and implying or explicitly offering to negotiate terms for payment), you have a good chance of getting a response, if not fast payment. If the customer's record is good enough to justify installment paying, you can at least get the process started:

> Although we have sent you two reminder notices, we still have not received payment of your account of $540.00, outstanding since April 30. Interest charges are accumulating. Since you are a trusted customer, we wonder what has happened.
>
> We would appreciate immediate payment or at least an explanation for your delay. We may be able to work out a mutually satisfactory plan for payment.
>
> We await your prompt response.

In asking for an explanation, be careful not to provide ready-made excuses for the customer, such as suggesting possible dissatisfaction with goods or services.

Positive Appeal

This appeal may take several forms, but essentially it appeals to the customer's better qualities or gives positive reasons for paying the bill. The emphasis in this and other appeals should be on the benefit to the customer rather than to the company. Depending on the customer, the central message may appeal to one or more attitudes or emotions:

- **Fair play**   Here you can point out what you have done for the customer, and suggest that it is the customer's turn to balance the equation. A majority of people think of themselves as fair and honest, and many will react positively to a call for fair play:

    Last July we sent you a shipment of lumber to help meet your cottage building needs. Now we in turn ask you for payment of your bill for $410.00, which was overdue as of August 30th. We have already sent you two reminders and a request for an explanation.

    We value your business and will continue to strive to give you prompt and efficient service. Please return us the favour by a prompt payment of the $410.00 still owing.

- **Pride in reputation**   People in the public eye or in positions of leadership are usually especially conscious of maintaining a good reputation. Many are justifiably proud of their reputation and do not want to be known for anything discreditable. These people will likely respond well to a letter which appeals to their pride:

    We are sure you value your reputation as a successful small business owner, and want to retain the respect of the business community by paying your bills promptly . . .

    or

    Through sound management, your company has acquired a good credit rating in the business community. In order to keep this rating and the respect that goes with it, please pay your bill promptly.

- **Practical self-interest**   In this appeal you simply show how prompt payment will directly benefit the reader — usually in avoiding extra expense, whether high interest charges or the legal costs of a suit. This is obviously less an appeal to emotion than an appeal to reason. You are counting on the reader seeing the sense of paying and avoiding more problems.

Negative Appeal

People who are normally good credit risks are more likely to be frightened of the consequences of non-payment than are poor risks. People with a history of defaults often try to get away with it again. An appeal to fear emphasizes the consequences of non-payment, such as loss of reputation, inability to get credit with other businesses, or costly court action. Take care that your tone is direct and matter of fact in laying out the consequences; let the threatened consequences rather than abusive or inflammatory remarks do the work:

> . . . Since we have received no money or explanation from you since the due date of April 30th, our next step will be to turn to your employer. We will be seeking permission to deduct a portion of the amount owing from your monthly pay cheques. To avoid this embarrassment . . .
>
> *or*
>
> . . . We are sure you realize the damage to reputation and credit rating that a court case will entail, as well as the extra cost in time and money. You can avoid these consequences by promptly settling your account.

You can emphasize the urgency of this kind of ultimatum by sending it through registered mail. You can also get someone in a higher position in your company to sign it.

Ultimatum

This letter of last resort is a straightforward warning to pay or be prepared for the consequences — either the intervention of a collection agency or immediate legal action. If you think the customer will fight the case, it's a good idea to mention your previous notices and appeals. You should also give the precise date on which you will take further action if the bill is not paid:

> On February 15, we delivered four new chairs to your office and sent you a bill for $540.00 at the end of the month. Despite four requests since that time, we have received neither the money nor an explanation from you. We have no option now but to take direct action.
>
> If we do not receive payment by June 30 of the total bill, including interest, of $578.00, we will instruct our lawyers, McBinn and Naylor, to start legal proceedings.

For small bills, the cost to you or your company of legal proceedings makes a final ultimatum of this sort impractical. Your only hope in these cases is to make the other appeals strong enough that the customer tries to pay the debt to you before paying any other creditors. If you are supplying a continuing service or product, such as garden maintenance or magazines, where you can stop the supply, you can effectively paint a picture of the pleasure or convenience which the customer will now lose — or could regain by paying the bill.

In any case, despite some bad apples, most customers and clients want to pay their bills and want the comfortable feeling of a transaction satisfactorily completed. Unless you have evidence to the contrary, you are best to be positive before being negative in handling collections. You will more likely get your money — and keep a customer.

EXERCISES

● Section A

1. Clip an advertisement in which there are at least three paragraphs of text, and make three photocopies. In groups of three, discuss the dominant motivator and the type of appeal used in the advertisement each of you has brought.

   Then think of a way in which the advertisement could stress a different motivator and use a different type of appeal.

2. In small groups or as a class, consider the type of appeal you would choose in each of the following situations:

   a) As the new accountant for your small company, you think buying a new accounting computer program would help you to be more efficient and would create a better internal control system. Your boss is known to be a penny-pincher, and does not yet trust your ability.

   b) As a way of increasing sales, the vice-president of your company has divided the sales force into four regional groups, with a promise of cash rewards to those groups that reach their new sales targets for the next six months, and a special prize to the group that does it fastest. As a regional sales manager, you want to write a memo to subordinates, urging them to strive for specific monthly targets.

   c) As the new Director of Outpatient Services for Children's Hospital, you want to hire a consultant to help reorganize the record-keeping and billing system in your department. You have in mind an aquaintance who was very successful in giving similar help to the much larger General Hospital in your city. The vice-president you report to has been very supportive in general. You know, however, that she is skeptical about consultants, having had several bad experiences with them.

3. A colleague has written the following draft of a letter appealing to fellow employees to join the company's United Way Campaign Committee. He is unhappy with the letter and has asked you to revise it.

   a) Discuss the weaknesses in class.

   b) Rewrite the letter.

   > Dear Fellow Employee:
   >
   > Will you become a part of our Company's United Way Campaign Committee? I know people are involved in so many activities these days, but I hope you will spare the time in the next few months to help this valuable cause. The United Way is an important part of our community and has done an excellent job for many years. Our company is trying to do its share of money-raising from employees.
   >
   > Please let me know soon if you can become involved.

4. The sentences here are all intended to be part of sales letters. Revise them, making them concrete, positive, and active. Try to put the reader into the action.

   a) The quartz battery in this clock makes winding unnecessary.

   b) A return trip to London can be had for $625 during the special earlybird sale, but the sale ends April 30th.

   c) With this wire whisk, there need be no more lumps in sauces but instead the sauces will be smooth.

d) Free bonus: a ball-point pen goes with every order, as long as the order isn't under $10.

e) The cost of this self-cleaning iron is more than that of a conventional one, but it avoids clogging and a lot of cleaning nuisance.

f) This cabinet for stereo components looks good and suits most living room decors.

5. Assess a persuasive letter or sales letter you have received recently. Note its strengths and weaknesses. Revise any weak parts.

6. A customer in your sportswear store, Mrs. Elsa Wilkes, bought $250 worth of clothing last June 15, and three months later she still has not paid her bill. Until this point she has been a reliable customer, paying her account on time. You have already sent her two reminder notes and have received no payment. Write the next letter in the collection series, as suggested in this chapter.

7. You are the owner of an accounting office that shares a driveway and parking lot with Handy Cleaners. Since the parking lot needed repairs, you talked to Sam Mavis, the owner of Handy Cleaners, who agreed to share the cost of resurfacing, estimated by All-Weather Paving to be $1000. You arranged for the resurfacing. When the job was completed, you paid the bill and sent a copy of the invoice to Sam Mavis, asking him to pay his share. Two months have passed and he has not paid. You have tried without success to reach him by phone (he does not work in the store) and left messages with his employees. Now you must write him another letter.

● Section B

1. As sales manager for Lancer Foods, you think that a mobile videotape monitor for the department would be useful. The unit could accompany sales personnel on visits to stores, so that store managers could see your company's upcoming advertisements for products. Such exposure would help to involve stores in your company's promotions and increase shelf-space for your products.

   The cost of such a machine would be about $1000.

   The controller of your company, Martin Tight, needs to approve the expenditure. He is known to be very cost conscious, but can be persuaded by good reasons.

   Write a proposal to Martin Tight. You may add any details you need.

2. As a summer assistant at your university's Career Centre, you have been asked by the director to write a letter to be sent to fellow students in the fall. You are asking for volunteers to work as career-planning assistants in the centre. The director gives you the following fact-sheet on which to base your letter. Organizing and rewording the facts as you see fit, write a persuasive appeal.

   Position: Volunteer Career Planning Assistant
   Hours: 4 hours per week during the academic session
   Qualifications: no experience needed — training provided
   Responsibilities: — direct students to Career Centre's resources;
          — critique student job-application forms;
          — plan career-talks, assisting in career workshops.
   Benefits: — learn effective job-search techniques;
          — develop leadership skills;
          — get work experience.

Information and application forms available at information desk, Career Centre, Room 202. Return application by September 30th.

3. You are heading the United Way Campaign in the office. Although the contribution rate is good (85 percent), you hope fellow employees will increase their donations this year, since the need for United Way services has increased dramatically in your city. Moreover, you know that most people have used or will use a United Way service at some point. You have heard objections that administrative costs of the United Way are too high, but have discovered that ninety percent of donations go directly into client services.

   Write a letter to all employees, to be accompanied by a brochure and a pledge card. You may add any realistic details that will help create an effective letter.

4. Assess the specific weaknesses in the following sales letter, according to the guidelines discussed in this chapter. Then revise it.

   > It's never too late! Just because you missed the after-Christmas sales doesn't mean you need to miss this bargain!
   >
   > We are offering to select buyers a unique pocket radio. It weighs barely 400 grams and fits into your pocket and yet gives magnificent sound. In both AM and FM! High-quality headphones are included.
   >
   > The price is only $29.95, as you can see from the order form below. Amazing value! Beat your friends to it and buy now! Don't delay!

5. Select an advertisement from a current magazine or newspaper. Ascertain the market for the advertised product or service, the image or selling point projected by the advertisement, and the special features mentioned. Now write a sales letter based on the advertisement. Use the AIDA formula discussed in this chapter. (Include the advertisement when presenting your letter.)

6. Last fall you began a winter snow-shovelling service. You offered customers a choice of a fixed cost of $100 to cover all snow removal throughout the winter or a fee-for-service charge of $10-15 per shovelling, depending on the size of the lot. You hired students to do the clearing, and you provided equipment and handled the sales and paperwork. Jennifer Harvey agreed to the fixed cost of $100 and paid $50 in advance. The winter had an unusually light snowfall and you only needed to shovel the small Harvey property four times. Mrs. Harvey has written to you and enclosed a cheque for $10, saying that she feels this is enough, considering the work done. You don't agree. Since Mrs. Harvey is out a lot and doesn't return your calls, write her a letter asking for the remaining money in a way that will not antagonize her. (The Harveys' neighbours are customers and potential customers.)

7. You have decided to set up a small catering business, operating from your house. You will specialize in casseroles and desserts for people who want to entertain without fuss. In testing your recipes on friends, you have discovered that two favourite casseroles are Beef Supreme (beef with hot peppers and mushrooms in a wine sauce) and Almond Duck (duck with almonds and wild rice in a subtle orange sauce). Your raspberry trifle and chocolate-mint cheesecake are dessert hits. You think that most of your customers will come through personal contact and word-of-mouth, but want to send an initial promotional letter to friends and neighbours. Included with it will be a separate menu and price list.

   Write the body of the letter.

CHAPTER 8

Informal Reports

Whether they are formal or informal, good business reports have a common quality: objectivity. The very name *report* suggests that they are not a vehicle for opinion but for cool-headed reflection based on facts. In writing a report, you will be providing material on which other managers will rely to make decisions. They will want information and advice they can trust.

They will also want a report that is easy to understand. Since managers have many demands on their time, they don't want to waste it sifting through an unnecessary clutter of details. Your job is to select and present the material in such a way that they can quickly grasp the essential features.

Informal reports are more common than formal ones, since they are internal — that is, sent to someone within the same organization. They are usually shorter than formal reports, often only two or three pages. They are informal not because of their brevity, however, but because of their tone. They are more conversational than formal reports, using frequent personal pronouns and contractions. Employees of a company like to think of each other as colleagues or associates, and an informal tone reflects this relationship.

As with every guideline, be prepared to make the odd exception. If you work for a conservative, hierarchical organization and are sending a report several levels up the line, or to someone you don't know well, you may prefer a more formal tone. (To recall the difference between an informal and formal tone, refer to pages 26-28.) Generally, however, internal reports are informal.

The beginning of a short report looks much the same as a memo:

Date:

To:

From:

<u>Underlined Subject</u>

The major difference in format is that a report is divided into sections, and occasionally subsections, with underlined headings for each. The pages (other than the first) are always numbered.

There are two main kinds of informal reporting:

1. **The Informational Report**   This simply gives the facts of a situation, often on a regular schedule; for example, a monthly sales report. Some companies have printed forms for regularly scheduled reports, and the writer has only to fill in the information required in specified categories. The details recorded on forms like these tend to be routine. As a consequence, the reader or readers may not really pay attention to the report, even though they are interested in having it as the administrative apparatus of the company. Such a report may be filed rather than read.

   A way to prevent regular informational reports from becoming mere bureaucratic busywork is to change the emphasis from the routine to the exceptional. Exception reporting is a way of highlighting the information readers ought to pay attention to. It reports on the significant changes from the routine — the achievements and the trouble spots.

2. **The Analytical Report**   In both large and small businesses, this is the more common kind of report and the more challenging to write. It is a problem-solving report, analyzing a situation and recommending a certain course of action. The primary reason for such a report is to help others make a decision; the writer wants to convince the reader of the appropriateness of the analysis and the recommendations or conclusions. Moreover, since presenting ideas or solutions is a harder task than presenting facts, the writer of an analytical report needs to take greater stock of the anticipated reader response in deciding how to organize the report.

Planning the Report

To make sure that a report is effective, you need to set aside a block of time for planning. Then when you sit down to write, you will have a firm idea of where you are heading and how you are going to get there.

Chapter 2 discussed the kind of assessment you should always do about the reader and the reason for writing. Remember that it's important to determine at the outset exactly what type of person you are addressing: consider the reader's position, knowledge, concerns, and possible objections or biases. In the same way, you should decide the precise reason or reasons for writing the report, including the results you hope to obtain from it. If you spend some time on this assessment, you will find it easier to organize and focus your material. In turn, you will find the report easier to write.

The next step is to work out in exact terms the subject of your study. In defining your subject, think of building a fence around a topic. What exactly are the boundaries of your discussion? What will be included and what left out? By being as exact as possible, you will create from the start a clear picture of the territory you are covering and make it easier to organize your analyis. Therefore "A Study of Cars" is too vague, whereas "A Cost-Benefit Analysis of Three Options for Company Cars" is more precise. The subject might not be the eventual title of the report: the title might in the end be "A Recommendation to Buy *X* as a Company Car." Nevertheless, defining the subject clearly will help keep the proportions of the study manageable.

You don't want to spend time on areas of marginal importance or on details that the reader won't care about. For example, if you are asked to write a report on the kind of car the company should lease for its sales force, you will be wasting time — yours and the reader's — if you examine every kind of car available, from sports cars to luxury sedans. It is better to establish in advance the kind or price of vehicle worth considering seriously, and then to analyze in detail the two or three most suitable options. You might also establish beforehand whether buying should be considered as well as leasing.

Ordinarily a short report does not require a great deal of research. Usually it is written by a person with expertise in the subject. Although the writer may have to gather some facts beyond his or her immediate knowledge, generally the information is the kind that can be collected with two or three phone calls. If you do have to do extensive research for an informal report, the next chapter offers some advice.

Choosing the Best Order

Two considerations will determine the best order for a report:

1. **What is the most important information?**   For an analytical report the most important information is likely to be the conclusion drawn from the investigation, or the recommendations for solving a problem. For an informational report, it may merely be a summative statement that generalizes from the facts or draws attention to the most important ones. In any case, construct a hierarchy of information or ideas; decide what matters most and what matters least. The information or ideas you select as being most important will become your key points.

2. **What is the reader's likely reaction?**   You can assume that readers of informational reports want to receive the information, even if it is routine. Similarly, most analytical reports are written at the request of a reader who will be interested in the conclusions or recommendations. In rare cases, however, the reader may be predisposed to reject your conclusions because of a personal bias or conflicting

interests. A manager who dislikes change or easily feels threatened can be negative by habit.

Direct and Indirect Organization

When the reader will be pleased or interested, put the key points before your explanation of how you reached them. This is the best order for most business reports. Specifically, for a short report try following this sequence:

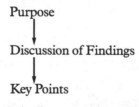

Purpose

Key Points

Discussion of Findings

Unlike an essay, a report needs no final, summary paragraph. As with a newspaper report, the vital information is at the beginning and the least important details are at the end. (Make an exception if you are sending a short report to an outsider in letter form, in which case you can end with a goodwill close.)

For those occasions when the reader of an analytical report will be displeased or skeptical, follow the path of least resistance. Build gradually towards the conclusion or recommendations, by following this sequence:

Purpose

Discussion of Findings

Key Points

Now let's discuss what goes into each section.

Purpose

Open with a short statement of purpose. At its simplest this may be a sentence that says "This report examines paper use in our office and recommends ways to reduce it." Or it can link purpose with recommendations: "This report on paper waste in our office suggests ways to reduce the amount we use." This statement can be worded differently if the subject line or title clearly reveals the aim of the report. If the method of obtaining information is important — if the recommendations are based on a survey, for example — you can include the method in the introductory statement.

Key Points

Most short reports have either conclusions or recommendations, depending on whether they are informational or analytical. In a short direct-order report, you can usually introduce these points in a short paragraph linking them to the statement of purpose. If there are a number of recommendations or conclusions, list them, with the most important first. You may also want to summarize the main findings that support the conclusions or recommendations. Sometimes you can indicate the main recommendation of a short report in the title; for example, "Recommendation to Install Skylight in Reception Area." In this case, merely summarize the findings leading to the recommendation.

You may find it easiest to write this section last, after you have completed the detailed discussion. It will then be obvious which points should be inserted after the statement of purpose.

Discussion of Findings

Here you show how the facts lead to the conclusions or recommendations. This is the most extensive part of the report and may have several headings. It can be divided in various ways, depending on the subject.

Order of Importance

Here you simply follow the direct approach again. For example, if you have determined the different causes or effects of a problem, start with the most important one and give the details. For each new point or finding, make a new section and heading. If the focus of your report is a list of recommendations, you can make each one the subject of a section.

Classification or Division

This method of organizing divides a topic into classes or component parts. Here are some examples:

- A report on the environmental damage to fish in a certain body of water could classify findings according to the different types of fish.

- A study of the recreational habits of people in an area might classify the target population according to age groups, income groups, or types of occupation. Alternatively it may be organized according to types of recreation.

- A marketing study for a new invention might be divided according to the traditional four P's: product, promotion, price and place.

When classifying or dividing the subject,

- **Do** incorporate *all* relevant information within the categories you have devised;

- **Don't** let information overlap categories. For example, a classification of stores shouldn't have small stores and department stores as two of the categories, since it's possible to be a small department store.

- **Don't** put vastly different amounts of information in each of the categories. If one category has most of the information and the remainder have little, you should try to create different categories, or to merge some of the small ones.

Chronological Order

This arrangement groups information according to time periods. It can be an effective way to report on trends; for example, the health problems of babies over the last fifty years, or house-construction needs for the next twenty years. It can also be the obvious choice for reporting a sequence of events or actions.

Take care that you don't choose this order just because it's easiest to arrange. Save it for when the sequence itself matters or for when a timeframe makes the information easier to understand.

Spatial Order

Here the division is according to geography or location. This would be an appropriate order for reporting on individual branch offices or for analyzing buying trends in various regions.

Comparison

The best way of comparing the merits of two or more options is to create an alternating arrangement. Use the criteria for judging them as the basis for division; then compare the alternatives within each section. For example, suppose you are investigating cars for a company fleet, and are comparing the two most likely cars on the basis of purchase price, maintenance record, and gas consumption. You can organize your findings this way:

1. Purchase price	a) Car X
	b) Car Y
2. Maintenance record	a) Car X
	b) Car Y
3. Gas consumption	a) Car X
	b) Car Y

Another way to organize comparisons is by parallel arrangement in which the various options are examined fully one by one.

1. Car X	— purchase price
	— maintenance record
	— gas consumption
2. Car Y	— purchase price
	— maintenance record
	— gas consumption

This arrangement is not as effective, however, since the reader has to skip back and forth to determine relative merits. Use it only when the things being compared are so diverse that it is impossible to establish common criteria.

Writing the Report

Overcoming Writer's Block

Some reluctant writers would do anything rather than put pen to page. They put off the fateful hour by inventive delaying tactics. One such tactic is to do yet another round of research and to build up such an array of facts that more study is needed. Of course such unnecessary analysis only leads to further writing paralysis.

If you recognize yourself in this description, take note that there's a better way. The cause of your reluctance to write is probably not laziness as much as fear that you won't do a good enough job. If this is the case, then remember that few successful writers get their results by sitting down and producing polished copy. Rather, they know how to rewrite and edit. Following their example, you should not aim for perfection on the first draft; as soon as you have decided how to organize the material in the report, just try to get it all down on the page as quickly as possible.

Here are three methods experienced writers have found useful in preventing or overcoming writer's block:

1. **Dictating**   People who have access to a dictating machine and typist often find that they can overcome writing paralysis by dictating the first draft. Speaking doesn't seem as formidable as writing. This method works best if you have already devised an outline for your report, and have mostly to fill in the details of sections. You should be prepared to do some heavy editing of the transcribed draft.

2. **Using a Word Processor**   This method is helpful even if you are not a good typist. Since it's easy to change what you have written — to add, delete, or move whole sections around — you will feel less constrained by your wish to write a perfect first draft.

3. **Free Writing**   Start with the part of the report you understand best or find easiest to explain and put your thoughts down on the page in any order that they come. Keep writing without second-guessing or criticizing. You might even begin simply by saying "The point I want to make is . . . " and continuing. The aim is to get the writing juices flowing. If you don't stop until your thoughts run out, you may be surprised at the amount of material you have written. This method requires more revision than most, but at least you have something on the page to work from.

Whatever method you use, don't worry about your grammar or spelling as you write: simply keep working until you've got all the ideas and information down. When you have a draft in front of you, you will be over the major hurdle.

Writing Objectively

The opening sentence of this chapter said that reports should be objective. A report that is free of personal prejudices and subjective opinion will surely have more influence than one that is not. Yet it's not easy to be objective, particularly if you have a special interest in your proposals or recommendations. Here are some guidelines that will help keep your reports as unbiased as possible.

1. **Identify your assumptions.** If you have assumed that some aspects of a given topic are not worth discussing in the report, say so. If you have chosen to limit the topic, give the reason. For example, you may have decided to limit your study of possible company cars to two-door models, based on the assumption that the drivers would rarely have more than one passenger. By identifying your assumption, you demonstrate your thoroughness — you have considered all the possibilities and have fixed upon the most appropriate ones.

2. **Substantiate your opinions.** Your conclusions and recommendations should follow from the facts. Personal opinion can have weight if the person expressing it is an authority on the subject, but in most cases opinion needs the support of evidence or explanation. Don't imply what you cannot prove. If your findings aren't foolproof, show where the uncertainty lies. In using statistics, show the level of uncertainty for any calculated values if you can.

3. **Avoid subjective language.** Words such as *amazing* or *dreadful* have an over-charged, emotional tone. Instead of saying, ''Ergon Products had a fantastic growth in sales last quarter,'' let the facts speak for themselves: ''Ergon Products had a thirty percent sales increase last quarter.''

4. **Be specific.** As discussed in Chapter 4, concrete language is more lively than abstract language. It can also be clearer. Although you needn't give specific details for every idea or fact you include in a report, you should try to be exact when referring to people, places, times, and amounts — especially when you think the information might be disputed:

   x   After the press contacted plant personnel, it was reported that some of the storage equipment was faulty.

   ✓   After *Globe* reporter June Fisher telephoned Harry Brown last Friday, she reported that two storage tanks had cracks.

   x   Plant management was involved in the safety discussion process.

   ✓   Jim Peters, the plant manager, and Helen Falt, the assistant manager, came to three meetings of the Employee Safety Committee.

Be especially careful with ambiguous phrases or words that can have more than one meaning. Terms such as *windfall profit* or *reliable* can have various interpretations, depending on the reader.

Effective Editing

When you have finished the first draft, it's time to take a break. Put the pages in a drawer and forget about them for a while. Meet some friends for lunch or go and play squash. Not only do you deserve a reward, but you will edit more effectively if you come back to the job refreshed. When you leave enough time before editing to forget what you have said, you will be able to assess the draft better. You will be able to spot the weaknesses and confusing parts in your report when you go through it as a relatively detached reader rather than as a harried writer.

The crucial guideline for editing is to put yourself in the reader's shoes. Just as you anticipated the reader's attitudes and expectations when you were planning the report, so in editing you should check whether you have adequately responded to them.

Experienced writers are sometimes able to edit different aspects of their writing at the same time, but if you are not experienced, your revisions will be more effective if you work through your report several times. The best place to begin is with the organization of your material. First ask yourself these questions:

1. **Is the report properly focused?**   Will the reader be able to state the central message in a sentence or two? Does the choice and arrangement of detail point to this message?

2. **Is the report complete?**   Has it addressed the reader's concerns? Will the reader have unanswered questions? Have I presented all the evidence, and put it in a form that is easy to follow? If I have not been able to provide some important details, have I explained why?

3. **Do the conclusions and recommendations fit logically with the findings?**   Are the links between them explicit? Have I considered all the evidence fairly? Would the reader be able to reach a different conclusion from the same evidence? In other words, do my conclusions seem objective or do they reflect a personal bias?

4. **Are there any inconsistencies, contradictions, or ambiguities in what I have said?**   Could the reader misinterpret any part?

Now you can turn to the surface structure of your report — to the grammar, punctuation, spelling, and style. Consider the kinds of mistakes you have made in past writing, and do a special check for these. If your special weakness is joining sentences with commas, for example, run through the report looking only for these faulty splices. The advice in Chapters 12 and 13 will help you to spot grammatical errors and to use punctuation accurately. Chapters 3 and 4 will help you improve your style. Underlying all your stylistic editing should be the three basic precepts of effective writing: be clear, be concise, be forceful.

Remember if you are a poor speller that a spell-check exists in most word-processing programs to help correct spelling and typographical errors. However don't depend on it entirely since, as mentioned in Chapter 5, it does not catch correctly spelled words that are incorrectly used.

Creating Visual Impact

Although you may not judge a book by its cover, you are probably influenced by appearance. The same is true for a report. If it appeals to the eye, the reader will be more inclined to read it. Since you will want your reports not only to be picked up but to be read through, they should have visual impact. Here are some ways to achieve the desired effect.

Use Space Creatively

Don't cram your writing all together, but leave space between sections and subsections. A densely covered page seems more formidable than one with some spaces. Leave wide margins — at least 3 cm (1¼ in.) at the top and right side and 4 cm (1½ in.) at the left side and bottom, as a way of framing the text. If you want to give a part of the report special emphasis, leave extra space around it, so that the white sets off the black of the text. You can also use a different typeface for that part or underline it if it is short.

Use Descriptive Headings

Each section and subsection of a report should have a heading. Try to make headings "high-information" — as descriptive and specific as possible — especially in your discussion of findings. They should tell the story of the report so that a reader glancing through it will know the important points. In fact, descriptive headings often reflect key points. Notice the difference between the following sets of headings for a short report comparing brands of office carpet:

Low-information headings:

a) Durability

b) Cost

c) Colour choice

High-information, descriptive headings:

a) Brand X is most durable.

b) Brand Z costs least.

c) Brands X and Y have most colours.

It's not always possible to make every heading reflect a key point. Occasionally a heading that simply tells the nature of the content will serve well. For example, if you must have a separate section explaining how you conducted research, it may be appropriate to call it simply "Method." On the whole, though, the more descriptive the headings the easier the report will be to read and remember. Descriptive headings are a decided advantage.

Although complete sentences are often useful for headings, keep them short. Point-form is preferable:

x   In the future, computers will show a substantial decrease in price.

⌁   Price of computers will drop.

Where possible, use parallel phrasing for the headings within the report.

With the new graphics packages for word processors, it's easy to use boldface, italics, and other typefaces for headings. With this candybox of options, however, there's a danger of using too much. For a clear and consistent approach, here is a guide:

- Capitals have more impact than lower-case letters.
- Underlining and boldface are more emphatic than italics.
- Italics are harder to read than conventional typescript and, therefore, are best reserved for short headings rather than long blocks of print.
- Frequent changes of typeface create a cluttered look. Keep to two at the most.

It's helpful, although not essential in a short report, to put numbers before the headings. Numbering lets readers easily refer to sections. Numbering also shows the relative importance of sections and subsections. You can choose from several numbering systems. Two common ones use a combination of numerals and letters:

```
I                              A
   A                              1
      1                              a
         a                              i
         b                              ii
      2                              b
   B                              2
II                             B
```

Increasingly, technical reports are using a decimal system:

```
1.
        1.1
           1.11
           1.12
        1.2
2.
```

Whichever system you choose, be sure to use equivalent symbols for sections of equivalent importance.

Vary Typeface and Position of Headings

If you look at a well-edited textbook or published report, you will notice that headings have different typefaces, depending on whether they introduce a chapter, a section, or a subsection. The varying positions of the headings also indicate their relative importance, although some reports keep all headings by the left margin. Systems can vary, but Figure 8-1 shows a common one, especially for typewriter users. For computer users, boldface can substitute for underlining.

FIG. 8-1   Format for Headings

FIRST DEGREE HEADING

Centred. Usually all in capitals. Sometimes underlined.

Second-Degree Heading

    At left margin. Underlined. Text is below. First letter of each word except an article or a preposition under four letters is in capitals.

Third-degree heading.   Usually at margin, but can be indented. Text follows on the same line. Only first letter of first word in capitals.

List Information

As well as having visual impact, lists allow for quick comprehension. They emphasize that you are making a number of points and help distinguish one point from another. Whenever you can simplify material by using a list, do so. As a rule of thumb, try listing three or more consecutive items or ideas. Conversely, if a list becomes too long — say, beyond six or seven items — try grouping some of the items to make a smaller list. If you will be referring to any items in a list later in the report, number the items. If not, you can simply introduce each item by a dash (—) or a bullet (•).

Use parallel phrasing for all items on a list. Notice the difference in readability between the first list describing problems with some machinery and the two revised versions, which have parallel phrasing:

Unrevised:
— breakdowns frequent;
— you will find servicing is slow;
— costly spare parts.

Point-form revision:
— frequent breakdowns;
— slow servicing;
— costly spare parts.

Sentence-form revision:
— breakdowns are frequent;
— servicing is slow;
— spare parts are costly.

Use Illustrations

Charts, graphs, tables and other illustrations clarify information and reinforce points. For best effect, design them so that they are simple and uncluttered. Provide a title, unless the text immediately before the illustration gives its purpose. Unless the details are self-explanatory, clearly label each part or axis. In a report on scientific or technical matters, where quantitative precision is vital, include error bars ($\pm$) if you can.

When the information is important, integrate the illustrations with your text; when the information is supplemental, put it in an Exhibits section at the end or in an appendix. When illustrations are in an Exhibits section or appendix, number each one so that it can be referred to in the text as "Figure 1" or "Table 3." With an integrated illustration, numbering is not essential, except where there may be confusion. The term *Figure* includes all illustrations except tables. Sometimes, writers use the term *Exhibit* to cover any kind of visual addition to the text. Whatever terms you use, explain in the text the main point of any illustration, so that the reader knows why it is included.

Charts and graphs have greater visual impact than tables and are often preferable. Different kinds suit different purposes:

1. **A line chart or graph** (Figure 8-2) is the simplest way to show changes over a period of time — to reveal trends and fluctuations, such as trends in sales or fluctuations in the real estate market. In devising a graph, be sure to use a scale that will distribute the data points over the total space. Put quantities on the vertical axis and time values on the horizontal axis. Try to shape the dimensions of the graph to give an accurate visual impression of the extent of change.

FIG. 8-2   Example of a Line Chart

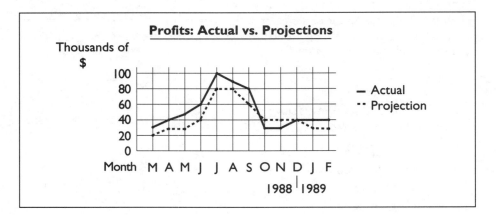

2. **A bar chart** (Figure 8-3) is best for comparing facts at a fixed point in time, such as the comparative training costs of several divisions within a company. The bars can be drawn horizontally or vertically, depending on the range of data. Bars can also be segmented to show different parts of the whole. As with a line chart, a bar chart

should use a scale that allows the data to spread over most of the total space, rather than crowding it in one corner. For ease of interpretation, make sure the distance between the bars is not the same as the width of the bars, so that the bars are readily distinguishable from the background.

FIG. 8-3   Example of a Bar Chart

Condominium Construction Spending in Metro

(Millions of Dollars)

Source: Contractor's Newsletter

3. **A pie chart** (Figure 8-4) emphasizes proportions. It draws attention to the relative size of parts that make up a whole — for example, the percentage of sales or the share of profit for each department in a store. Visual separation by use of colour or shading can emphasize any particular piece of the pie. Typically, a pie chart begins at the 12 o'clock position, putting the largest segment first.

FIG. 8-4   Example of a Pie Chart

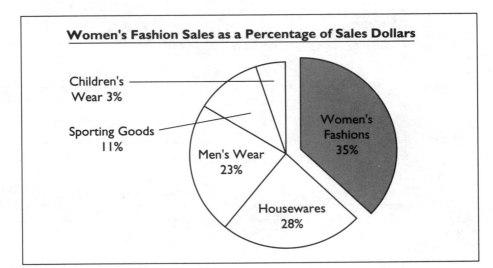

Women's Fashion Sales as a Percentage of Sales Dollars

Children's Wear 3%

Sporting Goods 11%

Men's Wear 23%

Women's Fashions 35%

Housewares 28%

4. **A table** (Figure 8-5) is useful to present a lot of different types of data that can't fit a simple chart. An example might be a cost breakdown of several advertising campaigns or the sale figures for a number of products in different regions. If a table is put right after the section of the text that describes it, the title can be omitted.

FIG. 8-5   Example of a Table

Seats Sold at City Theatres				
	Seat Capacity	1988 % sold	1989 % sold	% Change
City Centre	720	60%	62%	+ 2
Centennial Hall	950	45%	47%	+ 2
Princess Theatre	550	64%	63%	− 1
Tri-Plex	1000	28%	33%	+ 5

5. **A matrix** (Figure 8-6) looks like a table but usually presents an array of qualitative information rather than (or in addition to) quantitative information. For example, a matrix could be used to highlight the different features of several microcomputers or offices for rent.

FIG. 8-6   Example of a Matrix

Regional Tourist Activities				
	Summer	Autumn	Winter	Spring
Fishing	I-day trips		ice-fishing	
Camping	wilderness canoe trips			
Hunting	camera hunting	duck hunting moose hunting camera hunting		bear hunting camera hunting
Hiking	nature trail walks	nature trail walks	cross-country skiing	nature trail walks
Other			snow-mobiling winter carnival	

Reports can use other kinds of illustrations, from flow charts to pictograms to cartoons. Some reports use traditional charts and graphs creatively, changing the shapes to suit the topic. For example, a pie chart in the shape of a light bulb may show an electrical company's sales information.

Computer graphics packages are available that allow you to convert data into effective and distinctive visual aids. With software packages such as DrawPerfect, Harvard Presentation Graphics and Microsoft Chart, you can choose an appropriate design and have your data presented as an illustration on the computer screen before you print it. Once you have practised using these computer packages, you will be able to create your charts, graphs, and other varied designs much more quickly than you could by hand — and often more imaginatively.

Whatever forms you choose, don't dramatize the design of an illustration if the result is distorted information. Even without original design features, charts and graphs can easily mislead by the spread of distances or shapes. For example, a graph may exaggerate a trend by truncating the data — that is by showing only the part of the scale when there was great change and leaving out the time when there was little. It can also underplay a change by spreading the distance between points. Notice the different effects of the graphs in Figure 8-7, which use identical data.

Since illustrations can "lie" as much statistics, take care that the material you represent visually gives as accurate an impression as possible.

Two other guidelines will help make your visuals effective:

1. **Keep the visual clean.** Clutter complicates. If possible, round off decimals to the nearest whole number, and use as few lines as needed for clarity. Use strong bold lines or shading to delineate trend lines or the major point of the visual — for example, the slice of the pie you want emphasized.

2. **Present the data logically.** This means to organize the data either chronologically or by size — from largest to smallest.

Although informal reports may vary, here is an example of a short, internal report that uses a direct approach. In this case, the introductory paragraph serves as a summary, including the central recommendation and the criteria for making it along with the statement of purpose.

FIG. 8-7   Distorting Data

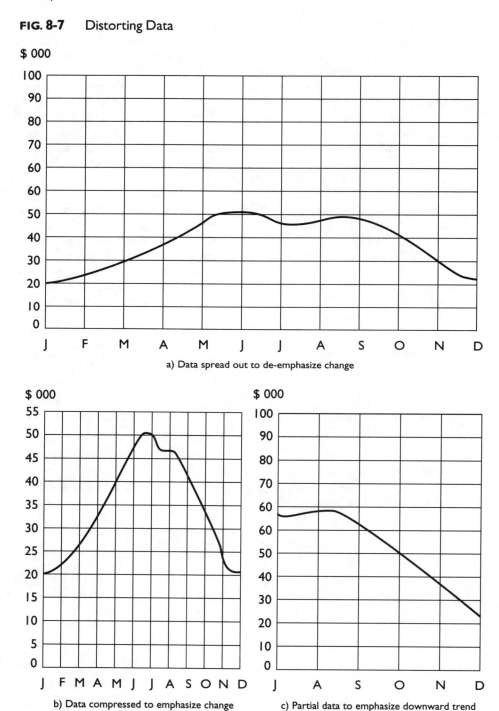

a) Data spread out to de-emphasize change

b) Data compressed to emphasize change

c) Partial data to emphasize downward trend

FIG. 8-8   Example of a Short Informal Report

February 10, 1992

To: R.L. Miller
From: J. Stone

Subject: ***Recommended Location for New Office***

As you requested, I have investigated several locations for our new office, including suburban and midtown sites. The space at 10 Civic Square in Mississauga is, I think, the best available location. My search was based on the assumption that we wanted to lease about 1500 square feet in an existing office building. The main criteria for selecting the Civic Square location were (1) cost; (2) accessibility; (3) quality of the building.

With the help of Gil Gordon of Royal Realtors, I narrowed the initial possibilities to two:
  — 10 Civic Square in Mississauga;
  — 451 Price Street West in mid-town Toronto.
Both of these meet our basic requirements.

1. *Mississauga Costs Less*

The low cost of leasing space in Mississauga as compared with mid-town Toronto figures is a major reason for selecting that area. As the following table of costs shows, the difference extends not only to the net rental cost for 1500 square feet but to the operating costs (maintenance, taxes, insurance) and parking costs, assuming that the company continues to pay parking costs for the sales force and top executives.

	Net Rent	**Operating**	**Annual Parking** (10 cars)	**Total**
Civic Sq.	@$16/sq. ft. $24 000	@$6/sq. ft. $9 000	@$360/car $3 600	$36 600
Price St.	@$20/sq. ft. $30 000	@$7/sq. ft. $10 500	@$600/car $6 000	$46 000

Since a long-term lease is better than a short-term one, the four-year lease available for 10 Civic Square, as compared with the three-year lease at Price Street, is a significant benefit.

The allowance for decorating and improvements is less at Civic Square than at Price Street. This is a one-time-only rebate, but it substantially reduces the first year rental cost.

	Allowance/Sq. Ft.	**Total**	**Year 1 Rental**
Civic Sq.	$10	$15 000	$18 300
Price St.	$15	$22 500	$23 000

2. *Both Locations Are Reasonably Accessible*

Since our present location is in the west end of Toronto, many of our employees live in that area. Other things being equal, it is sensible to choose a new location in the west rather than east or north end of town. Moreover, since many employees are living even further west in the suburbs, owing to the cheaper housing, Mississauga is a reasonable area in which to locate.

(a) *Public transportation*. Being close to good transportation is important for employees without cars. Since the Price Street location is within a three-minute walk of the St. George subway station on the Bloor Street line, it is easier to reach by public transportation.

While Civic Square is not on a subway line, Mississauga Transit runs buses from the Islington subway station right to the doorstep. Moreover, planners are talking of building a rapid transit line from the Islington station to Civic Square.

(b) *Car transportation*. Both locations are on major roads, and have ample parking facilities. Civic Square has easier access than Price Street to major highways — the Queen Elizabeth Way and Highway 401. It is also closer to the airport, a further advantage to some of our sales people and clients. Driving from Toronto to Mississauga in the morning and back to Toronto at night would be faster than the reverse route, because of the much lighter traffic.

3. *Civic Square's Building Is Better*

The attached pictures give some indication of the superior quality of the Civic Square building.

(a) *Office space*. The space available in both buildings is suitable for our offices, with good lighting and air conditioning. Both would need some changes in the partitioning walls, and new carpeting. Civic Square has vertical blinds on all windows.

The space we require (1500 square feet) would take up
— one-half of the eighth floor at 10 Civic Square;
— one-third of the tenth floor at 451 Price.

(b) *Quality of the building*. The fifteen-story Civic Square building is the more attractive and well-appointed of the two possibilities. It is only five years old and in excellent shape. The lobby is spacious and well-decorated, the four elevators are fast, and the washrooms are large and clean.

The twenty-story Price Street building is larger and older, having been constructed thirty years ago. Although it is clean, and has a large front lobby, it leaves an impression of relative dinginess. The lobby and halls are dark and the floor tiles are worn in spots. The four elevators are slower than at Civic Square and seem more rickety. The washrooms, however, are excellent; they were modernized last year.

E X E R C I S E S

● Section A

1. Decide whether you would choose the direct approach or the indirect approach for reports in each of the following situations:

   a) You are halfway through a landscaping job at a summer resort, and the absent owner asks you to send him a brief report on what you have done.

   b) After a lot of employee complaints, you have persuaded a reluctant boss to let you look into the matter of staggered work-hours. You find that staggered hours would improve employee performance and morale, and are going to recommend them.

   c) Your boss has asked you to investigate factory safety procedures and suggest ways to improve them.

   d) The sales manager has asked you to compare two possible choices for company cars for the sales force. You know he favours one, but you think the other is more suitable.

   e) You think your company's handling of customer relations could be improved, and you have some simple, inexpensive suggestions. You decide to write an informal report to put in the employee suggestion box.

2. You have been asked to investigate photocopiers for your office and prepare an informal report for your boss. You discover that the Beta brand costs no more than the Copyking, but produces faster copies. The copiers take up the same space. In checking further, you learn that both copiers are reliable. Copyking appears to have a slight edge over Beta in its record of servicing; its engineers are more prompt with repairs.

   Assess the following headings for your report. Are they effective and clear? How could you improve them? Consider weaknesses in the division and order of the sections as well as in the actual phrasing of the headings.

   1. **Beta**
      a) Cost
      b) Space Requirements
      c) Speed of the Machine
      d) Reliability
      e) Service Record

   2. **Copyking**
      a) Cost
      b) Speed of the Machine
      c) Space Requirements
      d) Reliability
      e) Service Record

3. Since the office you work in is too crowded, you have been asked by the manager to assess the physical environment of another open-plan office which occupies an entire floor in an old, downtown building. You discover that, although the space is big enough, it is very noisy since it has no carpets or acoustical tile. Lighting is poor in some areas. In the winter, the building is sometimes too hot and sometimes too cool. In the summer, the window air conditioning units are inadequate. Since your manager has said that he doesn't want to spend a lot of money renovating a space, you conclude that the office is unsuitable.

a) Write the subject heading and key points for the report.

b) Write descriptive, high-information headings for the detailed discussion of your findings.

4. The registrar, Dr. M.J. Cole, wants to make your college as accessible as possible to people in wheelchairs. You have been asked to write him an informal informational report on the college's facilities for students in wheelchairs. You are to consider such areas as:

— parking spaces close to buildings;

— exterior ramps;

— elevators to upper floors;

— space for wheelchairs in classrooms, cafeterias, and the library;

— washroom facilities.

Write the report.

5. Determine what sort of illustration would be most suitable for the following kinds of information. Create an illustration for one or two of them. (Establish with your instructor whether you can invent the data.)

a) The number of full-time students and part-time students in the last five years in your institution.

b) The number of defence dollars contributed to NATO by each of its partners last year.

c) A comparison of features, costs, and gas consumption on the four best selling pickup trucks in Canada.

d) The number of students enrolled in (i) colleges and (ii) universities in each of the provinces in the last year.

e) Stock prices of three leading oil companies over the last four months.

f) Unemployment and inflation rates in Canada, the U.S.A., Britain, and Japan over the last three years.

g) A breakdown of expenditures of four leading charities.

h) A comparison of the number of employees in the four largest departments of the provincial government.

6. Rewrite the following paragraph, using descriptive headings and lists.

Our buyers have now completed their monthly visit to branch stores across the province. Their buying decisions and suggestions reflect their observations about sales trends. They noticed that children's wear was selling well in all stores. They will have to restock playwear — specifically overalls and T-shirts — faster than anticipated. Clothes for children in all-cotton materials are more popular than they have been for the last five years, and they have ordered more heavy cotton clothes for fall. Sales for our line of cotton children's wear are up 10% this year. Of course, cotton clothes for adults, both men and women, continue to be popular in these summer months. In the women's fashion section, summer skirts and dresses had lower sales than they did at this time last year, probably because of some confusion over hemlines. The buyers want immediately to discount these summer items by 30%, in order to move them before our fall line comes in. They also have decided to increase our order of the Leslie line of lingerie. This luxury line is moving faster than the others. In menswear, overall sales figures are on target, and buyers plan to continue our normal volume of purchasing. Patterned sweaters continue to outsell plain ones. The only shift in our buying patterns will be an increase in natural fabric pants instead of wash-and-wear all polyester ones.

● Section B

1. The following comments were made to a travel agency by clients after a charter flight and package tour to a southern holiday resort. In small groups, organize this feedback into a clear outline which includes all comments without overlap. Put the outline on a flip-chart sheet or transparency. Compare your outline with those of other groups.

   — Bedrooms were not ready when tour group arrived.
   — Baggage was misplaced by airline.
   — Dining room had line-ups.
   — Hotel food was excellent.
   — Tennis courts needed new nets.
   — The swimming pool had no lifeguard.
   — Bedrooms were small.
   — The tennis instructor was first-rate.
   — Hotel-run tours of the area were overbooked.
   — Check out procedures should be simplified.
   — The dinner menu had too few choices.
   — The hotel manager made us feel welcome.
   — The airline served no meal on the five-hour flight.
   — Flights were delayed over four hours both going and returning.
   — Some dining staff were unattentive or surly.
   — The tour guide was well informed and helpful.
   — The swimming pool should have some adults-only hours.
   — The hotel floor show was very entertaining.
   — Group tennis instruction was overpriced.
   — Most of the exercise bicycles didn't work properly.
   — The area tour was well worth the extra price.
   — The golf course was uninteresting and in poor shape.

2. Using the information given in question 3 of Section A, and adding any details you need, write a complete informal report.

3. Helen Layton, the Dean of Students at your university, wants to find out about the quality of student life. Since she has come to know you in your time at the university, she asks you to write her a short informal report in which you assess one of the following: food services, health services, the sports program, social activities, or any other area you want to discuss. Dean Layton says you do not need to do any formal research, but should simply base your assessment on your experiences or those of your friends.

4. You have been appointed assistant to the president of Dominion Merchandise. One of your first jobs is to advise your boss, Arthur Sloane, on the type of present to give to the sales force at the annual sales dinner. The presents should be under $150 each. You are to pick two or three possible gifts that would appeal to various ages, sexes and types, and then write an informal report to Mr. Sloane in which you compare the features and attributes of each, and recommend which to buy.

5. Your employer, Tiny Tim Ltd., a large and successful manufacturer of children's furniture, donates money to many charitable causes. It has decided that, rather than giving small amounts to a lot of charities, it will give one half of its donations budget each year to a single charity with which it will become more closely identified. As a young man-

agement trainee in the company, you have been asked to select three worthy charities in the field of health, to describe their needs and the relative merit each might have as the special company charity, and to recommend one of them. Write an informal report to John de Wit, head of the Donations Committee.

6. As part of its community relations effort, the company you work for, Harkness Insurance, plans to participate in the community's "Let's be Beautiful" campaign. The company wants to sponsor some low-cost visual improvements to aspects or areas of the community. The director of public relations, Ann Medhurst, has asked you to investigate and recommend some low-cost projects, with the total cost not exceeding $15 000. Write her an informal report in which you describe one or more possible improvements and give some estimate of the money and time needed for each.

7. Oriole Food Products has recognized that profits for its Tasty Pudding line are declining. The Vice-President of Marketing, Al Fisk, has asked you for advice from the Sales Department.

Departmental figures show that sales for Tasty Puddings have not grown for the last three years and that for the past year there was a 5% decline in sales nationally. Trends in market share have remained constant for five years: sales declines are not the result of increased competition. A recent departmental analysis also shows that 70% of the buyers are at least fifty years old.

At a Sales Department meeting you have called to discuss the sales decline, several people suggest that the product could be repositioned for a wider market. Since it is a milk-based product, pudding could also appeal to younger women, who are looking for more calcium in their diet. Sales of calcium pills to women have grown dramatically in the last few years, since lack of this element has been linked to later bone deterioration.

Someone also suggests that the product could be altered slightly to include Vitamin D. This vitamin helps the body absorb calcium, and is added to many calcium pills. The addition would cost little but would increase the product appeal to health-conscious younger women.

There is general agreement that the package for the puddings could also be changed to give the product a less staid image.

You and your department conclude that with these changes the sales would increase over the long term. You also think that an aggressive advertising campaign will be required to generate awareness of the product among younger women.

Just as the meeting is about to finish, one member of your department suggests a promotional link with the annual Women's National Marathon. You think this suggestion has potential and is worth exploring.

Your task:

a) In small groups, create and organize headings for the report you must do for Al Fisk. Prepare specific, descriptive subheadings in the largest section.

b) *Either* write the report individually, *or* as a group make an oral presentation to the class.

CHAPTER 9

Formal Reports and Proposals

The distinctions between formal and informal reports are often blurred. Nevertheless, a formal report is usually written to someone in another company or organization. Occasionally it is written for a much more senior manager in the same company, or for someone with whom the writer has little regular contact. Usually it is longer than an informal report and requires more extensive research. Unless you are a consultant, you are unlikely to be asked to write a formal report often. When you are, there may be a lot riding on it — including your reputation.

The purpose of this chapter is to show you how to write a formal report and how to put together the kind of proposal that often precedes it. As Figure 9-1 shows, many of the elements of formal reports are the same as those for informal ones. You need to pay the same attention to headings, lists, and illustrations, for example. Although much of the advice in the last chapter could be duplicated in this one, the emphasis here will be on those areas where there's a difference.

The Four R's of Planning

As emphasized earlier, the first step in planning any piece of correspondence is to think about the reason for writing and about the receiver. For a long, formal report you need to add two more R's to your planning sheet: restrictions and research.

FIG. 9-1   Contrasting Features of Informal and Formal Reports

	Informal	Formal
reader	internal	external or distant within organization
length	usually short several sections	usually long (3 pages or more) sections and subsections
tone	personal contractions	more impersonal no contractions
summary	integrated	on separate page
introduction	no heading	can have one or more headings
title	appears as subject line in memo heading	appears on separate title page
transmittal page	none	covering letter or memo
contents page	none	useful if report is over five pages

Determining Restrictions

What are the limitations on the resources that will be available to help you with the report?

1. **Financial**   What will be your budget? What expenses will be involved and is the budget adequate to meet them?

2. **Personnel**   Will you have the services of a good typist or illustrator? Will outside help be required?

3. **Time**   What is your deadline? Create a realistic time-line on a graph with the various stages of the report plotted on it at specific dates — so many days or weeks for research, organizing, writing, editing, and final production. The larger the task, the more important these self-imposed dates become. In allocating time, you may be wise to leave a margin of error for delays, whether from bureaucratic mix-ups or postal problems.

Deciding on Research

Before beginning your research, explore the subject itself to avoid taking too narrow a path and overlooking important alternatives. Good questions are an effective stimulus for seeing different perspectives on an issue. Here are some ways to start:

1. **Brainstorming**   By yourself or with a colleague, blitz the subject. Jot down all the questions you can think of that relate to the topic, in whatever order they occur. Don't be negative or rule anything out at this point.

2. **Tree Diagram**   Assume that the subject is the trunk and add as many large and small branches as you can to represent the different aspects of the subject. Again, think of the branches as questions. Tree-diagramming can be useful by itself or as a second stage of random brainstorming.

FIG. 9-2   Example of a Tree Diagram

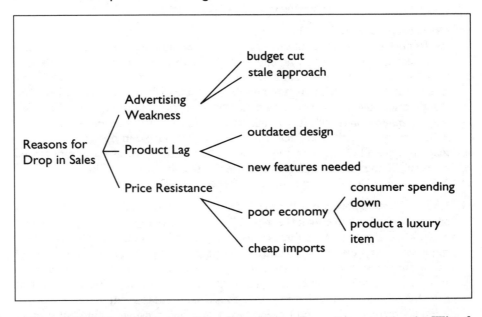

3. **Journalist's Approach**   In researching a story, journalists consider the W's of reporting: Who? What? When? Where? Why? For your research planning, try asking the same five questions and add another: How? Use these basic questions to formulate other subquestions.

4. **The 3C Approach**   A more thorough way to explore a topic is to ask questions about three areas:
   - *Components*   How can the subject be divided? How many different ways are there to partition it?
   - *Change*   What are the changed or changing elements of the subject? What are the causes or effects of certain actions? What trends are there?
   - *Context*   What is the larger issue or field into which this subject fits? How have others dealt with the problems associated with the subject?

Once you have stretched your mind exploring the possibilities of a subject, move in the other direction. Think of limiting the subject and working out the precise focus of your study. Weigh the time and expense of the research against its importance to the report. Remember that it's better to do a limited topic well than a broad one superficially.

Finding Information

1. **Use librarians.**   For some of your research information you may have to turn to government documents or academic studies. Librarians can be a great help in finding information or showing the fastest way to get it.

2. **Do a computer search.**   Most libraries now have access to extensive databases that can let you source needed information quickly by computer. For example, a computer search can show you where to find all the articles, books, and reviews on a topic. They can itemize certain kinds of transaction or economic activity over a given period of time. With many computer programs, when you enter the key word that describes the limits of your topic (for example, *free trade*, *auto parts*, *Canada*), the computer search will list the material relating to that combination of terms. Although much of the same reference material is available in books, your library may not have all of them, or they may not be as up to date as the computerized material. Besides, it's a much slower process to search through books.

    A librarian can guide you to the most relevant database for your topic.

3. **Look for inside sources.**   If you are doing a report on a particular company or organization, don't overlook the most accessible source of information — internal records and the employees themselves. Many an unsuspecting report writer has spent days searching for facts readily available in internal files. If the topic is one of continuing concern to the company, chances are that someone has looked at it, or an aspect of it, before. Some of the facts from an earlier investigation may be out of date, but it's likely that other information is timely and relevant.

    Even when an earlier report doesn't exist, it is still sensible to find out if other people have worked on the topic. They are usually glad to discuss the issues. A short telephone enquiry or memo may save you valuable research time or give you helpful suggestions for your exploration. Reinventing the wheel does nobody any good.

4. **Check the reliability of information.**   Establish whether any of the second-hand facts you get from research will need verifying. Remember that a source with a special interest may exaggerate or gloss over certain information, often unconsciously. Even statistical data should undergo scrutiny. Any observer of election polls and campaigns knows that statistics may not lie, but they can certainly distort. If you have to get fresh data through a questionnaire or survey, make sure the results are as reliable and valid as possible. If you are not familiar with proper sampling techniques and have no knowledge of statistical reliabilty, consult someone who is competent in those areas. The cost of obtaining outside help may be less than the cost of losing your credibility through faulty data.

5. **Try using file cards.**   In doing lengthy research, many people find that file cards are an efficient way to record and keep track of details. Use a separate card for each different item of information you gather — whether the item is an opinion or an important statistic. You can then shuffle the cards according to the order you have chosen for the findings. Drafting the findings section of a report is much easier if the sequence of information is already in front of you.

If you are gathering information from a published source, remember to include the bibliographical information on the card (author, title, publisher, place of publication, and page number) so that you don't have to spend time chasing down the reference later.

Organizing Formal Reports

Since a formal report is usually much longer than an informal one, its organization will require more thought. It will probably have both headings and subheadings. Although the sections will vary according to the subject, the basic principles of organizing are the same as for informal reports.

For readers who will be interested or pleased, use the direct approach. Here is the most common model:

Summary

↓

Introduction

↓

Recommendations and/or Conclusions

↓

Discussion of Findings

A less common variation of this direct approach is useful when there is a lengthy list of recommendations:

Summary

↓

Introduction

↓

Summary of Recommendations

↓

Discussion of Findings

↓

Details of Recommendations

When readers will be displeased or skeptical, the indirect approach will lead them gradually towards the conclusions or recommendations:

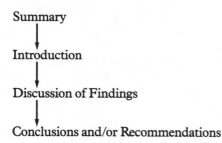

Summary

↓

Introduction

↓

Discussion of Findings

↓

Conclusions and/or Recommendations

The indirect approach is sometimes used in government and consulting circles, even when the readers are interested. The trend is towards the direct approach, however, especially for busy readers.

Writing: Filling in the Sections

The preceding suggestions are not an iron-clad prescription for every report. You may want to change or add some sections. You may also have to adapt the following advice about what to put in each section. Let ease of understanding be the guide.

Summary

A summary for a formal report — often called an executive summary — is really a condensation of the most important points. Unlike the introductory summary that begins most short informal reports, the summary for a formal report is put on a separate page with a heading. It's not an introduction to the report but a synopsis — the report condensed. It's a convenience for the reader and may be the only part that top management reads, but the report can make sense without it. For this reason, it's best to write the summary after you have completed the report.

The summary doesn't have to give equal weight to all sections of the report. It often has only a brief account of the background or methodology, and may even omit them if they are unimportant. By contrast, it usually pays most attention to the conclusions or recommendations. On rare occasions, if the list of recommendations is lengthy, the title may be simply ''Summary of Recommendations.''

Generally, in a summary, it's best to follow the order of the report. That is, if the report takes the direct approach, so should the summary. Similarly, if the report has an indirect order, the summary should be indirect.

In the interest of brevity:

— use lists where possible;

— omit examples, unless the example is a key finding;

— stick to the facts, avoiding unneeded references to the report itself. For example, instead of saying: "the Findings section reveals . . ." simply put a heading, *Findings*, and list the facts.

Since there is a subtle psychological barrier to turning a page, especially for a reader who is extremely busy, try to keep the summary to a single sheet. If this seems an impossible task for a complicated or lengthy report, remember Winston Churchill's instructions to the First Lord of the Admiralty in the midst of the Second World War: "Pray state this day, on one side of a sheet of paper, how the Royal Navy is being adapted to meet the conditions of modern warfare."[1] Is your task more difficult than this one?

Introduction

This section may have a heading other than "Introduction," depending on the focus, and may have several subsections. It can include several or all of these topics:

- **Purpose**   As in an informal report, a one-sentence explanation may be enough.

- **Background**   Many report writers make the mistake of giving too much background. Include only the information needed to put the report in perspective. If explaining the reasons for the report, a total history is rarely needed. Focus on those conditions that have influenced the purpose and design of the report. If you do have to include a lot of material, you should probably have a separate section on background.

- **Scope**   Here you define the topic precisely and reveal any assumptions you have made affecting the direction or boundaries of your investigation. If there are constraints or difficulties which limit the study in some way, say what they are. By doing so, you will help forestall criticisms that you didn't cover the area properly.

- **Method**   If your findings are based on a questionnaire or survey of some sort, outline the steps you took. Reports with a heavy scientific emphasis often include an explanation of the technical processes used in the investigation. The process of information-gathering is especially relevant when the data is "soft" — that is, open to dispute. Again, if the explanation will be lengthy, consider putting it as a separate section.

Discussion of Findings

This is the largest section in most formal reports, and discusses the details of your investigation, the facts on which you have based your conclusions or recommendations. It should be subdivided, with numbered and descriptive subheadings. (It may be possible to give the section itself a more specific heading than "Discussion" or "Findings.")

---

1   Quoted in David Ogilvy, *Ogilvy on Advertising* (Toronto: Wiley, 1983), 35.

In choosing the best arrangement for findings, remember that the most effective order is the one that most easily leads the reader to the conclusions or recommendations. As with informal reports, you can arrange findings by category or topic, by following a geographic or a chronological order, or by order of importance.

How many subsections should a report have? It's a matter of judgment. Don't have so many that the section is more like a long shopping list than a discussion. On the other hand, don't have so few that there's a thicket of information in each one.

Conclusions and/or Recommendations

While some reports have both conclusions and recommendations, many have one or the other. Conclusions are the inferences you have made from your findings; recommendations are suggestions about what actions to take. A long, research-based report generally gives conclusions; a problem-solving report, recommendations. Here are some tips for both types:

- If there are several recommendations or conclusions, separate them in a list or in subsections.

- Normally, put the most important recommendation (or conclusion) first. If you face a skeptical or hostile reader, however, you might make an exception, and put the most controversial recommendation last, even if it is the major one.

- Number the recommendations or conclusions, making them easier to refer to. Numbers will also reinforce the fact that there are more than one. Otherwise, in later discussions the reader may focus on the most important or controversial point and forget that there are others.

- Be as specific as possible about how each recommendation should be carried out and who should be responsible. Some reports have an implementation subsection for each recommendation. Others have a specific action plan at the end of the report, outlining all the steps that should be taken.

- If implementation details are not feasible, consider including a recommendation to set up an implementation committee or task force. If your recommendations do include the details of implementation, suggest a follow-up mechanism so that managers or departments will get feedback on the results.

Editing

The comments on editing informal reports also apply to formal reports. However, there are two particular considerations.

1. **Checking the outline**   Some writers find that they work best by banging out a first draft as quickly as possible without worrying about details. Others work best when they have a detailed plan in front of them. It doesn't matter what method

you choose, as long as at some point you carefully arrange the material so that each little bit is in the best place. Although with a short informal report you may not feel the need for an outline, with lengthy formal reports an outline is almost a prerequisite for avoiding muddle.

The outline can be in point form or in full sentences. Numbering each section will help you keep in mind the relative value of each. Whichever numbering system you use for your outline, you can repeat it in the body of the report and in the table of contents.

FIG. 9-3 Example of a Point-Form Outline

Reasons for Drop in Sales

1. Advertising Weakness   A. Budget cut
                                 B. Stale approach

2. Product Lag   A. Outdated design
                                 B. New features needed

3. Price Resistance   A. Poor economy
                                      i. consumer spending down
                                      ii. product a luxury item
                                 B. Cheap imports

2. **Using *I* in formal reports** As discussed in Chapter 2, formal reports are usually less personal than informal ones. They omit the contractions of personal conversation and tend to name fewer individuals. Traditionally, formal reports have tried to give a sense of objectivity by omitting the personal *I*. As a result, passages were often convoluted and difficult to read. While *I*-free reports are still the practice in some circles, business writers are increasingly using *I* in formal reports to produce clearer and more forceful writing. (In informal reports, personal pronouns are not only tolerated but recommended.) However, avoid "I think" or "in my opinion" phrases when you can complete the thought without them:

x   I found that the fittings were defective.

✔   The fittings were defective.

x   In my view, the market value will rise in the spring.

✔   Market value will probably rise in the spring.

If you are part of a group, you can also refer to *we*, since the collective weight of a group seems more objective than that of an individual. In any case, use *I* rather than refer to yourself impersonally as *the writer* or *the author*.

Additions at the Front

Title Page

Centre the information and arrange it so that it extends downward over most of the length of the page. Include

— the title of the report, underlined or in capital letters;
— the name and title of the intended reader;
— the name of the writer and the writer's title (or the name of the firm, if the report is by an outside consultant);
— the date.

FIG. 9-4   Example of a Title Page for a Formal Report

AN ASSESSMENT OF
ALLIED'S INTERNAL COMMUNICATIONS

prepared for

R.S. Millgate
Vice-President, Human Resources
Allied Chemicals Limited

prepared by

June Harris
Baker Consultants Limited

March 12, 1993

Table of Contents

This is useful if the report is over five pages. It follows the title page, and is without a page number. It may be labelled "Table of Contents" or simply "Contents." List the sections of the report in a column on the left, using the same system of numbering used in the body of the report. If the report has subsections, list these as well. (Subsection headings may be indented a few spaces from the section headings.) In a column at the right of the page, list the appropriate page numbers. If the report itself contains a number of tables or figures, list them on a separate page with an appropriate label — for example, "List of Tables."

FIG. 9-5   Example of a Table of Contents for a Formal Report

CONTENTS

Additions at the Back

References

If you have referred in your report to any facts or figures that are not general knowledge or part of the organization's internal operation, you should give the source in a reference. (A reference is unnecessary where the internal source is obvious, such as company sales figures or financial statements.) Acceptable form for references varies. The most important rule is consistency: whatever format you choose, stick to it.

Traditional Format

This format, using footnotes and a bibliography, is followed by many writers in the humanities and in some social sciences.

1. **Put footnotes at the end** of the report under the heading "References," "Footnotes" or "Endnotes," or put them at the bottom of the pages containing the references.

   - Put an arabic numeral at the appropriate reference point in the text, raised slightly above the line of the text, and at the end of a clause or sentence.

   - Number each footnote consecutively, using arabic numerals.

   - Single-space each entry, but leave a double space between them.

   - For a book, give name of author, title of publication, publisher, date and page number. Example:

     [1] Raymond W.Y. Kao, *Small Business Management: A Strategic Emphasis*, 2nd ed. (Toronto: Holt, Rinehart and Winston, 1984), 41.

   - For an article in a book, follow the above format, except put the author and title of the article at the beginning:

     [1] Douglas M. McGregor, "The Human Side of Enterprise" in Steve Altman and Richard M. Hodgetts, *Readings in Organizational Behavior* (Philadelphia: W.B. Saunders, 1979), 16-24.

   - For an article in a journal, give details about the journal issue:

     [1] Seymour C. Hamilton, "Scale and the Changing Nature of Development," *Journal of Small Business in Canada*, 1, no. 4 (Spring, 1984), 15-21.

   - For a second reference to an article or book, you may simply put the author's last name and the page number. If the second reference follows directly after the first, you may use the term *Ibid.*, meaning "the same," in place of the author's name.

2. **Provide a bibliography** (publication details) if your report uses a lot of published material or you think the reader may want to examine some sources not referred to directly in the report. Usually you will not need one, but if you do, put it at the end of the report after the footnotes, and on a separate page under the title "Bibliography."

- List items in alphabetical order, according to the surname of the author or editor; if there's no name, list according to the first word of the title. Do not number entries.

- Single-space entries, but leave a double space between them.

- Begin each entry at the margin, but indent any subsequent lines.

- Separate the main divisions by periods.

> Rosen, L.S. *An Introduction to Accounting Case Analysis*, 2nd ed. Toronto: McGraw-Hill Ryerson, 1981.
>
> Ross, Murray G. "The Non-Profit Board." In *Managing Voluntary Organizations*, 141-46, Mel S. Moyer, ed. Toronto: York University, 1983.

Simplified Format

Citations and an accompanying bibliography are used in scientific reports, in many social sciences, and increasingly in humanities papers and business writing. Although there are variations in this format, here is a common version:

1. **Use citations instead of footnotes.** In the body of the text cite only the author's name or the editor's, followed by the year of the publication.

   - If referring to a particular page, include the page number.

   - Enclose citations in brackets; for example, [Rosen, 1981, p. 33] or [Heller and Van Til, 1983].

   - When referring to institutional works, use acronyms or short titles, where possible (for example, UNESCO or IBM).

   - If the author's name is cited in the text itself, put only the date in the citation:
     > as Cohen says [1981],

   - For citations with more than three authors, use the name of the first author followed by *et al.* and the date.

   - If you are citing two works published in the same year by an author, use the letters *a* and *b* after the year.

2. **Include in the bibliography complete information** only on the works cited in the text.

   - List references in alphabetical order, according to the surname of the first author or editor. List works by the same author chronologically. Instead of *Ibid.*, use a blank line for subsequent references.

   > Drucker, Peter F. *Men, Ideas and Politics* (New York: Harper and Row, 1971).
   >
   > _____ . "How to Be an Employee," in N.B. Sigband and D.N. Bateman, *Communicating in Business* (Glenview: Scott Foresman, 1981), 453-60.

Kao, R.W.Y., *Small Business Management: A Strategic Emphasis* (Toronto: Holt, Rinehart and Winston, 1984).

Shapiro, B.P. and T.V. Bonoma, "How to Segment Industrial Markets," *Harvard Business Review*, 3 (May-June, 1984), 104-18.

Exhibits

When essential illustrations are not integrated into the text they may be put in this section at the end, as long as they are referred to earlier and numbered.

Appendix

This optional section appears at the end of a report, and includes highly specialized or inessential information that may still be of interest to the reader. Tables, technical information, and other complicated or detailed supporting evidence are often put in appendices so that the reader can quickly cover essential information in the report itself. If you do use an appendix, be sure to list it in the table of contents. If you use more than one, list them as Appendix A, Appendix B, and so on.

Finishing Touches

After putting a lot of time and effort into a formal report, make sure that its appearance complements the content. The advice on visual impact in an informal report (pages 120-128) also applies to a formal one. Here are two added suggestions:

1. **Consider using coloured paper.** If you are producing a long report, varied colours of paper will help to separate the different sections visually. A conservative organization, however, may prefer uniform white paper (along with a uniform dark blue or grey suit on the writer). In this case, at least consider using a colour to highlight the summary page.

2. **Provide an attractive cover.** A clear plastic cover will help keep a report clean and tidy. If the report is going to outsiders or if it is more than half a centimetre (about 1/4 in.) thick, consider having it bound with a specially designed cardboard cover. Copy shops can sometimes do this job for you at a small cost, and the result will be worth it. You will have the confidence of knowing that the report looks well put-together and will stay together when passed about.

For an example of a formal report, see pages 154-160.

Accompanying the Report: The Letter of Transmittal

A letter of transmittal is a covering letter, given in letter or memo form, depending on whether it is going to someone outside or inside the writer's organization. Put at the front or inside the front cover of the report, it provides the extra personal touch that formal reports generally lack. A covering letter is usually brief and follows this pattern:

— an opening statement, "transmitting" the report to the reader, and stating its title or purpose (for example, "Here is the report you requested on . . ."");

— a brief outline of the major conclusions or recommendations;

— a statement of thanks for any special help received from other employees;

— a goodwill close which looks forward to future discussion or opportunities to help.

Of course, a letter of transmittal can contain more or less than this model. Occasionally, a fairly extensive summary of the report in the covering letter will substitute for a summary at the beginning of the report. Sometimes, if the writer is an outside consultant hired for the job, the letter of transmittal expresses appreciation for the opportunity of working on the task. Whatever it says, however, the letter should have a personal, conversational tone. See Figure 9-8 (p. 161) for an example of a letter of transmittal.

Formally Presenting a Report

Sometimes report writers are asked to make a formal presentation to those who will be assessing its ideas. If you are in this position, remember that the presentation can never be a complete rerun of all that is in the report. Since speaking takes much longer than reading, the audience would be asleep before you were halfway through the material. Rather, think of your talk as another chance to emphasize the areas of most importance and to get some feedback. Alongside the advice on oral presentations in Chapter 10, here are some guidelines for this particular task.

• Determine whether the audience will already have read the report or whether they will receive a copy after the presentation. If they have already read it, do a little sleuthing and try to determine their reaction in advance. You can then aim to address any objections or uncertainties, and to shore up perceived weak areas.

  If the audience has not read the report, use the   presentation to reinforce its key points. The talk will have more impact if it does not mechanically summarize the report, but instead selectively emphasizes the most important or controversial areas. Usually the conclusions or recommendations should be the focus.

• Be wary of giving out a copy of the report just before or during your talk. The audience receiving such a hand-out will likely have their eyes on the text rather than on you and miss much of what you are saying.

• Make sure you use the opportunity for questions and discussion. If, for example, you have been allotted forty minutes for the presentation, plan to leave twenty mintues of the time for a spontaneous exchange. That way, lingering doubts in the audience will likely surface and you can respond. By forgetting to leave enough time for audience reaction, you run the risk of an objector raising an issue with others afterward, an issue that you could have addressed.

- Visuals, such as overhead transparencies, can be useful to summarize points or to give visual clarity to data scattered throughout the report. Remember to test in advance any technology you use, including a check on focus or sound, so that you do not waste valuable time fumbling during the presentation.

- If you will be pressed for time, it's better to ask the audience to hold their comments and questions until after you have finished. If the meeting is casual and you have lots of time, you might welcome queries as soon as they occur to the listener. Take care, however, not to let the questions run away with the presentation. If you sense the discussion is getting out of hand, ask that further discussion wait until you have finished.

- Since it's always an advantage to have the last word, make sure you bring a question-and-answer session to a close with some conclusion that reinforces your main argument or key points.

Formal Proposals

Proposals may be informal or formal. They vary from a one-page memo for a boss to a massive document for a government department. This section will show how to prepare a formal proposal, since it is usually more extensive than an informal one. If needed, the guidelines can easily be adapted for less formal circumstances.

Planning a Proposal

While proposals can be solicited or unsolicited, most are written in response to a formal or informal request. A formal "Request for Proposals" document outlines the specifications or requirements for the job. When a proposal is unsolicited, the task is more difficult, since the reader will have to be convinced there is a need to act. In either case, however, begin planning by considering

— the reason for writing;

— the reader's needs, concerns, and potential benefits;

— the competition.

Think of the reason for writing not in your terms ("I want to get the job for the money"), but in the reader's terms: the proposal is a way of solving a problem for the reader or giving a benefit, such as improved safety, increased productivity, or decreased accidents in the parking lot. Even if you don't mention the word *problem* in the proposal — and sometimes it's more tactful not to, if the reader hasn't indicated one — thinking of the subject as a problem will help you to focus your efforts on how best to approach it.

If you can choose your reader, make sure that he or she is the person who will make the decision. Then try to determine the most important criterion for making it. You may have to do some scouting to establish the reader's particular biases, attitudes, or special interests.

Order for a Proposal

Use the direct approach. Begin with a clear overview of what you propose. If cost is an important consideration, the reader will want to know "the bottom line" right away. The intended completion date of your work may also be significant here.

Follow with a discussion of the details. Determine what the reader needs to know to make a decision and then divide the discussion into several sections with appropriate headings. Here are the usual divisions:

1. **Method**   First outline the method in non-specialist terms. Then give a fuller account, in which you are as specific as possible about the various aspects of the proposal and the way you would proceed. Include any technical information which specialists in the reader's organization might want to know. If the proposal is a response to a formal request, check that you have addressed all the specifications.

2. **Timeframe**   If time is important, be sure to mention the projected dates for completion of each stage. For a complicated project, it's helpful to provide a time-line or flow chart on which you plot time periods for the various activities. Figure 9-6 is an example.

3. **Costs**   In a short proposal, the cost breakdown can be included in the discussion of method. For a long one, it may be simpler to have a separate section. Before putting down specific numbers, find out whether your total cost figure is an estimate of expenses or a competitive bid you will have to stick to. Then be as detailed as you can in listing costs, without endangering yourself. Admit to any areas where you cannot yet give a fixed cost. Realism is safer than optimism.

   It may be practical, especially in a proposal for an outside organization, to break down costs according to the various stages in a project. This method is often easiest for the contractor to follow and budget for, and will allow you some flexibility in allocating resources. By contrast, if you list the cost of each participant or function in the total proposal, you may face questioning and quibbling by the contractor.

4. **Qualifications**   This section can focus on your qualifications and experience or on the credentials of the organization you represent. The heading should reflect the emphasis. If the credentials of those who will do the job are a primary issue, you could summarize the important points and then attach résumés at the end. You should also consider providing references, including addresses and telephone numbers.

   Remember that past experience in which you or your organization did similar work can be an important factor in the decision to accept your proposal.

5. **Benefits**   This section highlights for the reader the benefits of acting on the proposal. If the benefits are intangible, they may not be immediately apparent to the reader. You should specify as precisely as possible the payoffs, both short-term and long-term.

FIG. 9-6   Example of a Proposal

PROPOSAL FOR FIFESHIRE & PARTNERS

<u>Objective</u>: Through design, furnishing and decoration of your new offices, to create for Fifeshire & Partners an environment in harmony with the values and business aims of the firm.

<u>How Irving Design will Proceed</u>

Keeping to your budget of $200 000, we will take the following steps:

1. Discuss with your decorating committee the firm's work patterns and needs, the committee's style and colour preferences, along with the image the firm wants to project.

2. Create alternative designs that meet your specifications and needs. These will include working drawings with sample materials and photographs.

3. After consultation with the committee, create final plans. If committee members wish, they can be taken to furniture stores to view or test the furniture.

4. Implement the designs, arranging for and overseeing the installation of all furnishings, including light fixtures, and the carpeting, painting or wall-covering of all office areas.

<u>Cost</u>

You will not be charged for our time, but only for the retail price of any purchases or services. Our payment is the difference between the wholesale or designer-discount price charged to us and the regular retail price.

<u>Time-Frame</u>

If the construction of our offices proceeds as planned and we can begin this month, we think that you can be enjoying finished offices by the new year. Since the time between furniture order and furniture delivery is often about two months, the sooner the planning begins, the better.

Here is the time-frame for completing the various aspects of the project:

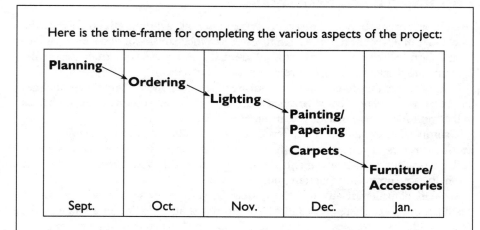

| Planning | Ordering | Lighting | Painting/Papering Carpets | Furniture/Accessories |
| Sept. | Oct. | Nov. | Dec. | Jan. |

Our Qualifications for this Project

The Irving Group is experienced in office design and decorating. Our work has often been featured in national design and decorating magazines.

Mary Hunter, Senior Designer, was a prize winner in the Interior Design Program at Ryerson Polytechnical Institute. She recently carried out design and decorating work for several prestigous professional firms in the city, including

- Lawlor, Bluestein, Foster;
- D.H. Deacon and Partners;
- Mills Thompson & Smith.

She understands the business environment of lawyers.

Why You Will Benefit From Our Work

- We will work from your needs, adapting tested design principles to create a unique environment that best suits Fifeshire & Partners.

- You will have undivided attention. Mary Hunter works on one project at a time. We pay attention to details.

- We are efficient. Since we do not charge for time, we all benefit from the speedy completion of work.

Presenting a Proposal Orally

Usually, a presentation is the second stage of selling a proposal and follows the acceptance of a written report. Often it serves as a mechanism for choosing a winner from a short list of proposers, previously selected after a review of written proposals. On large proposals, you may be presenting as part of a team.

The guidelines for presenting a proposal are much the same as the earlier guidelines for presenting a report. The difference is that in many cases you must sell yourself as well as your ideas, especially if you are an outside consultant.

It's important to be alert to the reactions of the audience, and especially the key decision-makers, if you know who they are. Use eye contact to spot any early signs of misunderstanding or disagreement. Be prepared to modify your presentation if that will help avoid opposition or strengthen your case.

As well, consider in advance those areas in your proposal where you can be flexible and those where you cannot. You do not want to look like a straw in the wind, yielding to any pressure. However if you can show your willingness to adapt details without sacrificing the basic plan of your proposal, you will appear responsive to customer or client needs. Such responsiveness, along with an underlying conviction about the benefits of your proposal, will help signal that you are an easy person to work with.

FIG. 9-7 Formal Report (Excluding Contents Page)

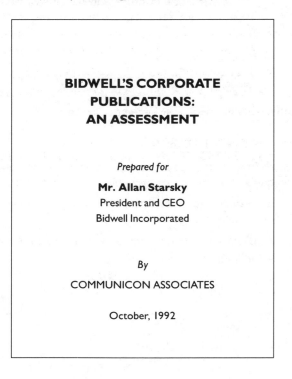

BIDWELL'S CORPORATE PUBLICATIONS: AN ASSESSMENT

Prepared for

Mr. Allan Starsky
President and CEO
Bidwell Incorporated

By

COMMUNICON ASSOCIATES

October, 1992

EXECUTIVE SUMMARY

Recent changes at Bidwell and a new strategy of customer service have led to this review of the current corporate publications. In a time of change, effective publications will help Bidwell employees to understand the changes and encourage active support. They will also enhance the company's marketing effort and its image.

As a result of our assessment, which included discussions with employee groups and major customers, we recommend four changes to the publications program:

1. Institute an electronic newsletter using the E-mail system currently being installed. It will provide brief, timely information to employees, and make feedback between management and employees easier to obtain.

2. Refocus the present print newsletter to emphasize discussion of policy issues. Rename it and reduce the number of issues to two a year from the current four.

3. Double the issues of *Rapport* to two a year, with the marketing becoming more involved in planning and getting feedback from customers.

4. Enliven the annual report by including colour photos of people in action, comments from employees or customers' quotations, and graphic illustrations of data.

The communications group can begin to implement these recommendations immediately, if approved, for an estimated added cost in 1993 of $24 000 over the 1992 budget of $126 000.

In its first year under new ownership and management, Bidwell Incorporated has undergone major changes, including adopting a new strategy of customer service. As part of Bidwell's company-wide review, this report presents our assessment of corporate publications and recommends steps to increase effectiveness in this period of change.

Our assessment included:

- extensive discussions with the communications department;

- meetings with senior managers in all departments;

- ten focus groups, each with 10 to 20 employees. Individuals in the groups were selected to represent the various functions and levels in Bidwell. We chose to use focus groups rather than conduct a survey of all employees, since in the preceding month employees had completed a human resources questionnaire and would likely not have welcomed a second one so soon after;

- eight interviews with Bidwell's major customers.

A. Summary of Recommendations

Based on our review, we recommend these changes to the present publications program:

1. Institute an electronic newsletter for topical news, using the electronic mail system now being installed.

2. Refocus the present print newsletter to emphasize company issues, reducing the number of issues to two a year.

3. Produce *Rapport* for customers twice a year, with increasing involvement from the marketing department.

4. Enliven the annual report through photographs, quotations and better illustrations of data.

B. Assessing Current Publications

Currently the communications group produces three publications:

1. *The Newsletter.* Produced internally in black and white through desk-top publishing, this 12-page publication covers a whole spectrum of topics, from employee news to industry matters. Our focus group discussions revealed that most employees read it and find it easy to understand. However, they find the news value is limited. Since it is published every third month, most news items have reached them through the grapevine before they read them in the Newsletter.

1

Our experience in other companies suggests that this type of publication is most useful for discussion of policies, issues, and ideas, for which the "news" element is not as important. It is also suited for complex items, such as changes in employee pension plan options, for which the ability of the communications department to write in simple, clear language is a great benefit.

2. *Rapport*. This glossy, coloured magazine for industry customers reviews new products and discusses industry issues. It has a high approval rating and serves a useful marketing as well as general public relations purpose. Customers say that this publication, with its review of new products as well as industry issues, gives Bidwell an edge over competitors. It is expensive — $18 000 to produce and deliver one issue of 3000 copies — but readers want more than one issue a year.

3. *Bidwell Annual Report*. The report, produced in two colours, performs a financial information function for investors. It also doubles as the Bidwell corporate brochure for people wanting general information about the company.

However, the impersonal focus, lack of photographs, and tabular presentation of data are conservative and leave a staid impression. The publication does not reflect Bidwell's new emphasis on customer service — on people serving people.

The annual report is relatively inexpensive to produce — $20 000 for 5000 copies.

C. Communication Needs for a Changing Company

Changes at Bidwell have created increased need for timely internal communication. The focus groups with employees indicated that at all levels they want to be informed regularly about new policies and planned changes. Without this communication, much productive time will be wasted on speculation and rumours.

As well, employees at all levels need to understand how the new customer service strategy translates into action. If they are to support it actively, they will need to know that management is responsive to their concerns and ideas. Although much internal communication with employees can and should take place informally through meetings and one-on-one discussions with others, written communications can also help. At the same time, external corporate publications can reinforce customer and investor perceptions of Bidwell's attention to customer service.

2

D. Details of Recommendations: A Communications Action Plan

1. *Create an electronic newsletter.* New information technologies are making it easier to send information quickly to many people and to have interactive communication. A weekly electronic newsletter would take advantage of Bidwell's highly computerized workplace, where 80% of the 1000 employees have a computer. The electronic mail (E-mail) system currently being installed on the computers, provides the vehicle.

   An electronic newsletter is useful for brief, timely items, not for lengthy multi-page discussions, which are harder to read off a computer screen. It can also foster a two-way flow of communication with management. For example, it can ask for quick feedback on plans, or respond to employee questions. Moreover, at Bidwell, it should publicly recognize achievements related to the customer service strategy.

   Be wary, however, of burdening the newsletter with information likely to interest only a few employees. E-mail can designate individuals or groups as receivers for information. However, information put out under the banner of the electronic newsletter, whatever it is called, should have broad interest.

   A print-out of messages should also be posted on bulletin boards, for those employees who do not have a computer.

   Since no added computer purchases are needed, the cost of creating an electronic newsletter will not increase the annual cost for the E-mail system of $60 a person.

2. **Refocus the present *Newsletter*.** If the E-mail system takes over the news function of the present print newsletter, the print publication will not have to be produced as often. Two issues a year will likely meet the need for the kind of in-depth discussion of policies and issues that the magazine format is best suited to.

   The name should be changed to reflect its new focus. The communications group has said it could hold a contest to choose a name — publicizing to employees the new approach.

   The present cost of $28 000 for four issues a year would decrease to about $14 000. The number of pages should remain the same.

3. **Double the number of issues of *Rapport*.** Concern for customer preferences as well as for costs suggests an initial experiment of two issues a year instead of one, with a re-evaluation of reader response after one year. Two issues will increase the present annual cost of $18 000 to $36 000.

   Since this publication provides an opportunity to market new products as well as enhance the company's image, the marketing department should be more involved in planning each issue as well as in getting regular feedback from customers.

3

4. **Enliven the annual report.** Three additions would help to produce a more dynamic, people-focused report, reflective of Bidwell's customer-service strategy:

- colour photographs of employees in action, interacting with customers and carrying out functions that help customers;

- quotations from Bidwell employees and customers, which illustrate good service and its benefits for customers;

- graphs and charts to present much of the quantitative data. They are easier to read and have more impact than tables.

These changes would likely increase the cost of the annual report to about $40 000.

E. Quick Benefits for a Reasonable Cost

Overall, the estimated increase in cost of implementing these recommendations is $24 000 over the current budget. As shown in the attached Exhibit of **Present and Projected Costs of Publications**, the current budget for 1992 is $126 000; the projected cost for 1993 is $150 000.

We have discussed our findings and recommendations with the communications group, who think realistically they could make the changes within six months. Moreover, they could do so with existing staff, adding nothing to personnel costs. Thus if management approves the proposed changes, for a reasonable added cost, Bidwell could benefit almost immediately.

EXHIBIT   **Present and Projected Costs of Publications**

$

	1992	1993
E-Mail, including newsletter	60 000	60 000
Print newsletter	28 000	14 000
Rapport	18 000	36 000
Annual Report	20 000	40 000
	126 000	150 000

5

FIG. 9-8   Letter of Transmittal

CRAWFORD & ASSOCIATES
34 Bay Street, Suite 12
Toronto, Ontario   M4T 3C5

October 9, 1992

Ms. Geraldine Connor
Vice President Human Resources
Lartex Inc.
100 Queen St., Suite 907
Toronto, Ontario   M5E 2T5

Dear Ms. Connor:

In September, you asked me to recommend procedures and a compensation package for employees you may encourage to take early retirement. Here is my report. It includes a financial plan with options for employees, as well as a suggested sequence of steps that will help you to introduce and implement the entire early retirement plan smoothly.

In undertaking this assignment, I was grateful for the support of your staff, and in particular for the continuous assistance of Helen Maxwell. It was a pleasure to work with such an enthusiastic group of people.

I look forward to discussing our recommendations with you when you return from your trip to Japan, and will be happy to help you in any aspect of the implementation.

Sincerely,

Peter Crawford

EXERCISES

● Section A

1. Write a one-page summary of a business article that is at least four pages long. Your instructor may select an article for the class or allow you to choose your own from a newspaper or business magazine. Assume that the summary is for a boss who wants to know the main points.

   Remember to avoid referring to the article by such phrases as "The article says. . ." Instead, report on the points themselves.

2. Ajax Corporation is a conglomerate in the chemical field. Among its holdings are two plants, Northfield Aluminum and Belmont Processing, both of which produce aluminum sulphite, as shown in the following chart:

COMPARISON OF NORTHFIELD AND BELMONT PROCESSES		
Item	**Northfield**	**Belmont**
aluminum sulphite production	intermittent batch process; considerable "down time"	continuous process
power consumption per ton of aluminum sulphate	110 kW.h	27 kW.h
insoluble (dirt)	8-10%	1-2%
water content	9-15%	4-5%
colour	grey-brown	white
uses other than water purification	none	pharmaceutical

In small groups, create and organize headings for one of the following formal reports. Give specific, descriptive subheadings in the biggest section. You may provide any added information you need to do a good job.

a) Ajax is concerned about Northfield's poor profit picture, as compared with Belmont's. It suspects that poor management is the problem, but hasn't been closely involved with the operation. You are a consultant for Ajax, investigating and reporting on the problem which you think is technical rather than managerial.

b) Domtech Corporation is another conglomerate in the chemical field, intent on expanding its holdings. Since it has heard that Ajax wants to sell some holdings, it has hired you to investigate and report on both plants.

c) Domtech Corporation is another conglomerate in the chemical field. It has heard that Northfield could be up for grabs and wants to buy it. As a consultant reporting to them, you have concluded that this would be a bad idea.

d) Ajax plans to close its Northfield operation (while keeping the Belmont plant open). Your job is to explain the reasons for the decision in a technical report, which will be made available to workers along with the company's plans for relocation and severance.

e) You are the manager of operations for Northfield. Through discussions with local politicians, you discover that Northfield may qualify for a plant modernization grant, but that Ajax would have to apply for it. Since Ajax will have to spend a lot of time negotiating such a grant and will have to make certain guarantees to the government, the president of Ajax asks you to write a formal report to him which shows why the plant needs modernization.

3. As a member of your college's Student Affairs Committee, you think it would be helpful if the college set up an information booth for the first month of the school year. The booth would be staffed five days a week by upper level students, who would be paid the minimum wage. They would help new students to find their way around the campus and let them know about the various student services available (such as sports facilities, health services, and clubs.) The booth would be located in the central meeting hall of the classroom building, where there is a lot of student traffic.

Since you think the information booth would make new students feel more at home, you want the administration to approve and finance the plan.

a) Write a proposal to your college principal.

b) Give to the class an oral presentation based on the proposal. It should be about three minutes in length.

Section B

1. Using the information supplied in question 2 of Section A, write a formal report for one of the tasks listed after the chart. Add information, if needed.

2. Individually or in small groups, prepare and deliver a short oral presentation based on one of the reports prepared for question 1. Have two or three members of the class play the role of the audience. Assume that they have not read the report and will have some questions. The length of presentation will depend on the number of presenters — a maximum of four minutes per presenter, including any response to questions.

3. Think of a way in which an activity you have participated in could be improved. The activity could be part of a paid or volunteer job, a sports team, a club, or any other aspect of student life. Write a formal proposal to the person in charge of that activity, suggesting why and how the change should be made. Assume that the person is open to suggestions.

4. Think of a problem area in a job you have held or in some aspect of student life. Write a formal report to the person in charge of that area, analyzing the problem and recommending changes. Assume that the reader is aware that the problem exists and has agreed to read your report, but is habitually cautious and nervous about change.

5. To help students earn money and gain work experience, the provincial government has agreed to pay 300 students up to $3000 each to devise and carry out civic service or civic improvement projects. The projects must benefit a needy area or group, or the community as a whole. The rules for the program state that the government will pay $5.50 per hour to a student, plus any material costs not exceeding $1000. Students may propose a joint project with up to four students participating.

Write a formal proposal to Arthur Belmont, Coordinator of the Student Summer Work Program.

6. Assume that the members of the class are the committee that selects the best projects for the student summer work program described in the preceding question.

Make a brief oral presentation (under four minutes), in which you try to convince the committee of the merits of your proposal.

CHAPTER 10

Oral Presentations and Meeting Management

Although in our daily work we speak more often than we write, many of us have not overcome the fear of having to speak to a group. Yet an oral presentation is an important part of business communications, whether it is a speech or proposal to some outside business organization or, as is more common, an outline of plans to an internal group of colleagues. The term *oral presentation* covers a variety of formal and informal speaking activities. For convenience, in this chapter the term *talk* will refer to informal presentations and the term *speech* will refer to formal addresses. Whatever the specific demands of your job, if you hope to rise up the managerial ladder, it's important to master the skill of speaking in front of others.

The advantage of speaking rather than writing is that it permits immediate feedback. The speaker can also respond to the audience's non-verbal reactions and clarify any confusing points. The listeners can often comment or ask questions. On the other hand, the audience cannot go back over material. Speaking is therefore not a good channel for conveying a lot of detailed information. The message in an oral presentation has to be relatively simple if it is to have an impact on the audience. Since simple does not mean simple-minded, planning for an oral presentation is just as important as for a written one.

Assessing the Reason and Receivers

Are You Informing or Persuading?

While humour can add spice to any business presentation, the main aim is usually to inform or persuade. Although professional speakers may also aim to entertain in their speeches, business people rarely have the comedian's gift — or the need to be funny. If your purpose is to inform, you should emphasize facts. If it is to persuade, you may consider an appeal to emotion as well as to reason. And even if you are selling a straightforward business proposition, you may have to overcome resistance. As a first step in planning, consider the results you want to achieve with the audience. What exactly do you want listeners to do, to think, or to feel?

What Kind of Audience Will You Have?

For most internal business presentations, it is fairly easy to assess the listeners. Most will be aware of your experience and why you are talking to them; you won't have to establish credibility. They will be interested in your subject, since it will presumably have a bearing on the business as a whole. And, as business associates, they will be fairly homogeneous in their backgrounds or experience. Still, it's worthwhile considering answers to the following questions:

- Who are the key decision-makers or opinion-makers, and what are their needs and concerns?
- What will the audience already know and what should I explain?
- Where might resistance to my ideas come from and how can I counter it?

With a formal speech to outsiders, the task of assessing the audience is more difficult:

- The listeners are more likely to come from diverse backgrounds or occupations. The only common bond you can assume is the one that draws them to the organization that has invited you to speak. It's a good idea, therefore, to try to pinpoint some shared concern they will probably have, whether it is economic, political, or cultural.
- Your speech may not be the attraction. The audience may be assembled for reasons other than to hear you — for example, they may be coming for some organizational business that follows the speech or simply for the fellowship of the group. You can't assume they will be interested in the topic. A light or anecdotal approach may be more appropriate than a speech heavy on specialized facts or subtleties.
- You may have to establish your own credibility. Although as a guest speaker you will no doubt be introduced by someone who will relate your background, you may still be wise to include in your speech a few indicators of your relevant experience — without blowing your own horn.

Assessing the Conditions

How Much Time Do You Have?

Whatever the length of time allocated to your presentation, stick to it. If an audience expects a half-hour talk and you speak for only fifteen minutes, they may feel somehow cheated, especially if they have given up valuable time — or paid money — to attend.

Far worse than being too brief, however, is being long-winded. Even ten minutes beyond the expected length can seem like an eternity to an audience. Psychologists have suggested that most people's attention span is not longer than twenty minutes, and many people's thoughts begin to wander long before that. If your presentation is scheduled right before a meal, the audience may be even more restless. (Can food for thought compete with lunch?) On the other hand, if it is scheduled right after a heavy meal, the audience may be sleepy. According to a survey by New Jersey-based Motivational Systems, four out of ten top executives admit to having dozed off — or "fallen dead asleep" — while listening to a business presentation, and others may have as well but are too embarrassed to admit it.[1] If you anticipate either of these problems, you can plan to counteract them by building more changes of pace into the presentation and accentuating possible dramatic elements.

Of course, it's difficult to tell in advance exactly how long you will take, but timing yourself in rehearsal will provide a guide. When preparing your presentation, mark off a rough timing guide and include in the plan some "nice to know" but not necessary detail. Then when you are speaking, you can choose to omit or keep the detail, depending on how close you are to your guide. If it looks as if you are going to be way behind, summarize the remaining material and end on time rather than push on relentlessly through the full speech.

What Is the Physical Layout and Technical Set-up?

- Find out how large the room is and whether you will have a microphone.
- If a door into the room is placed so that anyone coming in late will distract the audience, try to arrange for an alternate entrance during the presentation or see if latecomers can be kept out. Although these solutions are not always possible, it's annoying to see a good speech disrupted when all eyes turn to observe latecomers.
- Check to see that any audio-visual aids you need will be on hand and in good working order.
- Find out if you will be speaking in front of a lectern or a table. A portable lectern is usually available in most organizations where people give presentations. If you prefer one, ask for it.

    Using a lectern can be both an advantage and disadvantage. It allows a speaker to look at notes unobtrusively, to move just the eyes up an down rather than the head. It can also hide nervous hands. On the negative side, it presents a physical barricade between speaker and audience, increasing the sense of formality and distance. If you are giving a short, informal talk or presentation, you are probably better to do without a lectern.

---

[1]As reported in "Street Talk," *Marketing*, July 10, 1989.

Organizing the Material

A common prescription for speakers is, "Tell them what you are going to say, say it, and then tell them what you have said." If this sequence seems repetitive, remember that listeners, unlike readers, cannot review what has gone before. To help the memory, therefore, it's a good idea to build in some repetition. Think of a presentation as having

— an introduction that previews;
— a body that develops;
— a close that reviews.

Since the body takes up most of the presentation, it should be worked out before the opening.

Planning the Body

1. **Sort out the theme.**   Just as it's sensible to work out a thesis before writing an essay, or to clarify your subject before writing a report, so in a speech you should begin with the theme of your presentation. In an informative talk, it will be factual ("How we plan to market Softee Soap" or "Discoveries from our European sales trip"); in a persuasive talk or speech, it will have an argumentative edge ("Why we should move towards computer-integrated manufacturing" or "The need to improve internal communications"). The theme needn't be your eventual title; rather, it's a planning device, a linchpin to hold together the various facts or ideas you want to discuss.

2. **Choose the basic method of organization.**   Your options are similar to those available for a written report. Select whichever method makes your material most manageable for you as planner and most interesting and dynamic for the listener:

— order of importance;
— chronological order;
— geographic or spatial order;
— division or classification;
— comparison.

Another simple way to organize is to consider the message as a solution to a problem. It's the common "get'em on the hook, get'em off the hook" approach. The introduction points out the problem and the rest of the speech explains how to solve it. The explanation, however, will still need organizing in one of the preceding ways.

How direct or indirect you should be in your organization depends on your analysis of the audience. In most instances, the direct approach works best. When the receiver's mind has a sense of order, it more easily assimilates the details. For example, with a problem-solution approach, if you not only point out the problem in the introduction but indicate the solution, the audience will be prepared for the explanation that follows. The direct approach is especially useful for a business presentation when you and the audience are in general agreement about objectives and goals.

If the audience is likely to be opposed to your ideas, however, you may want to be more indirect. You may choose to build gradually to your solution, keeping the most effective argument to the last. Another option is to direct the audience, by pointing out in the introduction that you will be proposing a solution, but keep from disclosing the exact nature of the solution until you have laid the groundwork.

3. **Create three main sections.** Keith Spicer, an accomplished speaker, maintains that three is the magic number for an effective presentation.[2] Certainly students have long been accustomed to a three-part exam answer, and a three-part structure underlies much of our literature, music, religion, and art. Although two, four or five parts can also work, the three-part body is a good rule of thumb. You can organize around categories ("the three stages in our marketing campaign"), or points ("three ways to improve productivity").

4. **Help the audience remember your points** by using frequent numerical reminders. Describe them in full. Instead of saying, "Next" or "My next point," say, "My second discovery in reviewing costs," or "The third reason we need to enlarge the sales force."

5. **Support your points with specifics.** In an informative presentation you will naturally be presenting facts. In a persuasive one, anecdotes, quotations, and dramatic examples may be as effective as evidence or statistics. You may appeal to reason or emotion, but keep in mind that your aim is to gain support rather than simply to state what is.

   You may wonder: "Should I give evidence or arguments contrary to my position?" As pointed out in Chapter 7, if you are talking to the converted, to people who share your view, you can simply keep to the points that reinforce it. On the other hand, if you are talking to a group that is skeptical, you will add to your credibility by being balanced in your presentation. Discuss alternative points of view and give contrary evidence, while pressing your own case. Even if the audience is on your side, a two-sided argument will strengthen your case over the long term.

6. **Draw word pictures for the audience.** Your points will have more effect if you put them in visual terms. Let the listeners *see* the implications of your findings, or the consequences of following or not following your suggestions. Images have impact.

---

[2] Keith Spicer, *The Winging It Logic System: How to Think and Make Sense* (Toronto: Doubleday, 1984).

Beginning and Ending

When you have planned the body, you will easily work out the opening and close.

1. **Spark the audience's interest.**   The more captive the listeners and the less they know about your topic, the more you will have to work to capture their attention. If you are not well known to them, personally or by reputation, the opening lines are doubly important. Here are some common attention-grabbers:

   - *A joke*   This approach is only for people who have a good sense of timing. If you can't tell a joke well, don't try. Few moments are more embarrassing than the dead pause after a joke that doesn't work. A joke is not a mandatory opening; nor will any old joke do. While a good joke will warm a crowd, it must be related to the topic or the occasion for it to be effective.

   - *A topical anecdote*   If you do not feel comfortable telling a joke, a short description of an incident related to your topic or the context can build rapport with the audience. The incident might have something to do with the organization the audience belongs to, with your own preparation for the speech, or even with an occurrence earlier in the day — anything that is lighthearted and will bring you and your listeners together. Naturally, the more topical it is, the more the audience will appreciate it. And the more it will remove the impression of a "canned" presentation, one prepared well in advance for an unspecified audience.

   - *A startling fact or statistic*   This can be a dramatic opener, if relevant, and can help make the topic itself seem more important. For example, an opening statistic on the number of working hours lost because of alcoholism could raise interest in a speech on ways to combat alcoholism in the work place.

   - *A quotation*   This approach works well only if the quotation itself is startling or dramatic. Quoting the trite words of a well-known person will not do — unless your main purpose is to refute them.

   These are not the only ways to begin a speech or talk, but whatever tactic you use, think of your audience and what will draw them into your address.

2. **Reveal your plan.**   Tell how you are going to proceed and what the main sections of your presentation will be about. Not only does this help the listeners to remember main points, but it reassures them that you have a plan and don't intend simply to ramble on.

3. **At the end, close quickly.**   Simply summarize the main points of your presentation and then finish in a forceful way. The ending can be uplifting or funny, dramatic or moralistic, a quotation or a colourful phrase. But at least try to end with a flourish rather than a fizzle.

Using Audio-Visual Aids

Audio-visual aids help not only to clarify material and give it impact, but to keep an audience alert. Visual aids are especially useful for internal business presentations, which are often held in stark, single-coloured seminar rooms lit with fluorescent bulbs. The problem with these "classroom" surroundings is that sameness makes people drowsy: hypnotists know that a person who has a fixed focus over a period of time will begin to feel sleepy. Along with their other merits, visual aids force a shift in focus from the speaker to the medium and thus combat sleepiness.

Visual aids can have a negative side, however. If you are a dynamic speaker, they may lessen the momentum by shifting the focus away from what you are saying. They can also be over-used. A constant stream of transparencies, for example, can annoy an intellectual audience, especially if the message is readily understood without them. Despite these potential drawbacks, you should get used to handling visuals as a supplement to talking.

Various kinds of audio-visual aids have different advantages and problems:

1. **Overhead Projector**   This machine casts the images from transparencies onto a screen. Diagrams, charts, and lists are effective on transparencies.

   One of the advantages of an overhead projector is that the lights need not be turned off, but only dimmed slightly. Another advantage is that it's possible for the speaker to modify the transparencies on the spot, using a felt pen. These changes, even if they are only underlinings, add spontaneity to the presentation and keep the audience alert. If you are planning to use an overhead projector, make sure it has a spare bulb.

   When designing a transparency, remember these guidelines:

   - Keep the message or diagram simple and uncluttered. The audience should be able to understand it quickly.
   - Break complex points into simple ones. Use overlays to show any complex relationships.
   - Use letters large enough to be seen at the back of the room.
   - If possible, use a horizontal rather than vertical layout, so that heads in the audience don't block the view.
   - In a bland or monochrome room, colours in a transparency will add life. However, use no more than three in a single illustration. Avoid a combination of green and red, since many colour-blind people can't distinguish the difference.
   - If the illustration is a list, try placing a pencil or pointer by the item you are referring to.
   - Alternatively, you may slide a piece of paper under the transparency, gradually moving it down from the top as you discuss each point.
   - After checking the placement of the transparency, turn to face the audience before talking, or else your words may be lost. The same advice holds true for flip chart and blackboard illustrations.

- Turn off the projector when you are finished referring to the transparency. The light and noise of the machine can be distracting.

2. **Flip Chart**   This is simply a large pad attached to a stand. The speaker can draw or write on the pad while talking. There is no worry of machinery breakdown and no need for advance preparation of illustrations. The spontaneity of the process helps involve the audience. In a large room, however, the relatively small size of a flip chart is a disadvantage.

   If you are not a good artist or are too nervous to draw properly on the spot, consider drawing illustrations in advance. That way, you will still have clear visuals. To keep a sense of drama, you can draw on the second page of the flip chart, and use the top page as a cover until you want to remove it.

3. **Chalkboard**   This has most of the same advantages and disadvantages as a flip chart, but it is usually not as easy to read, especially if it is black or green. White boards are better, but they require special dry felt markers.

4. **Slide Projector**   Slides are invaluable for presenting photographs or subtle illustrations, since they have a degree of clarity not possible with transparencies. A series of slides can be run through quickly by means of a hand switch. If you plan to use slides, remember to check the order in advance and to find out how to turn the room lights on and off quickly with little disturbance.

5. **Movie Projector or Video Recorder**   Movies can have high interest value, since they combine sound, action and colour. Movie projectors can also break down at awkward moments. If you are going to use film in your presentation, try to have a technician present to work the machine. Failing this back-up, at least test the projector yourself, and set it up so that all you need to do in the presentation is push a switch and turn off the lights. While a videotape or television set is easier to use, the small size of the screen may be a disadvantage.

6. **Tape Recorder**   This is useful when sound can dramatize or enhance a point. Make sure that the listeners will be able to hear what is recorded. Small recorders may not have good enough speakers to project clearly to a large room. Also check beforehand that the lead-in is at the right spot, or that you have the exact spot on the tape marked. You shouldn't have to fiddle and fumble in the middle of a presentation trying to find the beginning of the excerpt you want.

   A final point: Never use audio-visual aids if they simply repeat the obvious. Rather, use them to emphasize, clarify or pull together important information.

Delivering the Presentation

There are four ways of speaking to a group:

1. **Reading from a prepared text**   Choose this approach when the exact words are important — when any confusion, ambiguity, or mistakes could have serious consequences. Academics usually read papers to other academics, who may query

the particular points or even the phrasing. Business and government leaders will usually read from a text when the issues are major ones and they want to avoid misinterpretation by the audience — and any reporters. People introducing guest speakers often read biographical information to make sure they have the correct details.

Unfortunately, unless the speaker is trained, a reading voice tends to drone or have a sing-song quality that can lull the audience. The presentation also lacks spontaneity, the sense of a speaker grappling to express ideas and creating a subtle suspense. Unless you have no other practical recourse, therefore, do not read. If you must read a prepared script, try these techniques:

— Type the speech on every third line in large print so that it is easy to read at a glance.
— Fill only the top two thirds of a vertical page with print, so that you don't have to bob your head up and down noticeably as you glance from page to audience and back.
— Underline the key words in each sentence, and practise emphasizing them.
— Mark on the script places where you can change your pace or tone to give variety and drama.
— Look up from the page as often as you can. Try to begin and end sentences while looking at the audience so that you can accentuate your message. In other words, look down between sentences to recall your points and then look up to deliver them.
— Practise reading the speech aloud beforehand so that you know the material well enough to keep visual contact with the audience.

2. **Memorizing** Although an actor can memorize speeches and deliver them flawlessly, few other people can. The danger is that in a rush of nerves a speaker may forget, and be more hopelessly lost than if the speech had never been committed to memory. If you have ever been in an audience when a memorized speech came unstuck, you will recall squirming at the speaker's silent agony. For most presentations, you are wise not to put your memory to the test by relying totally on it. It's better to memorize only the order of ideas and perhaps some colourful phrases or opening and closing sentences.

3. **Impromptu speaking** Few things are more nerve-wracking than those moments when you are suddenly asked to address a group on the spot, without any advance preparation. If you have the gift of the gab, you may rise to the challenge brilliantly; however, for most inexperienced speakers it's a matter of instant sweaty palms. Luckily, in business you will rarely have to do an impromptu presentation unless it's a very informal occasion (such as a birthday party or other celebration); for business meetings most organizers have the courtesy to give advance notice.

If you are asked to give an impromptu talk, remember that the audience will not expect much. Be short and to the point, making a few specific remarks that relate to the occasion. If you treat the task with good humour and pleasantness, the audience will likely respond to you the same way. You can also try to anticipate those occasions when you might be asked to say a few words, and plan your approach just in case. (As Will Rogers reportedly said, "A good impromptu speech takes two weeks to prepare.")

4. **Extemporaneous speaking** This kind of presentation is prepared in advance but delivered fresh — that is, the exact wording is figured out as the speaker goes along. It combines the benefits of prior organization and spontaneity. Whether the business occasion calls for an informal talk or a formal speech, extemporaneous speaking is usually the best method.

Sometimes, if you know the material well, you can speak without any notes, relying on your memory of a prepared outline. If you feel uncomfortable without some memory aids, try putting the outline on small cue cards. Don't try to squeeze the entire speech onto cards; use only the key points and any quotations. If it will give you more confidence, write out in full the opening and closing sentences. Then, if you have prepared well, you will probably find that you don't have to use the notes. The mere fact of having them there will relieve you of the anxiety of forgetting.

Delivery Techniques

Look confident. Don't worry about being nervous before a speech. Most speakers are, even seasoned public speakers. The trick is not to appear nervous, since speaker nervousness is somehow contagious. Conversely, a seemingly confident, relaxed speaker will make an audience relax. How do you appear confident? Here is a guide:

1. **Have good posture.**   A speaker who walks purposefully and stands erect conveys a sense of command. Try not to slouch or to drape yourself over the lectern.

2. **Wear clothing that is appropriate and comfortable.**   There's no point distracting an audience from what you are saying by what you are wearing. Unless special clothing is a deliberate part of the drama you are creating — a kind of costume — it's better to be on the conservative side. In any case, if you wear jewellery, avoid any that jangles; if you tend to put your hands in your pockets and can't break the habit, remove change.

3. **Establish eye contact.**   As you speak, think of the audience not as a group but as a number of individuals. (Some speakers say it creates confidence to think of the audience as individuals without clothes.) In any case, look for someone who is especially attentive and establish eye contact. Later, switch to other parts of the room and do the same with different individuals. Try to hold your eye contact for a few seconds with one person before moving to another. Eyes that flit about a room give an impression of nervousness.

This technique will help you to feel comfortable with the audience and to establish a rapport. It will also help you to adapt to audience response if necessary — to explain in more detail if you notice quizzical looks or even to leave out some details if you notice fidgeting.

4. **Slow down.**   It's natural, when you are nervous, to speed up your talking — to try to get it over with quickly. Unless you are normally a slow speaker, take the opposite tack. Before you start to speak, pause for a minute to get your bearings and look over the audience. Take a few deep breaths to relax. Smile. Then begin slowly and deliberately. At appropriate spots, when you are changing your emphasis, pause again. Silence can speak: an occasional deliberate pause will generate suspense over what is to follow — and wake up the audience.

5. **Speak clearly and with varied tones.**   Don't mumble. Articulate your words. When you don't have a microphone, project your voice to the back of the room. When you do have a microphone, stay about 15 cm (6 in.) away from it. If you are not in the habit of public speaking, you will likely have to concentrate on articulating the words, on pronouncing word endings so that your voice doesn't drift off into nothingness.

   Nervousness tends to flatten the voice. To counter this effect, deliberately widen your range. Exaggerate the tones, and stress key words in each sentence. In general, give a downward emphasis to the ends of sentences. Tentative speakers often let their voices rise at the end of sentences, suggesting that they are not confident. When you are rehearsing make sure that you have a downward thrust when emphasizing your points.

   Although you don't want to push beyond your natural range, remember to use the lower end of your natural register. A low-pitched voice is usually more pleasing than a high-pitched one, especially in women. Breathing from the stomach rather than the upper chest will help increase both the resonance and depth of your voice.

6. **Be natural with gestures and movement.**   Some people talk with their hands; other don't. While gestures can be an effective way of reinforcing points or expressing moods, there's no point trying to change your style to something you are not comfortable with. Artificial gestures can distract from your presentation. So can repetitive or fidgety movements. But if you like to use your hands, be assured that they will make you seem less stiff and constrained. In any case, keep from gluing your hands together throughout your talk or from planting them in pockets. If you leave them free, you will probably use them naturally for emphasis.

   A tip: If your hands feel awkward hanging at your sides — like five-kilo hams rather than helpers — try a tension-release exercise. Just before you walk up to speak, press your wrists hard against your sides for thirty seconds. Release. Notice how light your hands feel. They will seem to float up, ready for use.

   Is it helpful to move around while talking? Although constant walking about to no purpose can be distracting, taking the odd step here and there, if you feel natural doing so, can be useful. It makes the listeners shift focus and helps them stay alert. Don't feel you have to move during a presentation, however; many good speakers prefer to stand still the whole time.

7. **Practise.**   Go through your presentation as often as you can, not only to check the timing but to strengthen your delivery. If possible, rehearse in front of a video-recorder; playing the tape back will allow you to see and hear nervous mannerisms

and other weaknesses. If you don't have access to a video-recorder, try standing in front of a mirror with a tape recorder. The more you repeat the exercise and the more familiar you are with the material, the more confident you will feel about delivering it.

A practice tip: if you stumble, don't start again. Make yourself carry on through to the end, however badly you do it. The point is to get used to expressing your ideas in different ways, so that you relax with the wording of your thoughts. If instead you go back and keep repeating material until it is "word perfect," you will likely end up with a memorized tone to your presentation. Rest assured that if you have to struggle for a word during your actual delivery you will add to the sense of spontaneity.

Coping with Nerves

It's natural to feel somewhat nervous. It's even desirable. Top speakers and actors know that nervousness releases adrenalin, giving a burst of energy that will help them to perform well. Trouble comes with an excess of nervousness. It can produce not only mental stress but physical discomfort. Chest and voice muscles can tighten, making talking and even breathing seem difficult.

The strategy is to relax those muscles deliberately. Before you speak, practise breathing deeply from the stomach. Put your hand on your stomach to make sure it is expanding and contracting. Try to loosen the throat muscles by humming a song. When not in view of the audience, make exaggerated faces so that your mouth and jaw are loosened.

When you do get up to speak, stand and survey the audience for a few seconds before beginning. Take a couple of deep breaths, and establish eye contact with a friendly-looking face. Above all, don't apologize or say that you are nervous. If you look confident, the audience may never think otherwise.

By far the best strategy for stage fright, however, is to practise. You will find that the adrenalin rush is a little less each time you repeat a performance. You won't lose all nervousness, but you will feel in control of it.

Handling Questions

With many business presentations, getting feedback through questions will increase the likelihood of producing the desired results with the audience. When you are giving a speech or presentation, consider whether you should encourage questions, and whether they should be raised during the speech or afterwards. If you want to have questions, let the audience know at the start how you will handle the process.

The advantage of taking questions throughout a talk is that the audience becomes more involved rather than sitting back as passive listeners. The disadvantage is that constant interruptions can diminish momentum and a sense of focus. Probably a good guideline is to assess the formality of the occasion: save spontaneous questioning for the most informal talks and provide a question period for more formal presentations. For some highly formal speeches, you may choose to have no questions.

When you invite questions, it's important to control the process. Anticipate the kinds of question you might be asked and figure out how you would answer them. You may decide to have some extra back-up information on hand. Remember also what the purpose and focus of your presentation are and don't let yourself get sidetracked. Here are the main problems that can arise with questions, and some suggestions on how to handle them:

- **A confused question**   Formulate or paraphrase the question in simple terms before you answer it. This practice can be useful for all questions, since it gives both you and the audience time to think.

- **A hostile question**   The trick is not to be defensive or hostile yourself. See first if you can rephrase the question so that it is not emotionally loaded. Then try to use facts to answer it. If you appear unruffled and try to address the matter, the audience will appreciate your poise.

    When answering, address the audience as a whole, rather than look at the questioner. This will divert attention from the source of hostility, and reduce the chance of the questioner's persisting.

- **A two-part or complex question**   Separate the parts, and answer one at a time. If this sequence will take too long, answer one part, and suggest you will be pleased to discuss the other issues informally later.

- **An off-topic question**   Mention that you think topic X is an interesting one which you would like to answer if you had the time, but your focus at this presentation is Y. If you can, suggest that you might be prepared to handle topic X another time.

- **A question you cannot answer**   If you haven't got the answer, admit it. If possible, say that you will get a response to the questioner later.

- **A scene stealer**   Occasionally members of the audience will use a question-and-answer period as a platform to give their own opinions rather than ask a question. If someone starts to launch into a speech, try to take advantage of a pause and politely interrupt. Ask the speaker to state the question briefly, so that others have time to raise their questions. Then in your answer steer the audience's attention back to the points you want to stress — to the focus of your presentation.

- **An underground questioner**   This person can be disruptive. Instead of asking an open question, he or she will make critical comments or ask snide questions in an undertone loud enough for others to hear. The best approach if this behaviour persists is to single out the offender. You can, for example say, ''Do you want to ask something?'' ''Can you speak out so that everyone can hear?'' or ''Can the person giving a talk in the back row share his question with all the audience?'' Such a direct approach will usually silence disrupters.

- **A reticent audience**   Sometimes the process needs help to get started, particularly with a large crowd. If you anticipate that this will be the case, arrange for someone you know in the audience to ask the first question. Another option is to ask the first question yourself. For example, you can say "You may be wondering . . ." and then address the issue. Keep eye contact with all parts of the audience when responding, encouraging people sitting in different locations to speak up.

When a lengthy or contentious question-and-answer period finishes, it's a good idea to bring the audience's attention back to the main point of your talk. A brief closing statement will place the final emphasis where you want it to be.

Introducing and Thanking a Speaker

Introducing and thanking are the bookends of a formal speech. Unfortunately, people asked to perform these tasks often forget that their role is a secondary one. They talk too long.

Introducing

Your task is to let the audience know why the speaker has been asked to talk on the subject and to present the speaker to the group. When the topic is already known to the audience but the speaker is not, some introducers rely on the HAM formula:

— **home** (speaker's present hometown or birthplace);

— **accomplishments** of the speaker that are relevant to the topic;

— **moniker**, or name of speaker.

Leaving the name until last — "Please welcome Mary Hunter" — builds a little suspense in the introduction.

For other occasions, especially when the speaker is well known, you may choose to emphasize his or her experience or the importance of the topic. Whatever form it takes, a good introduction is courteous, specific, and brief.

As mentioned earlier, it is perfectly acceptable to read from notes when presenting the biographical facts about a speaker, since the details need to be accurate. Try to get away from those notes, however, at the beginning and end of the introduction.

Thanking

The most gracious thank-you's often take no more than a minute, but they demonstrate that the thanker has paid attention to the speaker. If your job is to thank, be alert during the speech and try to comment on one aspect or one point that was of particular interest to you and the other listeners. One concrete remark is better than a number of generalized phrases of gratitude. Conclude in the easiest way possible — by expressing your thanks on behalf of the audience.

By working on the techniques in this chapter and becoming comfortable with them, you will discover that oral presentations are not simply a way of dishing out information or ideas, but a means of interacting with an audience. You will discover how you can affect listeners not only by the words but by the manner of the delivery.

As in all other endeavours, however, you need to practise. Instead of shrinking from chances to speak to a group, plunge in and try. Brief informal talks are the easiest way to begin, but in more formal meetings you can also wet your feet by introducing or thanking a speaker or simply making announcements. Practice may not make you perfect, but it will certainly make you better. And who knows? When you do a lot of it, you may even come to like it.

Managing Meetings

Business managers often feel that their energies are trickling out in a continuous round of unproductive meetings. Bad meetings are enormous time-wasters. Yet when well planned and well run, a meeting has certain communication advantages. It's especially useful for:

— a question-and-answer or information-and-feedback session;

— group problem-solving and decision-making;

— face-to-face discussion;

— team-building.

Good meetings can improve morale, productivity, and commitment. Here are some guidelines for creating meetings that work.

Before the Meeting

Decide:

1. **What's the reason or expected result?**   If there is none, cancel the meeting.

2. **Is a meeting the most suitable channel?**   For example, a memo can convey information at much less cost, and may achieve the same results — if feedback is not needed.

   If individual opinions about an idea are needed, perhaps a few telephone calls or a conference call can get the result with less effort and time spent.

3. **Who are essential participants?**   Exclude anyone who cannot contribute, since a large group makes discussion more difficult.

   Generally, a meeting with between five and fifteen participants works best for problem-solving. If it's smaller, it may not include enough differing viewpoints to anticipate all the problems or possible solutions. A meeting with over thirty participants is effective only as an information session with questions and answers.

4. **When's the best time?**   Arrange a time that fits participants' schedules, so that some won't be wandering in late or leaving early. Consider the frame of mind of the participants — when they will be freshest and least distracted by other concerns. A meeting to develop new ideas would not be productive at the end of a busy week or right before another stressful or important event.

5. **Where's the best place?**   If a meeting is held in a private office, the person who "owns" the space will be perceived to be more in control of the meeting. This advantage may or may not matter, depending on the nature of the meeting and on how well the participants get on. A controversial subject is nearly always better discussed in a "neutral" space, such as a special meeting room. Some businesses schedule important meetings away from the office, so that participants won't be distracted or interrupted by telephone calls.

Check the size and shape of the room, and the seating arrangements. An overcrowded room can become hot and stuffy, even with air conditioning.

The seating layout can make a difference to the tone of the meeting. As pointed out in Chapter 1, a circular table for a small meeting gives a sense of equality and encourages interaction among participants. If the person chairing the meeting sits at the head of a long table, he or she will tend to dominate more.

In a large meeting, the more separated physically the leader is from the group, the more formal the impression. When there's a need for audience participation, the ideal seating arrangement is U-shaped or, at least, V-shaped. Either arrangement allows the leader to move into the group and encourage participants to talk to each other face-to-face. (See Figure 10-1.)

When booking a room, arrange for any audio-visual aids or extra materials, such as pads and pencils. Just before the meeting, double check that the set-up is satisfactory.

6. **What's the Agenda?**   Decide exactly the number of issues you want to discuss and rank them. Check with key participants to see if they may have other useful agenda items. Allocate a time period for each.

Ordinarily it's best to put the major item first, so that it will be discussed when participants are fresh. Alternatively, you might put first those items for which a quick decision can be made and then move to the major issue for discussion, followed by minor ones.

Occasionally you may even choose to leave until the end a controversial proposal you want passed quickly. This approach carries a risk. The participants may approve the proposal out of sheer meeting fatigue, but they may also be annoyed by the lack of discussion, or feel manipulated.

Distribute the agenda and any background reading material to participants before the meeting. That way they will have time to think about the issues and come prepared.

During the Meeting

If you are chairing a meeting, you have three essential tasks:

1. **Focus the discussion.**   Get participants to agree on the order and timing of the agenda. Then gently but firmly keep the meeting on target. Record ideas as they arise, preferably where others can see them — on a flip chart or chalkboard. (It's also appropriate and may be more efficient to assign someone else the task of

FIG. 10-1   Seating Arrangements

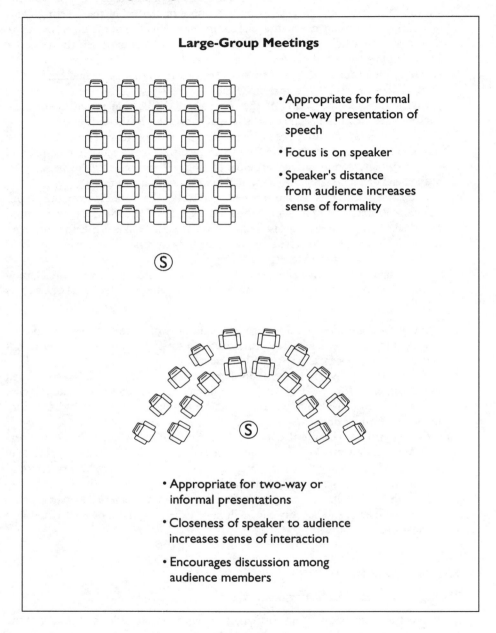

Large-Group Meetings

• Appropriate for formal one-way presentation of speech

• Focus is on speaker

• Speaker's distance from audience increases sense of formality

• Appropriate for two-way or informal presentations

• Closeness of speaker to audience increases sense of interaction

• Encourages discussion among audience members

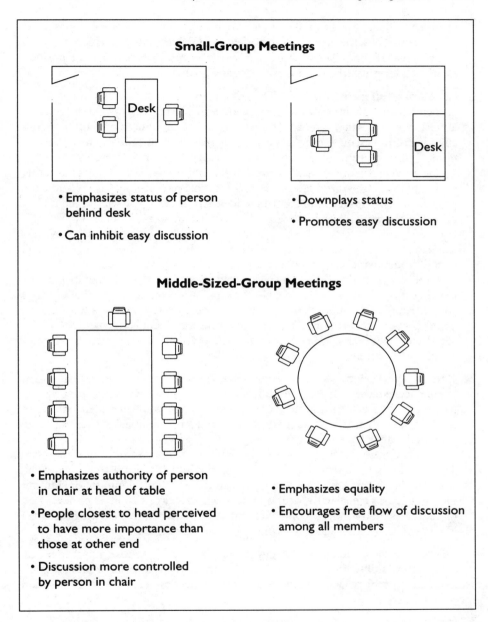

Small-Group Meetings

- Emphasizes status of person behind desk
- Can inhibit easy discussion

- Downplays status
- Promotes easy discussion

Middle-Sized-Group Meetings

- Emphasizes authority of person in chair at head of table
- People closest to head perceived to have more importance than those at other end
- Discussion more controlled by person in chair

- Emphasizes equality
- Encourages free flow of discussion among all members

recorder.) When time is running out for a particular item, see if the group is ready for a decision, or if the item needs to be deferred to a later date when more facts will be available. If consensus or a decision has been reached, reiterate the position clearly, and specify who is responsible for any further action.

2. **Encourage full participation.** The trick is to stimulate discussion and make participants feel their contribution is worthwhile. When the person in the chair also has the most senior position, there's a danger of domination, of unintentionally stifling discussion. Others in the meeting may keep quiet or stay with "groupthink," unless specifically encouraged to put forth alternative opinions.

One way to encourage participation, if you are the boss, is to appoint a meeting facilitator to run the meeting. The facilitator's sole responsibility is to handle the process of discussion, not to contribute ideas. Your authority will not be undermined, since you still set the agenda and contribute to the discussion. You still have responsibility for any decisions or plans coming out of the discussion. With a facilitator, you may see participation increase. Moreover, your organization will benefit from having a larger pool of experienced meeting managers.

If you do keep the chair, consider occasionally asking each member of the meeting in turn to comment on an issue. Explicitly encourage dissenting views. If you are running the meeting and the boss or someone several layers senior to the others is a participant, consider getting his or her argument beforehand to encourage the more junior members to voice their opinions early, so that they don't simply defer to rank.

3. **Control Aggression.** Sometimes emotions run high between individuals and, if left unchecked, they can create hostility. You can help by encouraging participants to stick to the facts, so that their comments don't become a personal attack on another member of the group. Try to remain neutral yourself, rather than take sides in the dispute.

If you anticipate conflict between two people, try to seat them beside rather than facing each other, so that they find it harder to do battle. Even when there's no open hostility, you should see that the vocally strong don't dominate or shut out the shy. Create a constructive atmosphere in which ideas are built up or developed rather than shot down. A process of recording all ideas before evaluating them can often work in meetings, as it does in brainstorming sessions.

Even beyond these three tasks, managing a meeting well requires a host of subtle communication skills. From time to time you are likely to find one or more participants creating problems for the most well-planned meeting. Here are some common meeting spoilers:

- **The interrupter** Sometimes people are unaware they are interrupting. Often they are simply enthusiasts, who do not mean to cut another off. In such cases, you can simply maintain eye contact with the first speaker while raising your hand in a "just wait a minute" gesture towards the interrupter. When someone interrupts repeatedly, you can politely suggest that you want to hear the rest of the first speaker's remarks. Such a comment is usually enough to stop interrupting behaviour. If it doesn't, speak to the interrupter privately, during a break in the meeting or afterwards.

- **The diverter**   This person brings up off-topic matters or breaks the flow with joking asides. Your job is to steer the discussion tactfully back on track, reminding the group of the issue at hand. If you think the diverter has a hidden agenda, you have several choices:
  - ask if there's another problem that should be taken care of immediately;
  - agree to leave time at the end of the meeting for new matters;
  - discuss the hidden concern privately at the end of the meeting.

- **The non-stop talker**   Some people seem to go on and on, sapping the forward energy of a meeting. They have trouble coming directly to the point. One way to respond is to listen attentively until the talker pauses for breath and then politely interrupt with a comment such as "Your point is that . . ." or "So you think we should. . . Would someone else like to comment?"

At the end of the meeting, if people are tired, you can simply adjourn. You can also provide a quick review. Focus on conclusions or decisions resulting from the discussion, and any follow-up plan. This review is especially important if there will be no written follow-up. It will give participants a sense of accomplishment from the meeting.

After the Meeting

Formal minutes are a useful follow-up to a formal meeting. Usually someone who isn't a participant in the discussion is the best person to record the minutes — to act as the meeting's secretary. If you have the job of writing minutes or overseeing the job, ensure that they:

- indicate the date, time, and place of the meeting;
- name the participants and person in the chair (along with the "regrets": names of any absentees who said they would be unable to attend);
- summarize the proceedings, following the order of items as they were discussed;
- record each proposal and amendment, and whether it was carried or defeated in a vote.
- name the proposer and seconder for every motion.

Informal meetings don't have formal minutes, but it's still often useful to send a brief report to participants, summarizing the conclusions and proposed actions emerging from the discussion. Be specific about who will be responsible for follow-up tasks.

Handling a Media Interview

When dealing with the media, it's important to establish an atmosphere of cooperation. Recognize that the job of journalists is to report a story. Your job is to help them get the facts right. If you treat them not as the enemy, but as people who, for the most part, want to be professional and report honestly, you are likely to establish the right atmosphere for an interview.

Most often the media will come to managers for a story when they sense a real or potential crisis or conflict in the organization. As a result, the manager being interviewed is under extra pressure not to enlarge the crisis or conflict — not to say something that will make matters worse. The temptation is to retreat to a "no comment" reply. However, such a response has two disadvantages:

1. It leaves a suspicion that the company has something to hide;
2. The reporter will likely produce the story anyway, with less reliable facts than the manager could have supplied.

Occasionally silence is essential as, for example, when a pending financial transaction has not been completed, or when comments could unfairly jeopardize a person's reputation or legal position. If you must be silent, it's a good idea to explain why you cannot comment, rather than simply issue an abrupt refusal. In any case, if you want to avoid disclosing something, do not lie. If you are found out, your credibility is destroyed.

Once you have agreed to a media interview, think of your task as being as open and honest as possible, while maintaining control of the exchange. The following suggestions will help you to succeed. They are directed more to the one-on-one interview than a press conference, but the advice applies in both cases.

- Choose a location that is to your advantage. Clearly most people will feel more comfortable in their own office than on a noisy factory floor or in the middle of a crowd of onlookers. If the interview will be filmed, decide whether you want to be sitting or standing, behind a desk or or a lectern, or even in front of a relevant backdrop, such as a sign or logo. The media may request a different venue, but you can disagree if the setting will undermine your effort.

- Establish the timeframe, but be considerate of media deadlines. You can set the time and length of the interview according to your need to prepare. However, reporters mostly work under inflexible time constraints. If you want your comments to appear in the next day's newpaper, find out when the journalist's story deadline is and meet it. Many an effort has been wasted because information came too late. Since old news is no news, the impetus to include the information has often disappeared by the time of the subsequent edition.

- Consider in advance the reporter's possible angle or perspective, and plan your answers to contentious or inflammatory questions. If you want to be quoted, short, direct, or colourful remarks are more likely to work than a long-winded or hedging discourse.

Remember that taped or filmed news interviewers are likely to choose clips of twenty seconds or even less, and try to give answers in one sentence. Some media experts suggest that you think of your comments as if talking in headlines. In other words, get to the point fast and with simple words.

- Try to shape the the story with your own simple message. The key is to bridge — to shift the answer towards the points you want to make. In other words, determine before the interview the key points you want to put across and try to get them into the conversation by linking them to some question. Of course, the more subtly you do this the better. Many politicans are good at bridging, but it takes practice.

- Take time to reply to a problem question. If put on the spot, pause for five to ten seconds before giving a considered reply. A delayed but clear answer is better than a quick one that is not what you really want to say. If you do make a mistake, correct yourself immediately.

- If you don't know the answer to something, admit it. Say you will get back with an answer later — and then do so.

- Don't repeat the interviewer's negative phrases or an incorrect statement while you are in the process denying them. Those phrases can find themselves in your mouth in the newsclip, giving added credence to them. Instead use your own words to give your message.

    For example, suppose as a result of a chemical spill, an interviewer were to ask: "Will your company accept the blame for the damage caused by the illegal spill of cancer-causing waste in Forestfield?" In your reply you would want especially to avoid the words *blame*, *illegal*, and *cancer-causing*. You might therefore say "We take responsibility and have established procedures for the safe disposal of our waste. We, and a team of government experts, are thoroughly investigating what happened at Forestfield, since we have a long record of safe disposal."

- Avoid giving answers to hypothetical questions, such as, "Will you shut down the plant if it's discovered that the chemical is damaging to health?" Speculation is dangerous. It can widen unnecessarily the scope of a story or lead you toward commitments you later regret.

- Treat reporters with respect, using their names. Try to figure out their level of knowledge, so that you can fill in the blank spots without condescension.

E X E R C I S E S

● **Section A**

1. In small groups, practise saying the following sentences with clear articulation and a downward thrust at the end:

   a) Right now, treasury bills are a sound investment.

   b) I feel confident of this talented candidate.

   c) We need to respond to employees' feelings.

   d) I suspect the union will now want to negotiate.

   e) Please correct the mistake on the second forecast sheet.

2. Take a short nursery tale or a passage from it, about a half a page in length. Underline the key words in each sentence. Then read the passage to the class, emphasizing the key words. If possible, photocopy the material, so that others can easily check your technique.

3. Prepare a short (two-or three-minute) informative talk on one of the following subjects:

   a) How to Build a Fire Outdoors

   b) How to Change a Tire

   c) How to Handle an Irate Customer

   d) How to Create the World's Best Sandwich

   e) How Not to Impress a First Date

   f) How to Dress for Business Success

   g) How to Be a Smart Shopper

   h) How to . . . (any other task)

   Give your talk to the class. Others in the class will make notes on (a) your organization; (b) your delivery; (c) audience awareness.

4. Pick a page of any published article. Practise reading it aloud clearly, varying the tone and speed so that it more closely resembles forceful talk. Read the page to the class and have it recorded on tape. Listen to your delivery. How could you improve it?

5. On a slip of paper write your name and a topic you know something about. Put the slip in a hat and draw another one out. Prepare a short introduction for the person whose name you have drawn. (You may have to talk to the person first for background information.) Then prepare a three-minute speech on your own topic. To complete this exercise you will have to

   — introduce your selected speaker and thank the speaker after the talk;

   — give your own short speech.

   If possible, presentations should be video-recorded for later playback and examination.

6. Select one of the following speech topics, create a theme, and select two different ways of organizing the material. Then plan a three-part structure for each method. (You need only give the headings.)

   a) Leisure Time and Lifestyle

   b) Business Opportunities: Where Are They?

    c) What Young People Want in a Job

    d) Trends in Health Care (or Manufacturing, or Technology)

    e) Why We Need to Act on Pollution

7. Have each person in the class write on a slip of paper and put in a hat the name of a well-known person from business, politics, or entertainment. Then in turn draw a slip from the hat and preprare to give a one-minute talk on the topic "If I were [name], I would change . . ." You are allowed five minutes to prepare. Remember that in such a short talk you have time to mention, explain, and/or illustrate only one point.

8. Select from a current newpaper a story or issue that could embarrass or damage an organization. Assume that you are the selected spokesperson for that organization, preparing for an interview with a newspaper reporter. Create a series of three questions that could cause a problem if answered badly. Include at least one hypothetical question or a question containing an incorrect fact or damaging accusation. Then write out your planned response to those questions. Keep your sentences as simple, short, and positive as possible. They must each be able to fit into a 20-second clip.

● Section B

1. Suppose a dinner is being given in honour of another member of the class who will be leaving an organization to which you both belong. (You are free to choose the person and the organization, whether it is a business, school, or club.) In front of the class, give a one-minute testimonial talk. Your talk may be serious or light-hearted.

2. Assume that a leading public figure is coming to talk to your college and you have been selected to introduce him or her. Create an imaginary topic for the guest's speech and then give a short speech of introduction to the class. Remember that this is a formal occasion.

3. For a report you have prepared for this class or any other, give a brief presentation in which you emphasize the important points. Assume that members of the class are interested colleagues. Use some form of visual aid in your presentation. If possible, have the presentation video-recorded. Other members of the class should mark down the positive aspects of the presentation and areas of organization or delivery where you could improve.

4. Put a light-hearted topic on a slip of paper which will be collected in a hat, along with slips from other students. Draw a slip and give a one-minute impromptu talk on the topic selected.

5. Working in groups of three, select a story from a current newspaper, the implications of which could damage or embarrass an organization. (Examples could involve environmental accidents; corporate mismanagement or fraud; factory closures, layoffs or strikes; or harassment or hazards in the work place.) Each member of the the group should prepare a series of questions that a reporter could use to interview a manager in that organization. Then, as if in a media interview, each will in turn respond to another member's questions. Afterwards, the third member of the group should comment on the strengths and weaknesses of the response.

    According to time constraints the interviews could last from three to five minutes. If possible, videotaping of the interviews would be helpful to the class.

11

Communicating to Get a Job

Job-hunting is a complex task, requiring both oral and written skills. As with any communications challenge, thought and planning can help you meet it.

Search and Research

Career counsellors say that only twenty percent of all job openings are advertised. The implication for you as a job-seeker is that you cannot simply look at the want-ads or check the job files of placement agencies. You will have to go out and search. But first examine yourself and the kind of job you are suited for.

Assess Your Qualifications and Personality

What kind of job do you want? What are your qualifications? Just as important, what is your personality? Peter Drucker, the internationally renowned expert on management, long ago pointed out that people who are unsuited for their jobs most often have the ability, but not the personality for them. In an article that still makes good sense, he suggested that before applying for any job, you should make some decisions based on your type of personality:

- Do you belong in a routine, secure job or a challenging, less secure job?
- Do you belong in a large organization with a hierarchy of regular channels or in a small organization with informal, direct contacts? Do you enjoy being a small cog in a big and powerful machine or a big wheel in a small machine?

- Will you be happier and more effective as a specialist or as a generalist?[1]

Analyzing your own personality and temperament — what you really like, as opposed to what others like or you think you should like — will help you decide the right kind of job to look for.

Research the Job Market

How do you find a job? Naturally you should look at the job advertisements in newspapers and keep an eye on the boards of employment agencies. Most academic institutions have job placement services. Take advantage of their contacts, counselling, and information about careers and specific businesses. But you need to go farther in the job hunt, and conduct your own research. Here are the most promising approaches:

1. **Read the financial section of newspapers and business magazines.** Most of these are available in local libraries. They often feature articles about up-and-coming businesses and about sectors that are expanding. These are areas where new jobs are likely to be created. You may find that a company has plans to locate in your area, in which case try to apply before an opening has been advertised.

2. **Obtain the annual reports of companies.** Visit a business library or try writing or phoning the company directly. In the interest of good public relations, many companies will be glad to send a copy.

3. **Conduct an information interview.** Talk to anyone you know who works or has worked in the field you are investigating. Review all friends and acquaintances for the name of a good person to contact. If you don't find any contacts this way, try a cold call yourself to someone in a position to help you. Most people will either spare a few minutes themselves or refer you to someone else in the company.

   When you come to the information interview, be prepared. Don't waste an employer's time on questions you could easily have found the answer to elsewhere. Here are some useful questions:

- How did you become involved in this type of work?
- What are the most rewarding aspects of the work? The least rewarding?
- Can you describe a typical day or assignment?
- What is the best preparation for this kind of job? What is the best kind of training or experience for it?
- What is the best way to gain entry to this kind of work?
- What is your opinion of the job outlook in this area?
- Would you advise young people to pursue this kind of career?
- Can you refer me to other people doing your kind of work or a specialty in it?

---

[1] Peter F. Drucker, "How to be an Employee," *Fortune* (May, 1952).

The Job Application

A job application is not so much an information sheet as a type of sales pitch, in which the product being sold is the writer. Like all persuasive communication, it requires some creative thinking.

Think of the résumé and covering letter as a package. Ideally, you should create a different package for each firm you apply to. Practically, this approach may be difficult if you are sending out a number of applications at the same time, as students often do. A workable compromise is to create a distinctive application package for each type of job, and then adapt certain parts to give an individualized look. A personalized application will be more effective than an obvious blanket one designed to cover a wide area of the job market.

Experts in job search and relocation say that scattering applications to a lot a companies seldom works. The most effective approach is to try to get a personal introduction to someone in a specific company. Face-to-face is the best way to sell yourself.

When contacts fail to get you in the door, however, a written application may be the only resort. Target five companies at a time, rather than send a "broadcast" letter to 150. Through research, determine what kinds of skills and experience the organization or the particular department needs. Get a sense of the corporate culture and of the ways you could contribute. Relate to the company's agenda, not your own.

The Résumé

Whether you send a résumé to get an interview or leave it behind after one, it is a vital part of the employment process. Write it before drafting a letter of application.

Although a résumé should give a lot of information about you, you need to determine your main selling points and then select and order facts in a way that will impress your reader. Here are some guidelines:

1. **Match your skills and experience to the needs of the organization.**   There's no point emphasizing talents that have no bearing on the job you want. This is where your earlier research helps; you have to determine what kinds of skills and experience are best suited to the job. On the other hand, many of your past accomplishments, which may on the surface seem irrelevant, can add to your qualifications if presented properly.

2. **Stress what sets you apart from the crowd.**   If an employer has a choice of applicants, all with much the same background — perhaps a teaching certificate, engineering degree, or experience in computer programming — personal attributes will make the difference. These attributes could be a high energy level, curiosity, leadership, and entrepreneurial spirit, or any quality that helps you to stand out.

3. **Remember that the primary aim is to rouse the employer's interest**, not provide a biography.

Format

The various categories of a résumé are not carved in stone. Some information is essential — namely an account of experience and qualifications — but the way the information is arranged and categorized is up to you.

Standard Format

Standard or traditional format emphasizes the record of employment, usually by making it the initial and largest category, followed by smaller categories covering education and other activities. This format gives the reader an easy grasp of your employment history; however, it also makes gaps in your employment record more obvious. If you have not had much work experience, or have had a variety of work experience that does not on the surface relate to the position you want, you are probably better to choose another format or to put another category, such as education, first (as in Figure 11-1).

An effective variation of this traditional format is to highlight only significant achievements under each category of work experience. This approach works well when past work involved many little assignments that aren't relevant to your present objectives. For each job, a subheading labelled "Achievements" will indicate that you are giving only a partial list of all you did.

Functional Format

This format emphasizes the type of functions you have performed or your relevant skills. You can organize information according to type of work experience, such as "Marketing Experience," "Accounting Experience." It's often more effective, however, to stress your skill or accomplishments, through headings such as "Initiative," "Creativity," or "Research Skill." This approach is especially useful for people whose experience primarily comes from activities other than paid jobs. (See Figure 11-3.)

Employers are sometimes wary of functional résumés, if they sense they are being used to distort an employment record. A way to avoid this problem if you do have a substantial employment history is to include at the bottom of the résumé a brief record of the jobs you have held. Under the heading, "Employment Record, simply state the name of the organizations you have worked for and dates you were employed. If you have not held many jobs, try to include dates when describing your skills and achievement.

Unconventional Formats

An unconventional format can be effective but it is risky. You must be cautious in assessing the reader. If the job is for an accountancy firm, bank, or a conservative organization where dependability, order, and systematic thought are more important than imagination, you are best to stick with a more conventional format. By contrast, if the employer is in advertising, promotion, or another occupation where imagination or innovation is a primary qualification, you might try to vary the format to

FIG. 11-1   Standard Format Résumé

BARRY LISTER

Address Before May 7, 1992	Address After May 7, 1992
Erindale Campus	24 Kilbarry Crescent
University of Toronto	Ottawa, Ontario
Mississauga, Ontario	K0B 1K0
L5C 1C6	(613) 632-2150
(416) 826-3000	

JOB OBJECTIVE: Junior member of a survey crew, with the ultimate goal of becoming an Ontario Land Surveyor.

EDUCATION

1992
— Will complete second year of a Bachelor of Science Degree at the University of Toronto. Specialist: Survey Science
Grade Average: B
Major courses — Introduction to Surveying
— Introduction to Survey Analysis
— Land Planning
— Survey Law

1990
— Completed one year of Architectural Science at Ryerson Polytechnical Institute.
Grade Average: B

WORK EXPERIENCE

Summer, 1991
— Tree planter for Roots Ltd. in British Columbia. Earned enough to pay for my year at university.

Summers, 1989-1990
— Hillsview Golf & Curling Club Ltd. Groundsworker. Maintained golf course, cutting grass, clearing brush, maintaining equipment.

— Previously earned spending money by taking care of neighbours' lawns and having a paper route for four years.

OTHER ACTIVITIES
— Captain, Erindale hockey team
— Treasurer, Survey Science Club

PERSONAL INFORMATION
Birth Date: September 30, 1971
Marital Status: Single
Height: 175 cm
Weight: 77 kg
Physical Condition: Good

FIG. 11-2   Standard Résumé Modified

JANE McGREGOR	914-55 Banrigh Road Scarborough, Ontario M1W 3V4 (416) 491-7124

Profile

Training and development specialist, with excellent communication skills and the ability to analyze needs and implement solutions for all levels of an organization.

Education

Bachelor of Arts: McMaster University
Les Cours spéciaux de la Faculté des Lettres: Université de Dijon, France
Data Processing Fundamentals: Seneca College

Experience

Infomarket   1990-92

Manager, Education Services

Established and managed the company's first education department.
Responsible for company-wide professional development in management and sales.
Reported to the Vice President, Corporate Development

Achievements:

- Directed a series of seminars for senior executives at the request of the President.
- Designed a sales program which benefitted the sales teams of six U.S. clients and the Infomarket sales force.
- Developed a basic computer course for all non-technical employees to increase staff morale and improve productivity.
- Created and managed a seminar to enhance product knowledge.

2

Datacrown   **1988-90**

Senior Education Analyst, Education Services

Responsible for the development, maintenance, and delivery of technical courses to Datacrown clients.
Reported to the General Manager, Plans and Controls

Achievements:

- Managed the activities of the Education Coordinator, the Technical Educator and the technical analysts who delivered the programs.
- Oversaw the design and implementation of new classroom facilities and a new calendar, two significant changes that enhanced the marketing of the product/services.

Edufax Learning Systems   **1987-88**

Training Consultant

Conducted skill development seminars for Edufax's clients including:

- Interpersonal Managing Skills
- Professional Selling Skills II & III
- Strategies for Effective Listening
- Account Development Strategies
- Focused Selection Interviewing

Interests

Watercolour painting, weaving, cross-country skiing, aerobics

FIG. 11-3   Functional Format Résumé

SUSAN HERTZ

16 Osler Street
Vancouver, British Columbia V6R 2T1
Tel: (614) 741-0329

Job Objective: Public relations trainee in a public relations firm.

Profile: An energetic and skilled communicator, with a
record of leadership and initiative.

Communication Skills

— B.A., Honours, in English, Queen's University, July,
1989; B+ average.
— Entertainment editor for Queen's *Journal*, 1991-92.
— debated regularly as a member of Queen's
Debating Society.
— gave oral presentations to public as guide at
Huronia Village in Summer, 1991. Described
background of historic site to groups of visitors and
demonstrated old equipment.

Leadership   — elected to Student Council in my last year at
Richmond High School.
— served as a Gael leader at Queen's, introducing
new students to university life.
— elected vice-president of English Club at Queen's,
1988. Planned and chaired monthly seminars.

Initiative   — founded my own home-baked cookie business,
Susan's Cookies, when still in school. Baked, sold,
and kept accounts, earning enough to pay for my
first year at Queen's.
— organized a bike-a-thon at university; proceeds of
$2500 went to the Cancer Society.

References

1. Professor Michael Hughs, Queen's University, Department of
English, Kingston, Ontario, K7L 3N6.
2. Mrs. Mable Williams, Administrator, Huronia Village,
Penetanguishene, Ontario, L0K 1P6.

suggest your creativity. In any case, your primary question to yourself should be, "How can I best reveal those qualities the employer is looking for?"

Whatever format you use, design the résumé so that it is easy to read:

1. **Create wide margins** and leave space between sections, so that the text stands out boldly — the black is set off by the white surrounding it;

2. **Underline** the section headings or use boldface;

3. **Be consistent** in placing and setting off the details for each section;

4. **Feel free to use boldface or italics** to set off an important point. If you choose to use different typescripts, take care that the overall impression is not one of clutter.

5. **Never put all the résumé in capitals or italics.** Both are more difficult than a standard typescript to read in large doses.

Desktop-publishing packages for word processors make it easier to create an effective design. Even without such a package, try to set up the résumé so that readers can glance down the page and spot the points you want them to notice.

Information

Your résumé should include enough information about you for the employer to feel that you are worth interviewing. Here is a list of the most common kinds of résumé information. Be prepared to omit, add, or alter according to the job and how you choose to present yourself.

Name and Address

Usually this information is placed at the top of the résumé, but the address can also be positioned at the end. Be sure to include the full mailing address, including postal code. You may also want to add your telephone number, if you don't mind being contacted by phone. If you are a student with a different mailing address for winter and summer months, give both addresses and the dates when you will be at each location.

Present Employment

This information helps the reader to grasp quickly the basis of your experience and the level of your responsibility. It is useful towards the beginning of the résumé, especially if you are not providing a sequenced record of employment, or if your format is unconventional.

Job Objective

This category is helpful if you are a student trying to suggest that you have definite career goals. It may also be useful if you want a specific job in a large organization with a number of different job openings. On the other hand, if you are willing to try a variety of jobs, you may omit this category from your résumé, as long as your accompanying letter gives a more specific focus to your search.

In any case, for an unsolicited application, it's usually better to give not the position you would like (for example, sales manager), but the area and general level of responsibility (for example, "a management position in marketing" or "management trainee"). Students who are willing to take a junior or entry-level position but expect opportunity for advancement can show this expectation. An application to a bank might say "management training position with the goal of future employment in the international banking department"; a student applying to an accountancy firm might say, "student-in-accounts with the goal of becoming a practising chartered accountant."

Summary of Qualifications

Some well-known job-placement consultants recommend that, instead of a statement of objectives, a capsule "Profile" of one or two sentences precede the more detailed listing of your experience or qualifications. This summary is your chance to hit the reader directly with your most important attributes for the job, an advantage if your application is one of a stack to be sifted. The résumés in Figures 11-2 and 11-3 provide examples. While it is perfectly proper to keep this kind of statement for your letter of application, if your résumé is separated from the letter when it is filed or passed on to others, it will benefit from having a compact summary of your "selling points" close to the top.

Education

For students whose job experience is scanty or nonexistent, this section usually comes first. Educational qualifications are most often the primary selling point. Begin with your most recent educational attainment or your most advanced or relevant degree or diploma. If you have post-secondary education, it's not necessary to include your high school, unless you have some particular reason for doing so. Be sure to give the date you obtained any degree or diploma, along with the name of the institution that granted it. If courses you have taken are a selling point, list those relevant to the job you are applying for. (This advice pertains especially to students seeking their first permanent job.)

Work Experience

In most résumés, this information is the major focus. In a standard résumé, the record of jobs held is given in reverse chronological sequence, starting with the most recent. In a functional résumé, experience may be arranged according to type of work; for example, sales, marketing, administration. Students should include all volunteer and part-time jobs.

However you arrange the section, follow this guide:

1. **Make the information action-oriented.** Use verbs as lead-ins to the facts. For example, say

   — *reviewed* customer service procedures and *recommended* changes;

   — *organized* employee training seminars;

— *prepared* budgets for the promotion department;

— *trained* new employees in the delivery department.

2. **Stress accomplishment.**   A job description hasn't much impact. Instead of listing your duties for each job, tell what you have achieved. After all, duties represent an employer's expectation; listing them doesn't necessarily signify that you have fulfilled them. Rather than say that your "*duties were* to supervise customer accounts and keep the books," say that you "*supervised* the customer accounts department and *kept* the books."

3. **Be honest.**   A small lie in your résumé is enough to wipe out the employer's trust in you, even if it is discovered well after you have the job. Integrity is an attribute never worth sacrificing. This advice does not mean that you should lay out your faults or draw attention to errors. It does mean that you should not misinform the reader.

Other Interests or Accomplishments

In outlining outside activities, you will have to use your judgment on what to include. Some employment counsellors say that a list of hobbies or activities simply clutters up a résumé, making it longer and therefore less inviting to read. Others maintain that a person with varied interests makes the best employee in the long run.

Clearly, you don't want outside interests to dominate your résumé. If you have a long list of possible items, concentrate on those which reveal unusual talents or personal qualities relevant to the work you want, such as leadership, imagination, or perseverance.

Personal Information

Most personal information, other than your address and telephone number, is unnecessary and should be left out. Employers are now forbidden by law to ask about religion or country of origin, and you have no need to provide the information. Neither do you need to give details about your health, marital status, or age for most jobs. However, if you think that listing some personal details will give you an advantage, by all means do so. For example, size might be an advantage in some kinds of heavy labour; being single might be an advantage for a job requiring a lot of travelling; citizenship might be an advantage for certain academic jobs.

References

You don't need to give the names of people who can supply references. Some applicants prefer to wait until the employer is seriously interested, especially if they are currently employed and don't want others to know they are looking around. If you don't want to provide names on the résumé, you can omit the category altogether or simply say that references will be supplied on request. If you do include references, give full name, title, company, and address. Telephone numbers may also be helpful if the people are easy to reach that way.

The Covering Letter

A covering letter should do more than state "Here's my application and résumé." It should be the primary attention-getter, making the reader want to examine the résumé and to give you an interview. Can you imagine a prospective employer, with a stack of applications on the desk, wanting to read the following applicant's résumé?

> Dear Sir:
>
> I am applying for the job in your sales department, which you advertised. I am graduating from college this year and would like a job in sales. The enclosed résumé gives my qualifications for that kind of work. I hope you will think I am suitable and that I will hear from you soon.
>
> Yours truly,
> Joe Sinclair

Not only is this an I-centred letter but it provides no particular reason for the employer to hire the applicant. Your covering letter must do a better job. Aside from what you say, the *way* you say it matters: a well-written letter reveals important communications skills.

The following guidelines for a covering letter, like the AIDA guidelines for other kinds of sales letters, are not hard-and-fast rules. Applicants should not be like cookie-cutters, producing identical products. Feel free to express your own personality, as long as you remember the reason for writing and the reader you hope to influence.

Get the Reader's Attention

Try to say something that will make the reader want to read on. This could be an outstanding qualification or a reason for your interest in the firm. Here are some examples:

> The article on your firm in *Canadian Business* suggested that you may be expanding. Are you looking for a dynamic sales person?

> As a prize-winning English student, I believe my skill as a writer would be a useful attribute in your public affairs department.

Name-dropping is another attention getter: if someone respected by the employer has suggested you make the application or is willing to vouch for you, mention the person right at the beginning; for example, "Arthur Stone suggested that I get in touch with you," or "Arthur Stone has told me that your company regularly hires students as summer office help."

State Your Purpose

You want the reader to know early in the letter that you are applying for a job. Don't beat around the bush and merely imply that you want employment — be specific. If you are responding to an advertised opening, say so. If your application is unsolicited, indicate the type of work you are applying for. Remember that a reader who is uncertain about your purposes is unlikely to act.

Give a Brief Summation of Your Selling Points

You may create a second paragraph for this part, but keep it as short as possible. A covering letter should not exceed a page. The shorter the better — as long as it creates interest in you. Here are some tips:

1. **Link your skills to the employer's needs.**   Don't just restate part of your résumé, but adapt it to the company or organization. Focus not on how the job would help you but on how you can help the employer. If you were a surveyor looking for summer help, which sentence from a surveying student would appeal to you most?

   > I would like to work for a surveyor this summer to up-grade my qualifications and gain some practical experience.

   > I believe the courses in surveying I have taken will help me to make a useful contribution to your summer surveying work.

2. **Sell yourself without seeming egotistical.**   This may seem a tall order, but you can emphasize strengths in a sincere way. First of all, don't boast. State your attributes simply, without exaggertion or a lot of intensifying adjectives. For example, instead of saying "I am extremely responsible," or "I can fill completely all your expectations" (a statement which presumes you can read the employer's mind), reveal why you can do the job well. In other words, try to use facts that speak for themselves rather than make claims:

   > x   I have extraordinary talent in mathematics.
   > ✓   I have consistently achieved high marks in mathematics.

   > x   I am a very good salesperson.
   > ✓   Last summer, although one of the youngest salespeople in the store, I had the second highest sales total.

3. **Try to bury the *I*'s.**   When writing an application letter, it's impossible to avoid using *I* repeatedly. After all, the letter is about you. You can make the first-person pronoun less prominent, however, by placing something in front of it. Rather than putting it in a position of emphasis at the beginning of the sentence, bury it in the middle.

   > x   I worked for an accountancy firm last summer.
   > ✓   Last summer I worked for an accountancy firm.

   You needn't switch the order in all instances, but you can easily prevent a string of *I* beginnings.

4. **Place any weaknesses in a subordinate position.**   Most of the time your covering letter or résumé will not mention the weak area of your background. In an advertised job opening, however, you may be asked to provide specific information that is not a selling point for you — information such as present employment or work experience in a specific field. If you must include something you don't want

to emphasize, try putting it in a subordinate clause, with a main clause emphasizing a more positive point.

> x Unfortunately I have never worked in a job requiring accounting.

> ✔ Although I have not had an accounting job, I have taken four accounting courses.

5. **Don't apologize.** If you don't think you can do a specific job, don't apply for it. If you think you can, be confident in outlining your qualifications. Avoid apologetic phrases, such as "I'm sorry", "I regret" or "unfortunately" when referring to your background or skills.

Ask for an Interview

Applicants often forget to do this directly. You need to press for one politely. You can indicate specific days or times when you will be available.

If practical, mention that you will telephone the employer rather than ask the employer to get in touch with you. Exceptions to this practice are the times when your application will be one of hundreds routinely received (for example, an application for a summer job with a government department or with a large manufacturing plant). If the hiring company is going through specific channels, such as a student placement service, you are also best to abide by their terms and not try to do an end run around the designated route. For the most part, however, a telephone call will not be considered a nuisance. As long as you are courteous, you will appear eager rather than pushy. In case you can't reach the person you want by phone, include in your letter some way to reach you.

Two final tips:

* **Don't** mention salary expectations unless asked to. The interview is a more appropriate time to discuss money, after you have had a chance to assess job opportunities; moreover, you will be better able then to gauge the employer's reactions.

* **Don't** thank in advance. Although intending to be polite, you may seem presumptuous.

Application Letters for Unusual Cases

In rare instances, a résumé may not be a benefit. If someone has been out of the work force for many years and has done little in the community, a résumé might be embarrassingly bare. Similarly, if a person wants to move to a completely different line of work from any past jobs — say, a sales person wants to work as a chef in a summer resort, or a stock broker wants to learn the theatre business — then a résumé may be unsuitable. In both cases, an extended application letter with explanatory comment may be a sensible substitute for a résumé and covering letter.

Follow this approach only as a last resort, if a résumé is truly unsuitable. If you are a student without much of a job record, or a homemaker who has not had paid

FIG. 11-4   Example of a Letter to be Sent with a Résumé

31 Lombard Drive
Edmonton, Alberta
T6H 1C3

April 1, 1993

Mr. R. Jones
Personnel Director
Computer Systems Inc.
125 Microchip Road
Calgary, Alberta
T2M 4H1

Dear Mr. Jones:

Since Computer Systems is a fast-growing company, you are likely in need of young and energetic people with a good knowledge of computers. In one month I will be graduating from University of Alberta with a Computer Science degree and would like to join your company as a programmer.

In addition to my university courses, I have had work experience in programming and operating computers. Last summer I implemented programs for the design of loudspeakers at Nortec Industries. In November I demonstrated Morris computers at the Alberta Computer Show. Throughout the school year I have worked part-time at the University Computing Center as an equipment operator.

At your convenience, I would like to meet you to discuss how my qualifications could benefit Computer Systems. Next week I will be in Calgary and will call you to try to arrange an interview.

Yours sincerely,

Helen Graham

Helen Graham

employment for many years, you do not necessarily fall into this category. Take some time to think about yourself and your experiences. In most instances you can create a good résumé by drawing attention to the skills and knowledge you have gained in other endeavours.

Handling a Job Interview

If you have been asked for an interview, you can usually assume that you are being considered seriously for the job; businesses don't want to waste time — and money — on people they have no wish to employ. In a buyer's market, you can also assume that you will be competing with others for the available opening. Preparing for the interview will help you to put your best foot forward.

Find Out About the Company

If you are going to an interview with a manufacturing company, learn all you can about its products and customers; if going to an advertising agency, know something about the advertisements for its main accounts; and so on. Annual company reports are a useful source of information for large companies. For large and small ones, you may find a receptionist who will help you, if you are polite rather than demanding. The local library, your college's library or career counselling service, or even a customer or supplier, are other useful places for research.

Consider Answers to Likely Questions

The University and College Placement Association recently conducted a survey of public and private employers across Canada to find out what they valued in prospective employees, aside from the technical ability to do the job. According to the 108 employers who responded, here are the five most important attributes and the questions often used to uncover them:[2]

1. **Ability to Communicate**   Almost any open-ended question will test this ability, but recruiters may deliberately ask some difficult ones just to see how well you can respond. Here are some common questions:

   - Tell me about yourself and why you think you can do this job.
   - Why are you applying to this company?
   - Why did you take your particular program of studies and what courses did you enjoy the most? The least?
   - What are your strengths and weaknesses? (Tread warily in revealing weaknesses; don't mistake the recruiter for a confessor.)
   - Tell me about your last job; what did you accomplish or learn in it?
   - Why did you leave it?

---

[2] This list of questions is based on a pamphlet distributed by the Career Centre, University of Toronto.

2. Willingness to Take Initiative

- What have you done that shows initiative?
- What do you do in your spare time?
- What accomplishments have given you most satisfaction?

3. Willingness to Accept Responsibility

- Are you self-supporting?
- When did you first start working?
- How did you obtain your jobs?

4. Leadership Potential

- What offices have you held at school or elsewhere?
- What has been your most difficult assignment in dealing with people?
- What has been the most satisfying?
- Describe a situation where you had to show leadership.
- What kind of people do you like to work with most? Least?
- How many people have you ever had to manage?

5. Ambition and Motivation

Recruiters like people who have a sense of purpose and have thought about their careers. They look for motivated employees. On the other hand, they are wary of a young employee who is an arrogant know-it-all and unwilling to learn. These questions are common:

- What would you like to be doing in five years? Ten years?
- How hard-working are you?
- How would you describe your energy level?
- What would you hope to accomplish in this job?
- What are your salary expectations?

Prepare a Few Questions

Be ready to ask the interviewer questions of your own about the organization you are applying to. The thoroughness of your research can be impressive.

Strive for a Poised Manner in the Interview

Even if your stomach is churning when you go for an interview, try to look calm and relaxed. Remember to smile, especially when you greet the interviewer and when you leave. If you seem pleasant rather than grim, the recruiter will naturally respond more favourably.

Here are a few more tips to impress recruiters:

- Dress neatly in a manner appropriate for the job.
- Shake hands firmly — no wet-fish handshakes.

- Look the interviewer in the eye, especially when greeting and thanking, and when listening to the interviewer's comments and questions.
- Speak clearly and correctly. Poor diction or grammar will be a strike against you in many managerial jobs.
- Project a sense of vitality in your voice and manner. A flat voice and lifeless manner are not impressive.
- Avoid simple "Yes" or "No" answers: your job is to communicate.
- Don't condemn others, such as former bosses or co-workers.

Final Task

When you have completed an interview, remember to send a brief thank-you letter to the interviewer. You can use this opportunity to stress a point you forgot to mention in the interview, or to emphasize a qualification the interviewer considered important. Even if you don't get the job this time, you will help create a positive climate for any future dealings.

EXERCISES

● Section A

1. Investigate the job market in an area where you are interested in getting employment. Compile a list of ten companies that would be good prospects for employment. Include the addresses and telephone numbers of the companies, and the names and titles of the appropriate people to apply to (for example, the personnel director). You may substitute the names of people with whom you would like to have an information interview. In compiling this information, you will find it helpful to use your college's career service, the library, and the telephone.

2. Draw up a list of questions that you would like to have answered during an information interview with a company on the list you have compiled for the previous question.

3. Using a standard format, create a résumé and accompanying letter of application for a summer job or permanent job in a field you are interested in. Be sure to include any volunteer work, part-time jobs, and positions of responsibility you have held at school or elsewhere. Remember: any work that shows you are reliable is useful information for an employer, and any accomplishment that shows initiative or leadership will help set you apart from the crowd.

4. With your résumé as a backup, write two separate application letters for two different employers or jobs. Change the emphasis or approach according to the differing needs of each.

    Remember that the letters must reflect the facts of the résumé. The point of this exercise is to show how your record can be adapted while sticking to the truth.

5. Using a word-processor, experiment with layout and typeface on the résumé you created for question 3. Select two variations. In small groups, compare résumés with those of other students, and discuss why some designs work better than others.

● Section B

1. In groups of three or four, take turns practising the interviewing process. Try forming a group with others who are interested in the same field of employment. One person should play the applicant and another the interviewer; the third (and fourth) should assess the positive and negative aspects of the applicant's performance. If possible, video-tape the role-playing so that everyone can view and discuss it.

2. Using a functional format, write a résumé and accompanying letter of application for a permanent job in a field you are interested in. In groups of three evaluate the application packages, pointing out possible improvements in the information provided, the order of information, the wording, and the layout. Make the needed revisions.

A Practical Grammar

You may sometimes say to yourself, "If only I'd learned more grammar when I was young, my writing would be fine!" Or, "If only I could remember the grammar rule!" Knowing the grammar of a language is certainly a help in writing, especially when you are checking your work, but it is less important to know the terminology — the parts of speech and their functions — than to appreciate that the essence of good grammar is clarity. The rules of grammar are really a description of how clear sentences work. If you don't know what your errors are, review the next section, which discusses the most common grammatical errors in business writing. Figure out which weaknesses apply to you. You can then check on your work with an eye to spotting and correcting them.

Lack of Sentence Unity

Rule 1   Sentences Must be Complete.

A complete sentence is an independent clause (able to stand by itself) containing both a subject and a verb:

> *I solved* the problem.
> The *report will be printed* tomorrow.

Sentence Fragments

A sentence fragment lacks a subject or a verb, or it contains a subordinating word making the clause dependent rather than independent. Remember this tip: an *ing* word, such as *being*, *by itself*, is not a verb.

> x   London *being* a good city to test-market a new product.

The verb is lacking, but *being* can easily become the verb *is*.

> ✔ London *is* a good city to test-market a product.

Words such as *although*, *while* and *whether* at the beginning of a clause make it dependent, unable to stand by itself.

> x   I was late. Although I solved the problem.
> ✔ I was late, although I solved the problem.

An occasional sentence fragment is acceptable, if it is used for emphasis and the rest of the sentence is easily inferred:

> ✔ How long can we continue with these losses? No more than six months.

Run-on Sentences

Sometimes called a fused sentence, a run-on sentence is the opposite of a sentence fragment; two sentences are improperly joined as one, sometimes without any punctuation.

> x   I like business this is why I enrolled at Western.

When the two sentences are joined by a comma, the mistake is called a comma splice:

> x   The sales figures are higher than last year's, they increased by ten percent.

Remember: Two independent clauses (clauses which can stand by themselves as sentences) must be separated by one of the following:

– a period;
– a coordinating conjunction (*and, or, nor, but, yet, for,* and sometimes *so*);
– a subordinating conjunction (*because, since, although*);
– a semi-colon.

Faulty Predication

Rule 2   The Subject of a Sentence Must Fit the Predicate.

Faulty predication occurs when the subject does not mesh with the predicate, which includes the verb and any direct object or complement.

x   The main point of the report examines the lack of adequate day-care as a cause of absenteeism.

✔ The report examines the lack of adequate day-care as a cause of absenteeism.

✔ The main point of the report is that a lack of adequate day-care causes absenteeism.

The first sentence is faulty because a *point* cannot *examine*. The first revision changes the subject to fit the predicate and the second changes the predicate to fit the subject.

Remember: If you use the verb *to be* by itself, follow with a noun phrase that completes the subject; otherwise change the verb.

x   The explosion was when the pipeline sprang a leak.

✔ The explosion occurred when the pipeline sprang a leak.

✔ The leaking pipeline caused the explosion.

Lack of Subject-Verb Agreement

Rule 3   The Subject Must Agree in Number and Person With the Verb.

This simple rule is most often broken when the grammatical subject has a modifier and the verb wrongly agrees with the modifier rather than the bare subject:

x   The *settlement* of Indian and Inuit land claims *are* likely to take several years.

Since the bare subject is the singular noun *settlement*, the verb should be *is*.

✔ The *settlement* of Indian and Inuit land claims *is* likely to take several years.

Compound Subjects

Two nouns joined by *and* take a plural verb:

The *carpenter and the bricklayer are* coming tomorrow.

When two nouns are joined by *or, either/or,* or *neither/nor*, the verb agrees with the last noun.

Neither my boss nor my subordinates *regret* the change.

If a plural noun precedes a singular one, however, a singular verb may sound awkward. If so, recast the sentence:

✔ Either the creditors or the bank *is* likely to act.

✔ Action will come from either the bank or the creditors.

Note: The phrases *as well as*, *in addition to* and *together with* do not make a compound subject.

✓ Jack and Jill *are* attending the meeting.

✓ Jack as well as Jill *is* attending the meeting.

Each, Either, Neither, Anyone, Everyone

These indefinite pronouns take a singular verb, not a plural one:

Each of the employees *is* contributing to the fund.

Neither of my colleagues *wants* the job.

In American convention, the indefinite pronoun *none* takes a singular verb, whereas in British uses, *none* can take either a singular or a plural verb depending on the context.

Names and Titles

Even if the name of an organization or the title of a book includes a plural or compound noun, it is considered singular and takes a singular verb:

Dominion Castings *has* a good pension plan.

Deloitte & Touche *is* the accounting firm we use.

Pronoun Problems

Rule 4   A Pronoun Must Refer to a Specific Noun, and Must Agree With It in Number and Person.

---

x When *office machinery* becomes costly to fix, *they* should be replaced.

✓ When *office machinery* becomes costly to fix, *it* should be replaced.

x When an *employee* has worked here for twenty-five years, *they* get a gold watch.

✓ When *employees* have worked here for twenty-five years, *they* get a gold watch.

The Person Dilemma

Our lack of a neutral personal pronoun causes problems in the singular: should a person be referred to as *he*, or *he or she*? Convention decrees that you still cannot mix singular and plural:

x When a *person* applies for a job, *they* should look their best.

The English rely on *one* and *one's* to get around the difficulty:

✓ When *one* applies for a job, *one* should look *one's* best.

Unfortunately, to a North American ear, a lot of *one's* in a sentence can sound pompous. Although many people now consider it sexist to refer to an unspecified person as *he*, good writers often point out that a repetition of *he or she* or *his/her* makes a passage stylistically awkward and therefore harder to read:

> When a *person* applies for a job, *he or she* should look *his or her* best.

What to do? A practical solution is to use the plural wherever possible for both subject and pronouns:

> When *people* apply for jobs, *they* should look *their* best.

Where the plural is not possible, you can occasionally use *he or she*, as this book does, but try to avoid a constant repetition of double pronouns. You should also make clear in your discussions or examples that you are referring to both sexes and, if possible, use neutral terms like *carrier* rather than *newspaper boy* or *supervisor* rather than *foreman*.

As in other areas of communication, be aware of cultural context. Although your writing and speaking should reflect the sensititivities of your community, these sensitivities are not always shared by others. Be careful, therefore, of attributing sexist attitudes to those from English-speaking cultures outside North America who may use "masculine" forms. Many other women and men still accept that these forms have double meaning (one specifically male and one general), as North Americans did in earlier years.

Vague *This* or *It*

The indefinite pronouns *this* and *it* must refer to a noun. When they don't have a specific reference, they can cause confusion:

> The supervisor decided to reprimand the workers, but *this* was not acted on.

What specific noun does *this* refer to?

> ✔ The manager decided to reprimand the workers but *this decision* was not acted on.

> ✗ Our plan was to conduct a seminar in the boardroom, but the advisory group considered *it* unsuitable.

Does *it* refer to the plan, the seminar or the boardroom? When a pronoun leaves any doubt about its reference, repeat the noun:

> ✔ Our plan was to conduct a seminar in the boardroom, but the advisory group considered *the room* unsuitable.

Woe with *Me*

Having been trained as a child not to say "Me and Sheila want to play outside," many adults wrongly use the subjective pronoun *I* when the objective pronoun *me* is correct. This mistake usually happens when two people are being referred to.

   x The congratulatory letter mentioned Helen and *I*.

A simple guide if you are not sure about what case to use is to try the sentence without the first name (Helen) and then use the pronoun that comes naturally:

   ✔ The congratulatory letter mentioned *me*.

   ✔ The congratulatory letter mentioned Helen and *me*.

Remember that the objective case follows a preposition:

   ✔ *Between* you and *me*, Bernhard is a blow-hard.

   ✔ She spoke *after* John and *me*.

One exception: When a pronoun following a preposition also modifies a noun or noun phrase, use the possessive form:

   x I worried about *him* losing the job.

   ✔ I worried about *his* losing the job.

Tense Troubles

Rule 5   Verb Tenses Must be Consistent With the Timeframe.

Tense Shift

A common error in business proposals is to switch constantly from the conditional *would* to the future *will*:

   x Implementing this idea *would* improve employee morale and in turn it *will* likely increase profits.

Either case will do, but be consistent.

Hypothetical Actions

The conditional verb (*would* or *could*) is often improperly used to describe a hypothetical action in the past. Use a conditional verb only in the consequence clause, not in the "if" clause:

   x If he *would have* smiled, I *would have* invited him.

   ✔ If he *had* smiled, I *would have* invited him.

When writing about a hypothetical action in the future — one that is unlikely to happen — use the subjunctive in the *if* clause and the conditional in the consequence clause:

   If meals *were* free, I *would be* fat in two months.

Writing About the Past

Actions that precede other past actions should have the past perfect tense — indicated by *had* and the past participle. Notice the ambiguity in the following sentence:

   x When the owners *toured* the plant, the manager *went* back to his office.

Did the manager avoid the owners? Or did he go back to his office afterwards?

   ✔ When the owners *had toured* the plant, the manager *went* back to his office.

Muddled Modifying

Rule 6   Modifiers Must Show Clearly What They Modify.

To modify a noun, use an adjective; to modify a verb, adverb, or adjective, use an adverb. (Adverbs are often formed by adding *ly* to an adjective.) Sportscasters seem to have forgotten this rule.

   x He played *good* today.
   x He threw the ball *real well*.
   ✔ He played *well* today.
   ✔ He threw the ball *well* (or *really well*).
   ✔ She threw the ball *accurately*.

Remember, however, to use an adjective after the verb *to be* (and its variations) as well as after some sense-related verbs — *taste, smell, feel, look, appear, seem, become*.

   The pie was *good*, even though it looked *burnt*.
   The material feels *soft*.
   I may seem *cranky* when I become *tired*.

Misplaced and Squinting Modifiers

Meaning in an English sentence is partly conveyed by word order. A misplaced modifier can cause confusion:

   x He made his brief to the commission, which was disorganized and long-winded.
   ✔ He made his confused and long-winded brief to the commission.

A squinting modifier seems to look two ways, creating doubt about whether it belongs to the phrase before it or after it:

   x She decided *after her vacation* to look for another job.

To avoid confusion, relocate the modifier:

✔ *After her vacation* she decided to look for another job.

✔ She decided to look *after her vacation* for another job.

A dangling modifier is not connected to anything:

✗   *Walking into the lobby*, the office was intimidating.

Who is doing the walking? Surely not the office.

✔ Walking into the lobby, *he* thought the office was intimidating.

Problems with Pairs (and More)

Rule 7   Comparisons Must be Equivalent.

The two parts of a comparison should match grammatically, whether the second part is stated or implied.

✗   Young employees often understand more about computers than their bosses.

This sentence unintentionally compares computers and bosses; it should compare employees' understanding with the bosses' understanding.

✔ Young employees often understand more about computers than their bosses do.

✔ Young employees often understand more than their bosses about computers.

✗   Baggs was a tedious man and so were his speeches.

✔ Baggs was tedious and so were his speeches.

Correlatives

The two parts of correlative constructions, *not only ... but also* or *both ... and*, should be equivalent. The coordinating term must not come too early: make sure both the parts following are grammatically the same.

✗   Margaret is *not only* good with figures *but also* with people.

✔ Margaret is good *not only* with figures *but also* with people.

✗   The manager *both* hired Heather for the marketing and for the sales jobs.

✔ The manager hired Heather for *both* the marketing and sales jobs.

Parallel Phrasing

Rule 8   Similar Ideas Should Have Similar Wording.

For clarity, items in a series need to be phrased in the same way.

   x We had increased sales, better productivity, and profits were higher.

   ↙ We had increased sales, better productivity, and higher profits.

Even when similar ideas take more than one sentence to express, your message will be more easily understood if you use similar wording:

   x Carolyn Fisher is a good manager. She is energetic and well-organized. The ability to motivate people is another of her attributes.

   ↙ Carolyn Fisher is a good manager. She is energetic and well organized. She also knows how to motivate people.

EXERCISES

● Section A

1. Correct faulty predication, sentence fragments, and comma splices in the following sentences:

   a) Since the train was late, we took the bus, however we arrived on time.

   b) The reason the report lacks information on the research is because of the secrecy surrounding so much of the activity.

   c) One example of faulty sampling is when the group sampled is not representative.

   d) Having little chance to upgrade her skills, on account of heavy family responsibilities.

   e) We were late for the meeting, we didn't miss much.

   f) Communications bypassing is when a word has a different meaning for the speaker than for the listener.

   g) I got the information I needed, you don't need to search for it.

   h) The campaign is important, therefore we should plan carefully.

   i) Although the meeting was adjourned early, since she felt ill and the important matters were covered.

   j) Please reread this file, it contains some mathematical errors.

2. Correct any problems with pronouns and pronoun-verb agreement in the following sentences:
   a) He explained the procedure again, for the benefit of Jean and I.
   b) The problem with him being ill is that we can't finish the report.
   c) Each of us have a different aspect of the case to research.
   d) The photocopier has broken down and this will cause a three-hour delay.
   e) Both of us have difficulty making early morning meetings, but neither of us have a problem with lunch meetings.
   f) Between you and I, the advertisement is a bad one.
   g) When one travels through the north in summer months, you need protection from black flies.
   h) I wonder if each of the partners are planning to attend the conference.
   i) When the invitation came to Pierre and I, I sent the reply on behalf of us both.
   j) The challenges are great, but it doesn't discourage us.

3. Correct any problems with verb tense and subject-verb agreement:
   a) When he ate the giant hot dog, he went back to playing baseball.
   b) Since the photocopier arrived, I no longer need carbon copies.
   c) If the manager would have talked to us earlier, the problem could have been solved.
   d) Either of the accountants are willing to check your books.
   e) Neither of the problems are too difficult; but either one or the other are likely to pose a challenge to students at your level.
   f) My supervisor, as well as the manager, are on holidays, but both are due back next Monday.
   g) We looked at several accounting firms, but Jones & Hume are best suited to our needs.
   h) Neither of the creditors have made an effort to pay us.
   i) Simplifying the process will create savings and would improve our balance sheet.
   j) If Canada was a part of Europe, we could increase our leather exports.
   k) We think that application of those new computer programs require a basic understanding of statistics.
   l) The latest version of the instructions haven't been translated yet.

4. Correct the faulty or confusing modifiers in these sentences:
   a) Although the interview was tough, fortunately I handled it good.
   b) In the consumer tests, the samplers said that the cake tasted well but the cookies were too salty.
   c) Talking to an angry customer, the experience was stressful and unpleasant.
   d) I want signs for the two entrances, which are inexpensive and easy to see.
   e) Thinking about the client's attitude, our proposal should be more detailed.
   f) Although she usually plays good tennis, yesterday the lighting was poorly and she couldn't hit good.
   g) The office in the west end of the city, which needs extensive repairs, is vacant.
   h) The Deputy Minister will talk about cleaning up the St. Lawrence River after lunch.

i) He almost ate the entire pie, but fortunately I arrived when one piece was still left.

j) She made arrangements at the morning break to have muffins with the coffee.

5. Correct the faulty comparisons and correlatives:

    a) She both handles promotion and advertising for our company.

    b) He not only designed the building but the landscaping as well.

    c) Fortunately, Bill's accounting problem is not as troublesome as my other clients.

    d) It's as important to keep the children's interest during the show as their parents.

    e) We hope that our sales for March will be as high as last year.

6. Use parallel phrasing in the following sentences:

    a) We want Mary to do the planning, Jerry to handle purchasing, and the books should be kept by Joan or Sam.

    b) Please make arrangements to paint the office this week, install the carpet next week, and by the end of the month see that you hang the new curtains.

    c) George and Peter are away at a conference, Jill is on holiday, and sickness accounts for the absence of five other employees.

    d) We have to develop a concept, devise a marketing strategy and create the advertising copy, but handling the client will not be our responsibility, fortunately.

    e) Writing the proposal will be fairly easy, but it will be more difficult to complete the job on time.

● Section B

1. Revise the following sentences, correcting the grammatical errors named.

    a) Sentence fragment: The new boss, having little time to spare for trivial matters, owing to a shortage of staff.

    b) Comma splice: We rushed to deliver the cheques, since it was Friday, unfortunately the bank was closed.

    c) Faulty predication: The subject of my report for Harry is about the advantages of microcomputers in a small office.

    d) Wrong verb tense: If the typist would have stayed longer and typed those three pages, I could have finished the project.

    e) Subject-verb disagreement: Our lawyer, together with his associates, have presented a formidable case for collecting damages.

    f) Pronoun disagreement: Despite a busy winter, neither of the partners are taking their holidays in the summer.

    g) No pronoun reference: Joan hasn't paid all her parking fines, and this will cause problems when she renews her licence next spring.

    h) Faulty pronoun case: After we had aired our grievances, our supervisor invited Ted and I to lunch at his club.

    i) Faulty modifying case: My old car ran as good as this one, but it didn't look as nice, even though it was painted fresh.

    j) Misplaced modifier: After weeks of partying and water-skiing, Mr. Smythe decided that his son should settle down to work.

    k) Dangling modifier: Walking along the dark street late at night, the tall buildings looked imposing and a little frightening.

l) Squinting modifier and faulty comparison: Although Jean is a better speaker as a result of training, I write better than her.

2. Although you don't need to name any grammatical errors, correct the following faulty or confusing sentences:

a) Since she finished the letter early, she went home.

b) You need more collateral, then we will be happy to increase the loan.

c) Neither of them remember, unfortunately, who was our third Prime Minister.

d) Squash as well as other racquet sports are good exercise and will keep a person fit.

e) Being good in mathematics, accounting was her best subject last year.

f) Payment of the expense claims for the last two months have been delayed, owing to a computer breakdown.

g) I wore my old Greb boots to the construction site, which kept my feet warm and dry.

h) Upward mobility, they say, is when you turn in jeans for a jogging suit.

i) When the office staff saw the auditors arriving, they knew they would take over their offices for the week.

j) Lawyers seem to have more financial problems than accountants.

k) We need to hire fewer people, encourage early retirement, and expenses should be reduced in office administration.

l) Jokingly, he said that the reason he needed glasses was not because his eyes were worse but because his arms were too short.

3. Correct the faulty grammar in the following memo:

Scott has decided not to hire more salespeople until spring at that time he will have a better idea of his sales picture. This fits in good with our overall budgeting plans, but I realize it may change if his departmental sales pick up much more. Scott reported last weekend he was understaffed.

Between you and I, I'm more optimistic than him about economic trends, however I appreciate him being cautious. If we would have hired more personnel last autumn we would have had a hard time keeping them through the slump. Moreover, comparing last year's forecasts with our actual sales, the experience is sobering.

This year, sales either will rebound over the Christmas season or we will be in the red again. We not only need to watch our internal costs but to keep a closer eye on cash flow. Like Scott, each manager will have to do their bit to avoid inessential hiring. I am confident, however, that with an improved economy, a lean staff, and by making a determined sales effort we will be profitable this year.

Guide to Punctuation

Punctuation marks are conventions — convenient, common symbols. Writers use them to give readers easy passage through a piece of writing. Long ago, when there weren't such conventions, it often took hours to decipher a page. Anyone who has read a piece of prose without punctuation will know the difficulty.

Punctuation gradually alters with the times, as does grammar. In some instances, it may also vary according to the writer's judgment of what is clearest. Yet the rules are still useful. Faulty punctuation can make a passage almost as hard to read as one with no punctuation, since it sends the reader the wrong signals. Ironically, although punctuation is probably the most frequent problem in writing, it is the easiest and most straightforward part of the writing process to learn. Most of the rules can be applied mechanically. For those that cannot, the sound of a sentence — its natural breaks and pauses — is often a helpful guide.

Marks Primarily to End a Sentence

. Period

1. Use a period to mark a "full stop" at the end of a sentence.
2. Use a period for an abbreviation: Mrs., Dr., P.E.I., Nfld. If the letters of an abbreviation form a word (an acronym), omit the periods: UNICEF, NORAD.
3. With some common abbreviations that don't form a word, you have the option of omitting periods: 3 am or 3 a.m. Whatever form you choose in these cases, be consistent.

? Question Mark

Use a question mark at the end of a direct question. Do not use it for an indirect one:

> ✔ How will you increase productivity?
> ✗ I wonder how you will increase productivity?
> ✔ I wonder how you will increase productivity.

Note: When phrasing a courteous request for which you don't expect a verbal answer, use a period instead of question mark:

> Will you please send me the form next week.

Never directly follow a question mark with a comma, period or semi-colon.

! Exclamation Mark

Use an exclamation mark for an exclamatory statement — a loud or dramatic utterance:

> What an impressive speech!

Be sparing with exclamation marks in business writing, or you will seem too excitable. Although exclamation marks can be useful in sales letters, a lot of them can create an impression of shouting at the reader:

> Last chance! Act now! Don't delay!

Marks Primarily to Separate Parts of a Sentence

; Semi-Colon

1. Use a semi-colon between closely related independent clauses (clauses that can stand by themselves). The semi-colon suggests a closer link than a period does and is especially useful before conjunctive adverbs, such as *thus, however, therefore.* Use it sparingly, however, or your writing will seem dense.

   > Preparing the lunch took four hours; eating it took forty minutes.
   > I realize I need exercise; however, I'll lie down first to think about it.

2. Use a semi-colon between items in a series if there are already commas within each each item:

   > ✗ The honoured employees were Helen Smith, the controller, Jean Hardy, her assistant, and Dr. Jack Hughes.
   > ✔ The honoured employees were Helen Smith, the controller; Jean Hardy, her assistant; and Dr. Jack Hughes.

(The semi-colons in the second sentence get rid of confusion about the number of employees.)

You may even use a semi-colon before a coordinating conjunction in a long sentence if there are internal commas within some of the clauses:

> The mediator settled the strike; but, despite their relief at getting back to work, not many workers were happy with the contract.

: Colon

A colon is a sign that something is to follow.

1. Use a colon after an independent clause, to introduce an explanation, expansion, or restatement of the clause. (Tip: if you can say "that is," or "namely" after the first clause, use a colon.)

> We made one mistake: rushing the job.

If the part following the colon is a complete sentence, you can begin it with a capital letter, although it's customary to use lower case except before a quotation:

> This is his advice: hire an accountant.
>
> *or*
>
> I remember Diefenbaker's scornful remark:"Polls are for dogs."

2. Use a colon before a list, especially if the list is arranged vertically:

> We transferred three employees to new branches:
> —Mary Aster to Victoria;
> —Hugh Koster to Calgary;
> —Max Cohen to Westminster.

If the list runs horizontally, use a colon only if the part preceding it is a complete sentence:

> x We want: three chairs, two desks, a credenza.
> ✓ We want three chairs, two desks, and a credenza.
>
> *or*
>
> ✓ We want the following furniture: three chairs, two desks, and a credenza.

3. Use a colon before a formal quotation:

> The Chairman said: "Either we work together, or we shall fail together."

4. Use a colon before a direct quotation of over three lines, and indent the quotation.

5. Use a colon after the salutation in a business or formal letter using closed punctuation:

> Dear Professor Hummel:

6. Use a colon between numerals when giving the time:

> 3:20 p.m. or 15:20

7. Use a colon between a title and subtitle:

> *Managing Change: A Guide for the New Leader*

, Comma

Commas are the most problematic of punctuation marks, not only because they have so many uses, but because they are sometimes discretionary. Although a long complex sentence with no commas is sure to confuse, a sentence with a plethora of commas will seem chopped up and jerky. The following guidelines will help you steer a course between too many and too few. Ultimately, however, the clearest choice is always best.

1. Use a comma between items in a simple series:

> Give me some felt pens, lined pads and an aspirin.

Although a comma before the final conjunction ("or", "and") is optional, it will sometimes avoid confusion:

> x The company suffered from old machines, inefficient manufacturing processes, increased competition and management turnover.

Had management turnover increased?

> ✔ The company suffered from old machines, inefficient manufacturing processes, increased competition, and management turnover.

2. Use a comma between adjectives that precede and modify the same noun:

> a heavy, unlabelled package
> her interesting, diverse responsibilities
> *but*
> favourite little restaurant.

In the last case *favourite* modifies not *restaurant*, but *little restaurant*; therefore, no comma is needed. A simple test is to see if you can reverse the adjectives. If you can reverse them, use a comma.

3. Use a comma before a coordinating conjunction (and, or, nor, but, yet) connecting two independent clauses:

> The pizzas arrived, and we ate them immediately.

If two independent clauses have a common subject, you may omit the comma and the second subject:

> Hawkins retired last June and [he] joined a consulting firm.

Note: *However, therefore,* and *thus* are not coordinating conjunctions, since they can go in various places other than between two independent clauses.

>   x   I felt like shouting, however I managed to stay calm.
>
>   ✓   I felt like shouting; however, I managed to stay calm.
>
>   ✓   I felt like shouting; I managed to stay calm, however.

The first example has a frequent error — a comma splice — since it wrongly treats *however* as a coordinating conjunction.

4. Use a comma to separate an independent clause from a preceding dependent one:

> When he had arrived, we toured the plant.
>
> Since it's late, let's have dinner.

When the dependent clause follows the independent one, the comma is often omitted:

> We found the lost ticket after the train had left.

5. Use a comma after a long introductory phrase:

> In the middle of the coldest winter on record, the pipes froze.

If the introductory phrase is short and connects smoothly with the rest of the sentence, you can usually omit the comma:

> In winter the pipes may freeze.

6. Use a comma to set off an appositive or naming phrase that gives inessential identifying information:

> My boss, Enid Miller, is on holiday.
>
> Mr. Hughes, our Vice-President, will make the decisions.

7. However, do not use a comma if the naming phrase is essential to identify the person:

> My daughter Brenda is a skillful promoter.

Use a comma on *both sides* of an interrupting phrase or a non-restrictive clause — one not essential to the meaning of the sentence:

> We suspect, as you have guessed, that the letter is lost.
>
> The appeal, so they say, is to teenagers.
>
> Mavis Jones, who comes from Halifax, will join the firm in June.

Important: If a relative clause is essential to the meaning of the noun phrase it modifies *do not* use commas to set it off. Failure to observe this distinction can cause serious muddles, as suggested by these two sentences:

All part-time employees, who aren't in the regular benefits plan, should obtain this insurance.

All part-time employees who aren't in the regular benefits plan should obtain this insurance.

In first sentence, all part-time employees are directed to buy insurance. In the second sentence, only those who aren't in the regular benefits plan are told to get it.

8. Use a comma before a short, direct quotation:

Duffy said, "Let's take a break."

Do not use a comma before an indirect quotation:

Duffy said we should take a break.

9. Use a comma before a tag question:

She's a good organizer, isn't she?

10. Use a comma between parts of

— an address (112 Queen Street South, Hamilton, Ontario);
— a date when the name of the day precedes it (Tuesday, February 3);
— large quantities, when using the imperial system of measures (3,000,000).

11. Note: In the metric system, spaces or hyphens rather than commas are used to separate the parts of a date; spaces separate quantities over three digits:

1992 12 03 or 92-12-03
$ 3 000 000

— Dash

Some people treat the dash as an all-purpose mark, and toss it into their writing frequently. A dash can effectively substitute for many other punctuation marks, especially the comma, but it should not be used constantly. A page full of dashes will make writing seem breathless; it won't give the impression of calm reason most business writing strives for. If a keyboard has no separate key for a dash, type two hyphens.

1. Use a dash to emphasize the phrase that follows. The dash will give a stronger emphasis than a comma or parentheses.

We got their approval — at last.

2. Use a dash on both sides of an interrupting phrase, if you want to emphasize the phrase.

The cheque was late — as usual — but at least it didn't bounce.

[( )] *Parentheses*

These are always drawn as curved enclosures, to be distinguished from brackets, which are square.

1. Use parentheses to set off incidental material or references:

> House starts were up 20% in March (despite gloomy forecasts), but are now levelling off.
>
> In his speech, Fraser predicted increased drilling activity (Empire Club, May 10, 1985).

If the insertion is within a sentence, put any punctuation after rather than before the parentheses; if the insertion is itself a sentence, put the period within the parentheses.

> Despite the gloomy economic forecast (see Figure 2), sales revenues are up 10%.
>
> Sales revenues this year increased by 10%, despite the forecasts. (See enclosure for a breakdown of forecast figures.)

2. Parentheses may enclose numbers or letters when listing material:

> (1) xxx
>
> (2) xx
>
> (3) xxx

Other Punctuation Marks

[[ ]] *Brackets*

Use brackets — they are always square — to mark any additions you make to a quotation. For example, if you need to insert words to make sense of a quotation, put those words in brackets:

> Jones said, "The costs of indexed pensions are more than they [taxpayers] realize, or their grandchildren will be able to afford."

Use brackets around the word *sic*, to show that any misspelling or misuse of the preceding word or phrase is in the original quotation:

> Their sign said, "Ban all nuclear missles [*sic*]. Ban the bomb."

Quotation Marks

Quotation marks may be single, following British convention, or double, following American convention. Canadians most often use double quotation marks, but you may use either form, provided you are consistent.

1. Use quotation marks to set off short quotations:

> Helen said, "Let's try and get that account."

For quotations within quotations, use the alternate form. For example, if you use double marks normally, use single marks for internal quotations:

> Helen said, "Let's follow Harry's advice: 'Reach for the brass ring.' "

Conversely, if you use single marks normally, use double marks for internal quotations.

2. Use quotation marks or italics to emphasize the word itself — as a word:

> American and Canadian forces traditionally pronounce the word "lieutenant" differently.

3. Use quotation marks around a slang or inappropriate word to show your awareness that it is not standard usage:

> Evidently he "misspoke" when he earlier denied the crime.

Use this intrusive device sparingly, however; often you can let the context show your awareness or you can choose a better word.

4. Use quotation marks to enclose the titles of poems (unless the poem is an entire book), short stories, journal articles, chapters in books, songs, and paintings.

Where exactly do quotation marks go? British and American conventions differ, but again Canadians increasingly follow this American pattern:

— Put periods and commas inside quotation marks;

> "Lend me your dictaphone," he said, "and I'll finish it now."

— Put colons and semi-colons outside quotation marks;

> He claimed, "I can double productivity"; only Sheila believed him.

— Put question marks and exclamation marks inside or outside, depending on the sense of the sentence:

> "Where are you going?" I asked.
>
> Do you agree with Carter that "A buck is a buck"?

| italics | ## Italics

Italics are slanted (cursive) letters, as opposed to ordinary roman letters. Since many typewriters don't have the capacity for italics, underlining is an acceptable substitute.

1. Use italics for the titles of books, a poem that is a complete book, films, and lengthy musical works.

> Please read *Megatrends* before the meeting.

If the title contains another title, put the internal title in a different type face or use quotation marks (single, unless the larger title has single ones).

> *The Implications of* Future Shock *for Business*
> *or*
> *The Implications of 'Future Shock' for Business*

2. Use italics to emphasize an idea.

> Given all the facts, we recommend that testing be abandoned *for now*.

This device is an effective way of stressing something, but don't use it constantly or your writing will seem over-excited. Intersperse it with other methods of creating emphasis.

3. Use italics for foreign words:

> Unfortunately, he resorted to an *ad hominem* attack on his opponent.

4. Use italics (or quotation marks) to emphasize a word — as a word.

> The term *parameters* has become a part of business jargon.

| . . . | ## Ellipses

1. Use ellipses (three periods) to show that part of a quotation is missing:

> He maintained that "Kelso is a profitable business . . . with a great future."

If the omission is at the end of the sentence, the ellipses marks are followed by a fourth period.

2. Use ellipses to show that a series of numbers continues indefinitely:

> 2, 4, 6, 8 . . .

| ' | ## Apostrophe

1. Use an apostrophe followed by *s* to show possession in

— singular nouns: cat's, house's, Mark's, Jess's
Exceptions: if the word always has two or more syllables and ends in *s*, and

the addition of another *s* would make an awkward-sounding word, you have the option of simply adding an apostrophe:

> Jesus' sayings, Saint-Saens' music, Mary Poppins' umbrella

— indefinite pronouns: one's, somebody's

2. Use an apostrophe by itself after the *s* to show possession for plural nouns:

> Canadians' attitudes, those businesses' profits, the Laytons' house

Exception: if a plural noun does not have an *s*-ending, add an apostrophe plus *s* to show possession:

> geese's, children's

Remember that possession may be shown without an apostrophe, if the possessor is preceded by *of*:

> the rules of the game, the pages of the report

This form is most often used with non-human entities or things, rather than with people

3. Use an apostrophe to show contractions of words or numbers:

> isn't, don't, I'm, it's, spring of '86

Caution: Don't confuse *it's* — a short form of *it is* — with the possessive pronoun *its*, which never has an apostrophe.

⊟ Hyphen

1. Use a hyphen to separate compound words:

> governor-general, fuzz-buster, father-in-law.

When used often, some compound words lose the hyphen and become one word. Check a dictionary if in doubt.

2. Use a hyphen to separate compound numbers under a hundred, when written as words: sixty-five, thirty-two.

3. Use a hyphen after the prefixes *self, all, ex,* and after any prefix to a name:

> self-sufficient, all-encompassing, ex-wife, pro-Conservative, anti-pollution.

Use a hyphen after any prefix if it aids clarity.

4. Use a hyphen to emphasize contrasting prefixes:

> The pro- and anti-strike groups agreed to talk.

5. Use a hyphen between compound modifiers — between two nouns or numbers used together as an adjective:

> twentieth century — twentieth-century discovery
> high profile — high-profile job

6. Use a hyphen to divide a word at the end of a line. Hyphens used this way can create difficulties when editing on a word-processor or when submitting work to be published, and it's best to avoid them. At least, do not hyphenate an end word if

— it has only one syllable;

— it is a proper name;

— it is at the end of a page;

— the page already has a number of hyphens.

Consult a dictionary for the proper division of words, but as a general rule,

— divide between syllables;

— don't leave a letter by itself;

— divide double consonants.

Exception: When double consonants come before a suffix, put the hyphen after the double consonants:

> stiff-er
> refill-able
> amass-ing.

However, if the second consonant has been added only because of the suffix, divide the consonants:

> thin-ning
> remit-tance

EXERCISES

● Section A

1. Put commas where needed in the following sentences:
   a) We need a new blue covering for that horrid uncomfortable chair.
   b) When I was away the office had a fire in its newly-furnished board room.
   c) I asked him to call my accountant Susan Hughes but he forgot to my dismay.

    d) Students who are caught plagiarizing assignments will fail the course.

    e) Last Thursday June 4th I held a meeting with Bill Hines Reg Hawkes and Sarah Rykert our new Research Director.

    f) The prospects are not good however despite our early optimism.

    g) Last week she said "Consumers are more confident" but this week she is predicting that the economy will soon be "sluggish."

    h) Your forecast is shocking needless to say but you are a pessimist aren't you?

    i) My boss who is always supportive suggested that I apply for the job in Lethbridge Alberta.

    j) I recommend therefore that we leave the machines buy the furniture and restore the old panelling and wood trim.

2. Add apostrophes where needed.

    a) Mr. Coates secretary is having lunch with the other bosses secretaries.

    b) Its a challenging job and Ill keep my fingers crossed that Marys application succeeds.

    c) The Hawkins house is located next to the Jennings property.

    d) A new womens club has opened downtown but its entrance fees are high.

    e) The fact that John Frasers little shoe store has grown into the Frasers huge chain of stores restores one confidence in the countrys spirit of entrepreneurism.

    f) My mother said "Mind your young sisters manners when you go to that reception."

3. Add quotation marks (and other punctuation where needed) to the following sentences.

    a) When he asked Are you free on Saturday night I replied No Im expensive.

    b) She said there was a good opportunity however I was not as certain.

    c) If you pay for the gas he said I will drive you to Montreal.

    d) Can we really believe the slogan Practice makes perfect.

    e) Have you read the article Managing Innovation.

4. In the places marked by a carat ($\wedge$) add a semi-colon, a colon, a comma, or no mark.

    a) We think $\wedge$ however, that the proposal is sound.

    b) I like Susie $\wedge$ however, she doesn't like me.

    c) For my presentation next Friday please arrange for $\wedge$ a flip chart, an overhead projector, and a tape recorder.

    d) He invited three guests $\wedge$ Mr. Jones, Mrs. Hunter, and Mr. Zavitz.

    e) My new book is called *Interaction* $\wedge$ *A Guide to Productivity*.

    f) My reason is simple $\wedge$ It's too costly.

    g) I called Arthur Hanna, the lawyer who works for us $\wedge$ but he was at a conference with Jed Hughes our accountant, and won't be back for a week.

    h) The press conference will take place at the Holiday Inn, Yorkdale $\wedge$ on Monday morning.

    i) Please send notice of the meeting to our lawyer, Jane Higgins $\wedge$ and her junior, Dan Spivak. (Assume the notice goes to two people.)

    j) A prompt reminder of their overdue accounts should go to our clients $\wedge$ who have not paid their December bills.

5. Hyphenate the following words:

meeting	market	mostly
running	arrest	according
agreement	passable	sorry
timetable	justice	notice

● **Section B**

1. Add semi-colons, colons, and commas where appropriate.

  a) We bid on the contract nevertheless we didn't get it.

  b) We invited three influential lawyers Harold Stark QC Melvin Thomas and Sylvia Raski.

  c) We plan to give long-term service pins to Ann Arbour our accounting supervisor Al Smith the sales manager and Pete Stuart head of maintenance.

  d) Last night I stayed up until 3 30 since I was engrossed in reading *Murder on the Metro A Tale of High Finance.*

  e) The plant will likely not need chemical engineers you should however check with Jim Jackson the general manager.

  f) Please paint the ante-room the manager's office and the computer room by next weekend one coat should be enough.

  g) Guy quoted Trudeau's remark "The state has no place in the nation's bedrooms."

  h) The woman who gave me the job is the aunt of my best friend who lives in Fredericton.

  i) The friendly old supervisor I've often talked to you about gave me a ticket to the hockey game between the Edmonton Oilers and Toronto Maple Leafs on Saturday night.

  j) Here is our strategy hang tough and keep cool.

2. Punctuate the following sentences.

  a) On Friday June 10 at 9 30 a m the premier will meet the union leaders however he is not expected to make an announcement afterward.

  b) The weary student asked whats the meaning of this assignment and I certainly didn't have an answer.

  c) Do women really believe that old slogan blondes have more fun.

  d) Jeffs article Magnum Corporation A Study in Entrepreneurship is a good one but its not likely to be published.

  e) When the Lewis car lost its muffler Sam had to take it to Susans fathers garage.

  f) Thats a nineteenth century attitude Ann said but at least its not hypocritical.

  g) On a cold winter night in March Mr Gallant went on a holiday his first in five years and he never returned.

  h) People who are shy often have spouses who do most of the talking for them or so it seems.

  i) The treasurers report see Appendix A gives details of our finances and unfortunately we still have a large debt to be paid off.

  j) What a disaster he shouted but then hes always overreacting.

3. Correct the punctuation in the following memo. Capital letters show where sentences begin, but you may create added sentence breaks if you wish.

June 3, 1989
To J Walker
From M Smythe
Subject *Date of Opening for New Office*

Alans plans for opening our new office make good sense however I think the date is not late enough Will it matter to you if we move the opening date back two weeks to Tuesday August 1

My concern arises from two potential problems First the furniture company cannot guarantee delivery of our order before July 28 Second Ace Movers is fully booked until the last week in July They may have cancellations for an earlier date but its safer I think to change our schedule I would rather not switch to another moving company because Aces prices are considerably lower than its competitors As well other companies who have used Ace report good results Reliable Movers who moved us last time have gone out of business I plan to hold the Ace people to their slogan let us take the fuss out of moving

Checklist of Misused Words and Phrases

accept, except   *Accept* is a verb meaning *agree* to something; *except*, when used as a verb, means *exclude*:

> I *accept* your offer.

> John's boss *excepted* him from the general criticism.

accompanied by, accompanied with   Use *accompanied by* for people; *accompanied with* for objects:

> She was *accompanied by* her assistant.

> The payment arrived, *accompanied with* an explanation.

advice, advise   *Advice* is a noun, *advise* a verb:

> He was *advised* to ignore the consultant's *advice*.

affect, effect   As a verb, *affect* means *influence*; as a noun, it's a technical psychological term. The verb *to effect* means *to bring about*. The noun *effect* means *result*. In most cases, you will be safe if you remember to use *affect* for the verb and *effect* for the noun:

> Interest rates *affect* our profit.

> The *effect* of higher government spending is higher inflation.

aggravate, irritate   To *aggravate* is to *make worse*; to *irritate* is to *annoy*:

> x He *aggravates* me.

> ✓ He *irritates* me.

> ✓ Your attitude will *aggravate* the group's anxiety.

all together, altogether   *All together* means *in a group*; *altogether* is an adverb meaning *entirely*:

> She was *altogether* certain that the supervisors were *all together* at that meeting.

allusion, illusion   An *allusion* is an indirect reference to something; an *illusion* is a false perception:

> In his speech he made an *allusion* to the president's report.

> He thought he saw a ship on the horizon, but it was an *illusion*.

alot   Write as two separate words: *a lot*.

alternate, alternative   Used as an adjective, *alternate* means *the other of two choices*. As a verb, *to alternate* means *to do first one thing and then another*; *alternative* means *a choice between two things*.

> She came by one route, and took the *alternate* route home.

> To prevent muscle strain, *alternate* hands on the lever.

> She faces these *alternatives*: retrain workers or hire new ones.

among, between   Use *among* for three or more people or objects, *between* for two:

> *Between* you and me, there's trouble *among* the maintenance crew.

amoral, immoral   *Amoral* means *non-moral* or *outside the moral sphere; immoral* means *wicked*:

> As an art critic, he was *amoral* in his judgments.

> Not to report the danger would be *immoral*.

amount, number   Use *amount* for money or non-countable quantities; use *number* for countable items:

> No *amount* of persuasion or *number* of petitions will budge him from his position.

anyways   Non-standard English: use *anyway*.

as, because   *As* is a weaker conjunction than *because* or *since* and may be confused with *when*:

> x   I left early *as* I was tired.

> ✓   I left early *because* I was tired.

> ✓   He arrived *as* I was finishing.

> ✓   He arrived *when* I was finishing.

as to   A common feature of bureaucratese; replace it with a single-word preposition such as *about* or *on*:

> x   They were concerned *as to* the new budget.

> ✓   They were concerned *about* the new budget.

> x   They recorded his comments *as to* tax changes.

> ✓   They recorded his comments *on* tax changes.

bad, badly   *Bad* is an adjective meaning *not good*:

> The meat tastes *bad*.

> He felt *bad* about forgetting the hand-outs.

Badly is an adverb meaning *not well*; when used with the verbs *want* or *need*, it means *very much*:

> She thought he managed the meeting *badly*.

> I *badly* need a new office chair.

beside, besides   *Beside* is a preposition meaning *next to*:

> She sat *beside* her assistant.

Besides has two uses: as a preposition it means *in addition to*; as a conjunctive adverb it means *moreover*:

> *Besides* recommending the changes, the consultants are implementing them.

> *Besides*, it was late and we needed a break.

between   See *among*.

bring, take   One *brings* something to a place where one is or will be and *takes* it when one is leaving for somewhere else.

can, may   *Can* means *to be able*; *may* means *to have permission*:

> *Can* you finish the job?

> *May* I have another look at your report?

In speech, *can* is used to cover both meanings: in formal writing, however, you should observe the distinction.

can't hardly   A faulty combination of the phrases *can't* and *can hardly*. Use one or the other of them instead:

> He *can't* balance the budget.

> She *can hardly* stay awake.

canvas, canvass   *Canvas* is a type of heavy cloth; *to canvass* is *to solicit votes*.

capital, capitol   As a noun, *capital* may refer to a seat of government, the top of a pillar, an upper-case letter, or accumulated wealth. *Capitol* refers only to a specific American — or ancient Roman — legislative building.

complement, compliment   The verb *to complement* means *to complete*; *to compliment* means *to praise*:

> His communication skill *complements* the skills of the engineers.

> I *complimented* her on her outstanding report.

continual, continuous   *Continual* means *repeated over a period of time*; *continuous* means *constant* or *without interruption*:

> The strikes caused *continual* delays in building the road.

> In August, it rained *continuously* for five days.

could of   Incorrect, as are *might of, should of*, and *would of*. Replace *of* with *have*:

> x   He *could of* done it.

> ✓   He *could have* done it.

> ✓   They *might have* been there.

> ✓   I *should have* known.

> ✓   We *would have* left earlier.

council, counsel   *Council* is a noun meaning *advisory* or *deliberative assembly*. *Counsel* as a noun means *advice* or *lawyer*, as a verb it means *give advice*:

>   The town *council* meets on Tuesday.

>   We respect his *counsel*, since he's seldom wrong.

>   As an employee *counsellor*, you may need to *counsel* some people after hours.

criterion, criteria   A *criterion* is a standard for judging something. *Criteria* is the plural of *criterion* and thus requires a plural verb:

>   *These are* my *criteria* for selecting the applicants.

data   The plural of *datum, data* is increasingly treated as a singular noun. However, this usage is not yet acceptable in formal prose: use a plural verb.

different than   Incorrect. Use either *different from* (American usage) or *different to* (British).

disinterested, uninterested   *Disinterested* implies impartiality or neutrality; *uninterested* implies a lack of interest:

>   As a *disinterested* observer, he was in a good position to judge the issue fairly.

>   *Uninterested* in the proceedings, he yawned repeatedly.

due to   Although increasingly used to mean *because of*, *due* is an adjective and therefore needs to modify something:

>   x *Due to* his rudeness, we lost the contract. (*Due* is dangling.)

>   ✓ The loss was *due to* his rudeness.

farther, further   *Farther* refers to distance, *further* to extent:

>   He paddled *farther* than his friends.

>   He explained the plan *further*.

good, well   *Good* is an adjective, not an adverb. *Well* can be both: as an adverb, it means *effectively*; as an adjective, it means *health*:

>   The apple cake tastes *good*.

>   She is a *good* tennis player.

>   She plays tennis *well*.

>   He is *well* again after his long bout of pneumonia.

hanged, hung   *Hanged* means *executed by hanging*. *Hung* means *suspended* or *clung to*:

>   He was *hanged* at dawn for the murder.

>   He *hung* the picture.

>   He *hung* to the boat when it capsized.

hopefully   Use *hopefully* as an adverb meaning *full of hope*:

>   She scanned the mail *hopefully*, looking for her cheque.

In formal writing, using *hopefully* to mean *I hope* is still frowned upon, although increasingly common; it's better to use *I hope*:

>   x *Hopefully* we'll make a bigger profit this year.

>   ✓ *I hope* we'll make a bigger profit this year.

imply, infer   *Imply* refers to what a statement suggests; *infer* relates to the audience's interpretation:

>His letter *implied* that he was upset.
>
>I *inferred* from his letter that he was upset.

irregardless   Incorrect; use *regardless*.

its, it's   *Its* is a form of possessive pronoun; *it's* is a contraction of *it is*. Many people mistakenly put an apostrophe in *its* in order to show possession:

>x   We can see *it's* advantages.
>
>⌐   We can see *its* advantages.
>
>⌐   *It's* time to leave.

less, fewer   Use *less* for money and things that are not countable; use *fewer* for things that are countable:

>Now that he's earning *less* money he's making *fewer* large expenditures.

lie, lay   *To lie* means *to assume a horizontal position; to lay* means *to put down*. The changes of tense often cause confusion:

present	past	past participle
lie	*lay*	*lain*
lay	*laid*	*laid*

like, as   *Like* is a preposition, but it is often wrongly used as a conjunction. To join two independent clauses, use the conjunction *as*:

>x   I want to develop *like* you have this year.
>
>⌐   I want to develop *as* you have this year.
>
>⌐   Arthur is *like* my old boss.

majority, plurality   *Majority* means *more than half*; *plurality* means *the highest number of votes*.

media   A plural noun requiring a plural verb. The singular noun is *medium*.

might of   See *could of*.

myself, me   *Myself* is an intensifier of, not a substitute for, *I* or *me*:

>x   He gave it to Jane and *myself*.
>
>⌐   He gave it to Jane and *me*.
>
>x   Jane and *myself* are invited.
>
>⌐   Jane and *I* are invited.
>
>⌐   *Myself*, I would prefer a swivel chair.

nor, or   Use *nor* with *neither* and *or* by itself or with *either*:

>He is *neither* overworked *nor* underpaid.
>
>The file was *either* lost *or* destroyed.

off of   Remove the unnecessary *of*:

>x   The fence helps keep trespassers *off of* the premises.
>
>⌐   The fence helps keep trespassers *off* the premises.

phenomenon   A singular noun: the plural is *phenomena*.

principal, principle   As an adjective, *principal* means *main* or *most important*; a *principal* is the head of a school. A *principle* is a law or controlling idea:

Our *principal* aim is to reduce the deficit.

Our *principal*, Prof. Smart, retires next year.

We are defending the policy as a matter of *principle*.

rational, rationale   *Rational* is an adjective meaning *logical* or *able to reason*. *Rationale* is a noun meaning *explanation*:

That was not a *rational* decision.

The president sent around a memo with a *rationale* for his proposal.

real, really   The adjective *real* shouldn't be used as an adverb in Canada, although this use is common in the United States; use *really* instead:

x It was *real* valuable.

✔ It was *really* valuable.

✔ We had *real* value for our money.

set, sit   *To sit* means *to rest on the buttocks; to set* means *to put or place*:

After standing so long, you'll want to *sit* down.

Please *set* the machine on the desk.

should of   See *could of*.

their, there   *Their* is the possessive form of the third person plural pronoun. *There* is usually an adverb, meaning *at that place* or *at that point*:

They parked *their* cars *there*.

to, too, two   *To* is a preposition, as well as part of the infinitive form of a verb:

We went *to town* in order *to buy* equipment.

Too is an adverb showing degree (the soup is *too* hot) or meaning *moreover, also*. *Two* is the spelled version of the number *2*.

while   To avoid misreadings, use *while* only when you mean *at the same time that*. Do not use it as a substitute for *although, whereas,* or *but*:

x *While* he's getting fair results, he'd like to do better.

x I left the meeting *while* she decided to stay.

✔ He glowered *while* he was listening.

-wise   Never use *-wise* as a suffix to form new words when you mean *with regard to*:

x *Sales-wise*, the company did better last year.

✔ The company's sales increased last year.

your, you're   *Your* is a pronominal adjective used to show possession; *you're* is a contraction of *you are*:

You're likely to miss *your* train.

Index